Parliamentary Government

IN ENGLAND

Parliamentary Government

IN ENGLAND

A COMMENTARY

BY HAROLD J. LASKI

NEW YORK · THE VIKING PRESS · PUBLISHERS

1938

To my friend
MAX LERNER
with warm affection

Preface

It is important for me to emphasize that this book is not a formal description of the working of parliamentary government in England, but, essentially, as its subtitle states, a commentary limited to certain aspects of its working. I have tried, as best I can, to present those aspects of its working which are most relevant to the pressing problems of our time.

I owe many debts to friends for help in writing it. Among the dead, Lord Haldane and Mr. Arthur Henderson were good enough to discuss with me on many occasions some of the problems here treated; and I have, I hope, learned a good deal from Graham Wallas in long years of eager colleagueship. Among the living, I should like particularly to mention Mr. and Mrs. Sidney Webb, to whom, like all of my generation, I owe an unlimited debt, and Dr. W. I. Jennings, whose work on *Cabinet Government* has already taken its place as the classic on the subject. None of them, of course, has any responsibility for the views I have expressed. Perhaps I may add that parts of the book have benefited greatly from the friendly, if vigorous, criticisms of my students in the London School of Economics and Political Science.

H. J. L.

July 3, 1938,
Little Bardfield, Essex

Contents

Introductory

1

NO system of representative government has a history so continuous or so successful as that of Great Britain. It was born of a revolution which, in any real sense, may be said to have lasted almost fifty years. Yet if it was the deposit of a grim civil war, for two hundred and fifty years all its fundamental changes have since been effected by peaceful compromise. It has stood the strain of two wars of world importance, and it has been able to adapt itself to a condition in which the form of its political institutions has been successfully adapted to the substantive distribution of its economic power. In the century and a half of its modern history, the government of France has been reshaped by three violent revolutions; while the constitution of the United States was challenged, half-way in its evolution, by four years of civil war. If we date the history of representative government in Germany and Italy from 1870, the one lasted for sixty-three years, the other for fifty-two.

The contrast is, on any showing, a striking one; and it is tempting to attribute it, as eulogists are wont to do, to some special British genius for the difficult art of self-government. That explanation, however, is an unsatisfactory one, since, obviously, it is a deduction from the history rather than a principle informing it. A passion for simplicity usually works havoc with political philosophers, and it is rare indeed for a phenomenon so complex as the success of the British government to be capable of explanation in terms of any single principle. Explanations that base themselves upon some supposed virtue in a national character rarely deceive any save those who are responsible for their making. Anyone who compares the impression produced by Englishmen upon Frenchmen in the seventeenth and eighteenth centuries, respectively, will recognize at once that judgments of national behaviour are always a dangerous enterprise. There is a presumption in them both of unity and of objectivity which rarely coincide with the facts themselves.

The "prerequisites," as Bagehot called them, of successful representative government are, indeed, both manifold and complex. It requires something more than intelligence and virtue. It presupposes a body of citizens who are fundamentally at one upon all the major objects of governmental activity; so fundamentally at one, it may be added, that the thought of conflict as a way of change is incapable of entering the minds of more than an insignificant portion of the nation. It requires, in the second place, a sense in the nation that no single class of any importance in the community is permanently excluded from power. For it has been not less true of the British than of other peoples that the possession of power over a long period is corrupting in its nature; so that, in the long run, exclusion from power tends naturally to mean exclusion from benefit also. The rule of an aristocracy has always meant rule in the interest of that aristocracy; the rule of business men has always taken a narrow view of the interests both of agriculture and of the poor. Unless a body of men feel that their place in the society is, granted that they are numerous enough, either certain to receive consideration, or, alternatively, that its refusal will jeopardize the position of those in office, they are unlikely, if the object involved is one to which they attach any profound consideration, to acquiesce at all easily in the maintenance of social peace.

A third condition of successful representative government is that it should be built upon widely diffused habits of tolerance throughout the nation. Men who are to live together peacefully must be able to argue together peacefully. They must not run to suppress criticism of things as they are; rather they must be willing, if pressed, to invite examination of them. They must refrain from imposing upon a significant minority principles of legislation by which the latter is outraged. Without this tolerance there is no prospect in the society of compromise, and every subject of division then becomes a highroad to disruption.

It is, I think, historically obvious that the habits of tolerance are born of a sense of security. By that I mean that the members of the society are confident, above all in matters of economic constitution, that their established expectations will be fulfilled. For tolerance depends on the existence of a mood in which men are susceptible to rational argument, and nothing is so destructive of this temper as the fear that is born of the disturbance of a wonted routine. Political reform in England was postponed for forty years by the terror born of the French Revolution, and there was a moment when it seemed not unlikely that the compromise of 1832 would not be effected peacefully. Men cannot settle their differences by reason when the passion of fear hangs over their lives. It may be the outcome of defeat in war. It may come through a wholesale disruption of the currency. It may be the invasion of some custom or right held specially dear by those to whom it is denied. Whatever the causes, the deeper the disturbance of the atmosphere of security, the less likely will it be that a free system of representative government can be successfully maintained.

When, seventy years ago, Bagehot made his famous analysis of the English constitution, he added two further conditions which he regarded as essential. The people, he thought, must, as a mass, have the habit of deference; and he regarded the institution of the monarchy as a "myth" which, by its magic influence, persuaded them to accept the rule of their betters. "They fancy," he wrote, "they are governed by an hereditary queen, a queen by the grace of God, when they are really governed by a cabinet and a parliament—men like themselves, chosen by themselves. The conspicuous dignity awakens the sentiment of reverence, and men, often very undignified, seize the occasion to govern by means of it."

We need not deny the influence of the monarch's person in unifying the sentiment of a nation. But it is obvious enough that Bagehot's myth, in fact, goes a very little way. For, historically, myths of this kind are successful only so long as, beneath their ægis, the "efficient" part of a constitution, as he termed it, is able to do its work successfully; and this, in its turn, depends upon the ability of the system, as it functions, to satisfy the legitimate expectation of citizens. Where it does not, as with Charles I or Louis XVI, or Nicholas II, the ability of the myth to do its work of conviction vanishes pretty rapidly. A successful myth operates only where a regime is secure; it collapses as that regime is undermined.

Underlying Bagehot's insistence on the importance of the "dignified" part of a constitution, there was a deeper apprehension, hardly, perhaps, made fully articulate, which is more important. Bagehot, it must be remembered, wrote before the maturity of trade unions, also before the Education Act of 1870 had exercised any effect upon the population. He doubted the compatibility of representative government with universal suffrage. He was afraid of the ignorance of the multitude. The combination of the lower classes might, he thought, drive their "betters" from power, and he urged a coalition of the aristocracy and the wealthy against this danger. It is clear enough that what he had in mind was a situation—like that of Chartism, or the French Revolution of 1848—in which the masses would use their political power to undermine respect for property. Particularly, he feared a situation in which the masses should find "two combinations of well-taught and rich men constantly offer to defer to their decision, and compete for the office of executing it. *Vox populi* will be *vox diaboli* if it is worked in that manner." "A political combination of the lower classes," he wrote, "as such and for their own objects, is an evil of the first magnitude; a permanent combination of them would make them (now that so many of them have the suffrage) supreme in the country; and their supremacy, in the state they now are, means the supremacy of ignorance over instruction, and of numbers over knowledge."

That fear of the brute force of numbers is a characteristic of the generation in which Bagehot wrote. Mill and Maine and Lecky are all, in different degrees, pervaded by its influence in their writings. It is, of course, clear now that in some ways their fear was greatly exaggerated. They underestimated the power of education to make men take long views; they underestimated the influence of propaganda in maintaining ancient routines of thought. But, at least from one aspect, their fear of a democracy based on universal suffrage has a significance in which their warnings are of great importance.

For it is certain that in any society where men and women enjoy universal suffrage there will be a persistent urgency to use their political power for the improvement of their material conditions. So long as the economic system is able continuously and measurably to respond to their demands, they are unlikely to discuss those foundations which, as Burke insisted, it is always dangerous to examine. They will want security, higher wages, shorter hours, better housing, more ample education and opportunity for their children. So long as the system is able to provide them with these things, so long, in Bagehot's own phrase, as the "better" classes can "remove not only every actual grievance, but, where it is possible, every seeming grievance, too; they must willingly concede every claim they can safely concede," all will be well. But the essential and central problem of representative democracy is the question of what the "better" classes can do when some claim is made which, in their judgment, they cannot "safely" concede. For Bagehot, no doubt, the idea of "safety" was an objective one, something, perhaps, that could logically be deduced from the postulates of that political economy of which he was so brilliant an exponent. Yet it is clear enough that those postulates were, in fact, the half-conscious assumptions of a class which had made them work and built its conceptions of "safety" upon the fact that it had come to think of no others as possible.

The real problem was one which was confronted in this period only by Tocqueville among liberal thinkers, and by Marx and his disciples among socialist thinkers. It was the consequences of the situation that might arise if the conception of "safety" in the granting of concessions was viewed differently, even antithetically, by the different parties to the political equation. Men would then be in disagreement about exactly those fundamentals unity upon which, as Bagehot saw, was the condition of successful government in representative democracy. "Our whole political machinery," Lord Balfour has written, "presupposes a people so fundamentally at one that they can safely afford to bicker; and so sure of their own moderation that they are not dangerously disturbed by the never-ending din of political conflict." It is that unity which explains the remarkable contrast between the political history of Great Britain and that of its continental neighbours.

It is a unity born of economic success, of success in war, of success in empire-building. Out of these came an expanding volume of wealth which permitted the policy of concessions that Bagehot recommended to be continuously applied. Moments of danger, like those of the Chartist movement, were transcended peacefully because each of them broadly synchronized with a great economic move forward which permitted the conference of increasing material benefit upon the masses. That conference, moreover, in no wise endangered, at least until the close of the war, the privileges or the security of the "better" classes; even so late as 1908 an eminent American observer could see no future for the Labour Party save as a minor partner in the liberal alliance. It was widely held, until the outbreak of the war, that the capitalist foundations of society were not seriously in question. It was believed that the new socialized liberalism, of which T. H. Green was perhaps the most notable exponent, had built a philosophy of state-intervention which would safeguard in perpetuity at least the large outlines of the Victorian compromise. The main bulk of British socialists themselves hardly doubted the validity of this view. Nourished, directly or indirectly, on the views of the Fabian school, they thought of the state-power as a neutral force which responded objectively to the will of an electoral majority. They had no doubt that reason was on their side, and they assumed that they had only to persuade that majority that they were right, to proceed to use the power of the state for the socialist transformation of economic institutions.

This simple theory, no doubt, is still the predominant view in England, though it has received some rude shocks in recent years. Its acceptance is built, in fact, upon a long series of assumptions none of which has been adequately tested. It believes, clearly, in the existence of an objective reason which compels men to peaceful acceptance of its conclusions whatever be their interest in the result of its application. It regards democracy as the supreme good, and it refuses to visualize the operation of democracy in the framework of the capitalist system to which it is so vitally related. It differentiates between the experience of continental countries and that of Great Britain on the ground that British national character and historic traditions create decisively different possibilities; British capitalists, in view of that character and those traditions, will not, it is assumed, act like continental capitalists when their privileges are threatened. It is, moreover, a purely rationalist interpretation of political action; it hardly considers at all the degree to which, in politics, reason has its opportunity only where men have an equal interest in its findings. Above all, perhaps, it has never seriously examined the relation between economic power and political power, the degree, that is, to which the authority of the state is subordinated to the logic of the economic foundations upon which it rests.

As Bagehot and, indeed, most of his generation saw, the position is far more complicated. Constitutional principles and forms do not operate in a vacuum of abstract reason. They are a method

intended to secure the triumph of certain ends; they are shaped
to the attainment of those ends. The English state of the past two
hundred and fifty years is the institutional expression of that liberalism which received its first classical expression in Locke. It was
the affirmation of the right of the property-owner to be protected
against arbitrary interference in the enjoyment of his property.
The business of the state was to find the terms upon which that enjoyment could be most amply protected. How narrow was this
conception of the state's function Adam Smith was not slow to
admit; for him the main function of justice was the protection of
property. "The affluence of the rich," he wrote, "excites the indignation of the poor, who are often both driven by want and
prompted by envy to invade their possessions. It is only under the
shelter of the civil magistrate that the owner of that valuable
property, acquired by the labour of many years, or perhaps many
successive generations, can sleep a single night in security." That
the protection of property was the main end of the state was also
the view of Burke. "To provide for us in our necessities," he said,
"is not in the power of government. It would be a vain presumption in statesmen to think they can do it. . . . It is in the power
of government to prevent much evil; it can do very little positive
good in this, or perhaps in anything else." The underlying assumption of this attitude was, perhaps, put most clearly, if somewhat starkly, by Arthur Young. "Everyone but an idiot," he wrote
in 1771, "knows that the lower classes must be kept poor, or they
will never be industrious."

The English liberalism of the last century has, in outward
form, departed widely from that attitude. It has built a state in
which freedom of speech and association, equality before the law,
universal suffrage, compulsory education, and religious liberty are
postulates to which all parties give adherence. More: the police-
state of the early nineteenth century has given place to the social
service state of the twentieth. Upon a scale of which Bagehot could
not have dreamed the state has used its supreme coercive power
deliberately to mitigate, by its conscious intervention, some of the

harsher consequences of economic inequality. The improvements
in public health and education, in housing and the facilities for
recreation since Bagehot's day, are quite literally immense. The
assumption made by most politicians is that there is no reason to
anticipate any permanent suspension of this progress unless there
supervenes some unlooked-for catastrophe. Social progress, no
doubt, will have its ups and downs; we are not yet, for instance,
the masters of the consequences inherent in the trade-cycle. But,
given goodwill and patience, there is, it is argued, no inherent
reason to suppose that our constitutional system is not elastic
enough to provide for the peaceful achievement of any social
transformation upon which the electorate has decisively made up
its mind.

There is, I think, in that confidence a neglect to pay due attention to the generalization Saint-Simon made in one of the
most remarkable of his prophetic insights. "The law," he wrote,
"which constitutes the powers and the form of government is
less important and has less influence on the happiness of nations
than that which constitutes property and decides its use." Our
political system takes for granted the private ownership of the
means of production; the consequences of that assumption cover
every nook and cranny of the law. All the great categories of our
jurisprudence are soaked in the traditions of individualism. They
assume property-rights which, save in the absence of direct contrary prescriptions from Parliament, are to be safeguarded from
invasion. They are based, not upon the collectivist and corporate
habits of the twentieth century, but on the liberal-atomic principles worked out from the seventeenth to the mid-nineteenth
century. They were the work of men who believed that, with the
triumph of the business man, a term had been put to the need of
revolutionary change. For, in their eyes, his victory ended the
power of those barriers of race and birth and creed to its place in
the sun. The true freedom was the freedom he had won—the
freedom to acquire property and to be safeguarded in its acquisition. This was the magic that had turned sand into gold. This

was what had brought the relations of production into harmony with the forces of production. Religion, ethics, political philosophy, all contributed to its sanctification. It was the "simple system of natural liberty" which had at long last enabled man to enter into his Kingdom.

The essence, at least, of this outlook was not touched by later changes. The concessions Bagehot recommended were made; they have not touched the class-relations of English society. Fundamentally, it still remains divided into the two nations of rich and poor. Fundamentally, also, any approach to equality of opportunity does not exist within its confines. Fundamentally, once more, the motive to production is not the need of the society but the ability of the owners of the instruments of production to make profit from their effort. Our society, as Mr. Keynes has insisted, has, upon this basis, become "absolutely irreligious, without internal union, without much public spirit, often, though not always, a mere congeries of possessors and pursuers." The political constitution it built is, in form, one which leaves the substance of governmental action at the disposal of that party or parties which command a majority in the House of Commons. But it is vital to realize that all the pivotal positions in the judiciary, the civil service, the defence forces, the police, are occupied by members of the governing class. The rules and habits in which they have confidence are those which do not disturb the social order they dominate. Here, as elsewhere, right and wrong, wisdom and unwisdom in public action, are established in terms of the effect they have upon the existing social order. The question it raises is whether its framework, not seen abstractly, but in terms of the social order of which it is the protective envelope, is elastic enough to admit changes that seek its basic transformation.

For, at this stage, both the method and the dynamic of change are different from anything known in the past two hundred and fifty years. Party government is still today, as it was in Bagehot's time, the vital principle of representative government. But both the principles and the interests underlying party structure have undergone a radical change. On the one side, there stands a party which, broadly speaking, represents a faith in the private ownership of the means of production; on the other is a party committed to the view that the system of private ownership has broken down and that the socialization of those means is fundamental to national well-being. It is, of course, true that the first is willing to continue the policy of concessions in so far as, within the limits of the national economy, this appears to be a feasible adventure; and it is also true that its opponents are eager to carry out the policy of socialization with the minimum detriment to existing interests. Each is eager, in fact, to discover the maximum common ground because neither desires to pursue a policy which would be regarded by the other as a challenge to democracy. But neither has seriously confronted the issue of whether the uneasy marriage between capitalism and democracy is psychologically possible in the period of capitalism's decline. While the party of the *status quo* remains in office, it is constantly outbid by its rival in what is offered to the electorate in return for its suffrages. Granted the nature of the party system, the Opposition will one day become a government. But it then meets a situation when the changes it will recommend are not such as can, in Bagehot's phrase, be "safely" conceded by the party of property. That sense will inspire in business men a lack of confidence which may well go so deep as to provoke, as it did in 1931, a grave financial crisis. Can representative government work if one party to the political equation provokes by its policies a situation in which the economic stability of the society is threatened?

As the issues are now set, in fact, the problem that confronts us is the problem of whether our people is so "fundamentally at one," as Lord Balfour put it, as to be able to "safely afford to bicker." It is a test to which the parliamentary system has not had previously to submit. It threatens the general sense of security; thereby, it weakens the power of reason to maintain its empire over men's minds. The great characteristic of the previous period has been the general ability of each party to accept without undue difficulty the legislation of its predecessor because this left undisturbed the foundations of the state. The perspective that now comes into view is one in which this characteristic can hardly obtain. Neither in the diagnosis nor in the cure for our difficulties is there any basic agreement between parties; and the remedies proposed by socialists seek nothing so much as the transformation of the state. Not that only. They insist that necessary ameliorations must accompany the process of transformation. From the point of view of a capitalist society, the bill of costs for these is a staggering one; as in 1931 its impact is the disturbance of business confidence and the prospect, above all in a time of economic difficulty, of budgetary disequilibrium. Are the psychological strains and stresses of such a programme not greater than a system of representative democracy can bear? If they are, it goes to prove that the British constitution, in the form in which we have known it, is merely an expression in political terms of a special parallelogram of economic forces. If they are not, then the British constitution will be the first to witness a change made without violence in the class-structure of society. If they are, then the maintenance of parliamentary government in its classic form is no longer a feasible adventure. It then becomes a type of government suitable to capitalism in its period of expansion, but incapable of maintaining itself in the period of capitalism's decline. It would be one more illustration of the general thesis that forms of government are contained by the economic principle they express, and that they disappear as that principle ceases to meet the needs of a new time.

It is important for us to remember that the changes we are witnessing in Great Britain are universal in their nature. We assist at a spectacle as momentous in its implications as the transition from feudalism to capitalism. Abroad, at least, the pressures resulting from the differences involved have been everywhere threatening, and sometimes fatal, to the parliamentary system. Even here, in the brief period since the war, they have brought about significant changes. They have resulted in an eclipse, which seems likely to be permanent, of the historic Liberal Party. Its members have discovered that in a choice between the defence of capitalism, and the acceptance of socialism, their real interest, and, they would add, the interests of the nation, lie with the former. More than this: the acceptance by a great mass of Liberals of the policy of Conservatism has resulted in the formation of a "national" government which regards the classic technique of opposition quite differently from its predecessors. For where, before the war, the idea that it was the duty of an Opposition to oppose was regarded as of the inner essence of the parliamentary system, now it is increasingly urged that opposition as such is merely faction; and the tendency is to discount the whole validity of the party conflict as in and of itself a detriment to national unity. At bottom, of course, this criticism is no different from that made by Fascists of the parliamentary regime. A nation, they say, struggling to maintain its competitive power cannot afford the luxury of an organized brake upon the power of its government.

Nor is this all. It is significant that our time has seen the first legislation against the trade unions in more than a century. It has seen an urgent movement for the reconstruction of the House of Lords, not simply because, as a form of legislature, that chamber is now an admitted anachronism, but in order, as its proponents have avowed, to provide as strong a safeguard as is available against the success of a socialist government. There has been not only a deliberate and intense effort to revive and extend the prestige of the monarchy; even more significant is the revivification of the theory that the Crown is the guardian of the constitution—a theory which leads straight to the notion that, in a period of crisis, it is the arbiter between parties; a position which, in an emergency, may easily become Bolingbroke's idea of a Patriotic King. For reasons that I shall explore in detail later, the effort to exploit the personality of the monarch is of exceptional importance. It is not only a complete reversal of the classic Whig doctrine so painfully established in the two centuries after the

Revolution of 1688; it is also a recognition that the prestige of the Crown—Bagehot's dignified part of the government—is a weapon of immense contingent value in future political conflicts, a weapon, it must be added, of which all the emphasis is necessarily on the side of the *status quo*. Nor is it in this context irrelevant that a prime minister has warned the Labour Party of the danger it would run if, as a government, it were to follow the advice of those who urge it to make a frontal attack on capitalist foundations. On Lord Baldwin's view, the safety of democratic government in Great Britain seems to involve a willingness on the part of the Labour Party to be an instrument of social reform on the old model. But that is to say that any attempt on its part to attack the foundations of capitalism, even when there is an electoral majority behind that attempt, is to put itself, as a government, outside the understandings upon which the system rests. Once more we are back at the conception of things that cannot "safely" be conceded. We are warned, in fact, that the maintenance of representative government depends upon the willingness of the victor in a general election to respect the private ownership of the means of production. But that, obviously enough, would be the frustration of the whole purpose of such a victory.

"So strong," wrote Bagehot, "are the combative propensities of man, that he would rather fight a losing battle than not fight at all." But it is not at all certain that the mere force of numbers is as decisive in constitutional struggles as he appeared to imagine. The temptation to a party of property to use all its influence, direct and hidden, to rid itself of its opponents in an epoch of challenge appears to be immense. As a rule, it is integrated in opinion, while its foes are divided. The technique of modern administration, moreover, gives it an advantage in initiative and striking power that it would be difficult to overestimate. Its control of the forces of opinion is far greater than that at the disposal of its critics. It has, while it remains a government, the immense advantage that it can abrogate the spirit of representative government under the cloak of constitutional forms; that was an important aspect of Herr Hitler's arrival at power. I am not, of course, maintaining for a moment that the Conservative Party desires to destroy the constitution in its historic form. I am arguing only that men value the forms of government at least as much for what they do as for what they are. It is the results of their operation, as these are translated into their daily lives, which create loyalty to the forms. Men did not go out to battle for an abstract dislike of the royal prerogative under Charles I; it was the result of its operation on merchant and nonconformist which sent them out into the field. Men, similarly, will respect the British constitution so long as they respect what it does. And their respect will be a function of its ability to satisfy their established expectations. Once it begins to fail in this, they begin to doubt the validity of its forms.

That, surely, is the implied presumption of the warning explicitly made in Bagehot's essay. He was sceptical of the extension of the franchise because he did not like what he believed an extended franchise would involve. He was no democrat; and he believed that the wider the foundations of political power, the greater was the chance that ignorance would gain the mastery over reason. For intelligence, in his opinion, stopped broadly with the "successful" classes; the men who had a banking account could alone appreciate the mysterious laws of political economy upon which the welfare of the nation depended. That was why he recommended a combination of those classes to inhibit the thrust to power of the ignorant multitude.

Bagehot wrote in a generation that was still oppressed by the fears of 1848. As those fears faded, men became more reconciled to the notion of a democratic society. They had the confidence which came from an ever-increasing volume of trade. They found that the trade unions could, without undue sacrifice, be reconciled to the foundations of the existing order. Not, perhaps, until the turn of the century was there any revival of the doubts to which Bagehot gave expression. After 1906, they can be detected in an increasing degree as the demands of the working-class begin to be emphatically made. There is a period from 1906 to 1914 in which it seems that, despite critical moments, the alliance between liberalism and labour will keep the latter in safe leading-strings; as late as 1911 Mr. Ramsay MacDonald was discussing the possibilities of coalition with Mr. Lloyd George. But, as we now look back upon those years, it is clear that the unrest of 1911 in industry was not a superficial phenomenon but the index to a deep dissatisfaction on the part of the workers with their material condition. There was a new trade unionism abroad as militant and determined as that which, after the dock strike of 1889, had given birth to the Independent Labour Party. That unrest made any permanent reconciliation between Labour and Liberal capitalism an impossible adventure. For the latter was already deeply involved in those diplomatic difficulties of which the war of 1914 was the outcome. That war ended an epoch; for its result, psychologically intensified by the Russian Revolution, was to breed in the Labour Party a conscious determination for an independent position in the state. Once it had come to this decision, an abyss had opened between itself and the older parties. The question was posed for the first time since 1832 whether the constitution could successfully bridge that abyss without violent disruption.

This is, I think, evident upon any analysis. In no period since 1832 have so many concessions been made to the workers by their masters; in no period, either, has the response to those concessions seemed so unsatisfying. The socialism which, before the war, was hardly more than a pious resolution for conferences, has become, since the peace, an active slogan of battle. Whole areas of territory, the mining districts and the East End of London, for example, have been lost, it appears permanently, to the forces of conservatism. The need to maintain an army of unemployed which has never been less than a million and a half and has risen, in economic crisis, to more than three millions, has put the problems of order and taxation in a new perspective. The growth of

economic nationalism has struck a grave blow at the basis of the
English export trade; that has created special areas of distress in
Great Britain which no government has yet been able seriously
to tackle because, at every point, the vested interests of capitalism
stand in the way. At some point, this is true of all the major economic and social problems of the post-war years—housing, education, cotton, coal, iron and steel, agriculture. In all of them,
the contrast between the demands of labour and the relevant
government action has been grave. If a Conservative government
has been in power, the cause of the contrast has, of course, been
either the conviction that the demands of labour were wrongly
conceived, or, as in the case of mining amalgamations, the inability of a Conservative cabinet to transcend the opposition of
its supporters. If a Labour government has been in office, it has
lacked the power, and so far, at least, perhaps the will, also, to
fight against the refusal of its opponents to accept its solutions.
In the result, while, in all these years, there has been a great mass
of social and economic changes, the constitutional system has
not, save in the single instance of the protective tariff, given rise
to any major reconstruction in the realm of our national life.

The effect of this has, I think, been serious in many ways. In
the first place, it has lowered the prestige of the parliamentary
system in the eyes of the public. A member of Parliament, even,
with rare exceptions, a member of either of the front benches of
the House of Commons, has much less hold upon the interest of
the nation than in the pre-war period. The power of the debates
themselves to influence public opinion has deteriorated also.
They are less fully reported than in the past, with rare exceptions; there has even grown up a section of the public press which
barely attempts to report them at all. I add that this is not, in
my judgment, the result either of a decline in the quality of
members of Parliament or of any diminution in the interest or
significance of the debates themselves. It is rather due to two
things for neither of which can the institution of Parliament be
held responsible. On the one hand, the nature of the subject-

matter with which Parliament has now to deal rarely lends itself to the direct solutions, the dramatic clashes of personality, which were characteristic of the pre-war period. Franchise reform, the principle of national education, Home Rule for Ireland, at least the large outlines of these issues could be seized by every responsible citizen; and then could be dramatized by men like Gladstone and Disraeli so that they appeared an intimate part of everyone's life. As soon as an issue capable of being so seized by the public emerges—the Revised Prayer Book, divorce-law reform, the Hoare-Laval proposals—it makes the House of Commons at once the centre of the national interest.

The second cause is related to the first. Most of the questions now discussed by Parliament are of a quasi-technical character. Their very nature does not lend itself either to dramatic debate or to simplicity of journalistic interpretation. The details of a tariff schedule, the principles of a derating scheme, the terms of a subsidy to agriculture or shipping, these affect, by their character, less a general than a specialized public; their inherent news value is profoundly affected thereby. To get into the press, therefore, they need the accompaniment of some external incident; otherwise they are crowded from the page by the superior interest of a dramatic murder, the presence in London of a famous film star, or the newest excitement in a dictatorial country. The result is the important one not only that politics is not the staple of popular discussion in the proportion that obtained in the Victorian age; the result is that the public is less interested in politics because, partly, it is less educated by immersion in the political process, and partly because it is less able to follow the results of a body of legislation less easily susceptible of discussion than in the past. A Parliament which is to interest an electorate of thirty millions must deal with objects that will arouse their attention. It has rarely been able to do so in the post-war years. For, if it did, it would be dealing with the foundations of the national life, and it is a major object of the Conservative Party to prevent such an effort; while in so far as the Labour Party seeks to deal with such issues, being in a minority, the result is a foregone conclusion when the division is taken. The result of a debate has little popular interest when it is a foregone conclusion.

A further fact has contributed to the decline in the status of Parliament. It is, necessarily, a far more overburdened body than in the past, because the area of its activities is so much wider. The result is a great increase in the governmental control of its processes. The initiative of the private member has diminished. The intensity of party organization has increased. Practically all political bills of any importance now emanate from the Cabinet; and the pressure on the time of the House of Commons is so great that the process of debate must be rigorously controlled. This means two things. It means, first, that, with exceptions I shall note later, the House of Commons has largely been transformed into an organ of registration for the will of the Cabinet; it means, secondly, that party discipline, owing to the exigencies of the situation, is now so strict that only when a minority government is in office is there any serious likelihood of a government's being compelled to resign or dissolve on defeat there. The contrast between this position and that of Parliament before the war is striking. It means that its processes are much less dramatic because the results there effected are, from a spectacular point of view, much less impressive. Governments are now made and unmade by public opinion outside the House of Commons rather than by parliamentary opinion inside it. In those circumstances, the picture painted by Bagehot of its impact on mid-Victorian opinion could hardly be true of our own time.

I emphasize the view that this is not a consequence of any inherent defect in the system itself. A Parliament with great principles to debate will still debate greatly; a Parliament that so acts as to jeopardize the existence of a government will still arouse widespread interest. In either case, it will create intense discussion outside; and that process of public education which is one of Parliament's most important functions will be resumed. It is notable that when the Labour governments were in office, both

in 1924 and 1929–31, the galleries and the lobbies of the House
were thronged with interested crowds; and it is worth remarking
that few elections have been able to attract meetings so numerous or so full as those of 1929 or 1931 when it was realized that
momentous issues hung upon the result. The same is true, it is
worth adding, of the Popular Front elections in France in 1936
and of the Blum chamber which followed on it; and the general
truth it implies is emphasized once more by the fact that the
drama of the Roosevelt experiment has created more interest in
the proceedings of the American Congress than at any time in its
history since the Civil War.

The inference, I think, is clear. Parliamentary government, to
retain its hold, must give the promise of great results. If it fails
to do so, the electorate will look elsewhere for them. Nothing is
more dangerous in a democratic state than a condition in which
the people is persuaded that the fundamental instruments of its
government are not equal to the tasks imposed upon them. A
habit of lethargy is thereby induced which easily persuades a
people to lend a ready ear to the siren voices of dictatorship. This
is especially true in a time like our own. For we have reached the
stage where the parties of the Right deny the premises upon
which the politics of the Left are conducted. The result of that
division is simple. When capitalist democracy is challenged, it
has to be enormously successful in the economic sphere if it is to
maintain its authority. For the contrast it provides between its
economic and its political configuration of power is, at best, a
startling one. To maintain the loyalties of men it must be able
continuously to satisfy their hopes. It must, that is to say, be capable of one of two things. Either the possessing class by which
it is controlled must be willing to tax itself on a constantly aug-
menting scale for the benefit of the masses, or its volume of
production must so constantly expand as to make possible an ever-
greater standard of life for the ordinary wage-earner. This second alternative, obviously, must be achieved on the basis of at
least a maintenance of that level of profit which persuades the

capitalist to perform his function. If either of these alternatives fails, the power of the capitalist system adequately to exploit the forces of production is then stricken at its base; and no system is likely long to survive which produces the spectacle for the masses of a poverty which is not their own fault suffered in the midst of a potential plenty to which access is not possible under the system. They are then bound ultimately to consider whether that system itself is not the cause of the dissatisfactions from which they believe themselves to suffer. In those circumstances it is in the long run inevitable that they should turn to the party that advocates a change in the system itself.

Something like this, at least, is the condition in which we find ourselves; and it is important to think of its repercussions upon the economic basis of parliamentary government. For the parties of the Right such a change implies not merely a surrender of great privileges. It implies also the acceptance of a transformation which they have been taught by two and a half centuries of power to be fatal to the national welfare. They regard the good of the nation as bound up with their own good. Their defeat would be, accordingly, such a hazard of vital principles as to make impossible the old continuities of governmental policy upon which the parliamentary system has been built. They cannot be neutral in such a contest, when they believe that all they have and are is being called into jeopardy. At the best, they will lose that confidence in the government which is always the condition of a successful transition from one economic system to another. At the worst, they may hold the right of the government to make such changes one that they cannot permit without challenge. The first mood leads directly to what is nothing less than sabotage of the government. Investment halts, business is withheld; the economic strain leads to a growing exacerbation of temper. In that mood, for a government to go on with its programme is a challenge to its opponents unlikely to promote the spirit of compromise. In that mood, also, for it to withdraw is to admit that, whatever the will of the electoral majority, the owners of economic power are the permanent masters of the constitution. For it then becomes obvious that they are, by reason of that ownership, in a position to dictate the possible limits of change. The state is their state, and its supreme coercive power can be directed only to those objects of which they are willing to approve.

The second mood, not less obviously, leads directly to civil war. It is the policy of Franco, who refuses to abide by an electoral decision on the ground that its results are impossible to contemplate. It is ridiculous to argue that such a condition is unthinkable in a country with the political traditions of Great Britain. It is exactly such a condition that, in the Home Rule controversy of 1912–14, Sir Edward Carson deliberately organized with the full and conscious assent of the Conservative Party. He built and munitioned an army, not hesitating to seek the assistance of a foreign power for its equipment. He jeopardized the loyalty of the British army. He compelled the surrender of Parliament to the will of the forces he represented as the alternative to civil war. What was possible over a relatively minor controversy like Ulster is certainly not impossible over a major controversy like the foundations of the economic system. Once more, it is necessary to affirm that the strength of parliamentary government is exactly measured by the unity of political parties upon its fundamental objects. Once that unity is broken, the fragility of the assumptions upon which it rests is even more obvious than it was when the Reform Act of 1867 awakened Bagehot to their implications. No subject is so likely to break down the barriers of mutual self-restraint as property; and what has now moved into the foreground of debate is the rights that attach to its possession.

2

The British constitution, moreover, is the expression of a politically democratic government; it is not the expression of a democratic society. The implications of that distinction are important. In Great Britain not only is there a contradiction between our economic power and our political power; what Mr. Tawney has called "our religion of inequality" has made a contradiction between our political democracy and the hierarchical character of our social system. It is, no doubt, true that wealth in Great Britain can purchase for itself access to the highest social place. But it is also true that, save for a favoured few, any serious approach to equality of opportunity does not exist. There are barriers in the way of ascent to the highest places in the state which the possession of ability alone is not sufficient to overpass.

There is little approximation to equality in educational opportunity, and that means that the main positions in the state are closed to the great mass of the nation. Access to them is largely a function of parental circumstance. Whether it be the law or the civil service, the armed forces of the Crown or the professions, the conditions of entrance to them are a heavy tax upon all not born into the middle or the upper class. Anyone who studies the composition of boards of directors in public companies, or appointments to such bodies as Royal Commissions, the British Broadcasting Corporation, the London Passenger Transport Board, will see that, for the most part, working-class representation is virtually excluded from them. It is the same with important positions within the Empire or in British embassies abroad. It is the same with membership of the House of Lords. Even in the House of Commons, the average age of membership in the Conservative Party is less by ten years than that of the Labour Party; that is the price of the struggle the working-class has to endure. It is particularly notable that in the hundred years which have passed since the Reform Bill of 1832 not half a dozen working-men have been chosen by the Conservative Party to represent it in Parliament.

Nor is this confined to politics and industry. It is true, also, of the state church; in 1937 all but one of the bench of bishops were educated in the great English public schools. It is true of the whole machinery of the Palace: the entire surrounding atmosphere of its operation denies the essential thesis of democracy. The universities will recognize distinction in politics or scholarship; they will hasten to bestow their doctorates on rich benefactors. But there have not been half a dozen occasions in a century when service to the working-class has been a passport to an honorary degree. Anyone, moreover, who studies the honours list will realize that, direct service to the state apart, what is really recognized there is the inherent right of wealth to position; the modern House of Lords reads like a summary of the *Directory of Directors*. And perhaps the profoundest irony of it all is when we are asked to view with admiration the occasional visit of a member of the Royal Family to some working-class area or institution; or to perceive in a holiday-camp where sons of workers mingle for a brief fortnight with public school boys the proof that class-barriers have broken down.

No doubt there has been a real change in social temper these past hundred years; the reader of Dickens and Thackeray, Trollope and Meredith, can perceive a significant movement of opinion in a democratic direction. The status of the aristocracy is far less important now than then; though it would be legitimate to argue that the real change is the enhanced status of the plutocracy as such in its place. Oxford and Cambridge are no longer places where the sons of the wealthy only are trained. The scholarship system brings the children of the working-class to the universities, even to Oxford and Cambridge, who would not have made their way there fifty or even thirty years ago; there is far less chance than there was of a tragedy like Jude's. But here certain things must be remembered. The percentage of working-class children who get the opportunity of that secondary education which is the necessary passport to the university is pitifully small; the demand for economy makes it still smaller. It has, for example, shrunk appreciably since the call of 1931 for "equality of sacrifice." And evidence goes plainly to show that the barriers which exist are largely unrelated to natural differences of ability;

they are, rather, the result of the reimposition of traditional differentials upon successive generations. Bad housing, weak health, defective nutrition, out-of-date school buildings, excessively large classes, uncertificated teachers, all these represent denials of opportunity to the workers' children.

| The result of this situation can be put quite simply. Our society is, overwhelmingly, what Mr. Tawney has called an acquisitive society, and its main governmental apparatus is in the hands of those who have been themselves successful in acquisition. It is they who determine what the state shall do with its power. It is they who examine the needs of our society and decide to which of those needs, and in what degree, response shall be made. Very largely, indeed, the workers have to trust their ability imaginatively to enter into conditions of life of which they have, quite naturally, no first-hand knowledge. Almost all of them enjoy security and a standard of living far beyond anything the great mass of the workers is likely to know. Almost all of them, also, enjoy that security and that standard by reason of the circumstances into which they were born. They tend, therefore, not only to think differently of the foundations of our society from those over whom they rule; because they are, so to say, the conquerors, they tend to believe also that the system is justified merely on the ground that they are the conquerors. The implications of the idea of equality cast no shadow of serious scepticism over their social horizons. They are Bagehot's "better" class; they expect to receive—it should be added that they largely do receive—respect and deference from their inferiors. It is not unnatural for them to infer from their experience that the rejection of their social philosophy is the outcome either of ignorance of the "natural" laws of social organization or of envy from the defeated at the higher return to superior talent.

And all the emphasis of our social life is used to impose this point of view on the masses. In the large contours of its substance, our educational system is nothing so much as a gigantic training in habits of obedience. The press, the cinema, the thea-

tre, the church are all, in their total effect, agencies used for a
similar purpose. They invest, for example, the inept routine of
what is called the life of "society" with a glamour intended to
conceal the price the masses have to pay for its fantastic cere-
monies. They teach them to believe in the obligation to show
gratitude to their industrial masters. They convey the impression that all industrial unrest is not the revolt of sober-minded
working-men against conditions too often intolerable, but the
work of "agitators" betraying their pathetic victims. They make
heroes of working-class leaders who desert the socialist movement. They utilize every rare instance of working-class ascent to
their own ranks to misrepresent the proportions in which the
career is open to the talented. They fight fiercely against every
scheme of social reform; a century ago Bentham listed the whole
armoury of fallacies they employ in defence of their privileges.
Their whole outlook is still based upon the notion that the problem of poverty is insoluble even while they boast that capitalism
has given to man an undreamed-of control over nature. They
believe in their hearts that their wealth is justified, in part as a
return to their talent, and, in part, by reason of the charity they
so gracefully confer.

Yet in their hearts they hate and fear the poor. Nothing is
so striking in our civilization as this one inexpugnable fact. It
emerges in every great strike. It emerges, also, in the constantly
reiterated belief that unemployment is the outcome of defective
character. It emerges in the professionalization of charity, and it
lies at the base of the philosophy of bodies like the Charity Or-
ganisation Society. It can be seen in the widespread belief that
there is too much education, or that our education is too "literary"
in character; it has even been urged by an eminent Dean that
our national education system must have gone too far, since it
has begun to enable the children of the working-class to compete
with the children of the privileged. It can be seen in the attempt
to draw a distinction between "safe" and "unsafe" trade-union
leaders. It was not a socialist but Mr. Gladstone who said that

"when the people of this country is silent, you say they are contented; when they are disorderly, you say you must not yield to violence." "Our streets," Mr. Shaw has written, "are fuller of feuds than the Highlands or the Arabian desert." It is so because our religion of inequality breeds fear and hate and envy. There is goodwill, but there is not justice; and there is an uneasy feeling abroad that the denial of its justice is increasingly apparent to the multitude.

We cannot understand the parliamentary system in Great Britain unless we recognize that, beneath the appearance of democracy, this is the economic and social system it is intended to uphold. It was made by the owners of the instruments of production in the interest of their property; and the safeguarding of their conception of their rights is inherent in all the rules by which it moves. It has been compelled to confer the franchise upon the masses; it has been careful to maintain for property the substance of effective authority. For those who own decide what shall be produced, and their claim to rent and interest and profit is, as it is satisfied, the chief thing that determines the way in which we live. Without the power to command property, the citizen has nothing but his labour-power to sell. Whether he shall work or no is settled not by his will, but by the decision of the employer as to whether there is profit in his employment. He cannot demand work. If he does so alone, he is helpless. If he does so in concert with others, he is threatening the structure of law and order; and the coercive power of the state will be used to bring him to his senses. What we mean by bringing him to his senses is that he is compelled by force to recognize the rights of property. This recognition is called the will of the people.

But all this is to say that a political democracy which rests upon capitalist foundations has war, open or secret, in its midst. The distribution of wealth is deemed unsatisfactory. Capitalists are always striking to maintain what they have; the workers are always pressing to obtain more. That is why each demand of the workers for a higher standard of life is first of all rejected, on the ground that it is impossible, and then, if it is urged with sufficient strength, as a rule grudgingly conceded in part. So it has been with factory regulation, with safety in the mines, with the hours of labour, with the establishment of a minimum wage. Nor has this resistance been confined to the purely economic relations of master and man. It has affected, also, the social relationships of rich and poor. The former have resented the need to tax themselves for measures like education, public health, facilities for recreation. One has only to watch the habits of rich taxpayers when some large municipal amenity is proposed to realize that for them it is psychologically impossible to understand why the state should provide for the poor services that their property enables them to purchase for themselves. The historic environment has so accustomed them to assume that the poor must remain poor as almost to compel them to resent provision which mitigates their poverty.

As I have said, the system worked well enough so long as it was in a condition of expansion. The problem for parliamentary government is what is to happen when, as now appears certain, the period of expansion is drawing to its close. The necessary effect of this is to exacerbate that latent war which lies at the heart of this society. The search for profit becomes increasingly more difficult. Concentration of capital becomes ever more intense. Technological revolution, with its multiplication of the unemployed, is quickened by the need to reduce the costs of labour in a competitive economic market. The balance of agriculture and industry is disturbed. The necessity to protect the home producer, with its consequent impact upon the export trades, develops increasingly. The power to produce rapidly outdistances the power to distribute, since the massive inequality of incomes involves an inability in the poor to meet the costs of purchase. And since, year by year, also, technological change increases at a revolutionary rate the productive power of our machines, the deliberate organization of scarcity becomes a necessary feature of the system. We adopt, on all hands, a deliberate policy of restriction-quotas and the like. But the inevitable result of this is an increase of price, and the consequence of that increase is a demand for higher wages in order to offset a threatened decline in the standard of living. Within the ambit of the capitalist system, there is no way of breaking this vicious circle save by the discovery, either at home or abroad, of new markets capable of the profitable absorption of our productivity. But, on any considerable scale, the poverty of the masses makes this impossible at home; let us remember that in Great Britain nearly ten million people spend a shilling less per week on food than the minimum laid down by the British Medical Association as required for reasonable physical existence. The conquest of markets abroad is possible, but that, as we have grimly learned, involves the international rivalry of states. They have to be strong in order to safeguard their markets, and their access to them, whether actual or potential. They arm in order to be strong. This has two inescapable results. On the one hand, it means a scale of taxation which inhibits the state from embarking upon alternative schemes of social reform; on the other, it means a competition in armaments which breeds distrust and insecurity. At the end of that grim highroad lies war.

Now parliamentary government, as I have said, involves the principle that citizens can settle their political differences by the compromises of consent. It assumes not only that they are rational creatures; it assumes also that they discuss their differences by accepting the same premisses of discussion. There is no great difficulty in achieving that result so long as everyone can see that the society steadily satisfies the wants of its members. There is profound difficulty in achieving it when there is serious division within and the threat of war without. The division within means that the contrasts of an unequal society do not appear just to those who believe themselves excluded from its benefits. The threat of war from without means the need in the society to organize itself for a defence the technical preparations for which are likely in the long run to sharpen the very divisions that provoke disunity. The power of reason to survive in this atmosphere is not likely to be great. The social tensions are such that what in an earlier period appeared abstract arguments now appear as threats to public order. Passions begin to rise. What seemed harmless becomes, in the context of passion, a danger to the wonted routines. And because the power of the state is behind those routines passion drives its possessors to its exercise. They seek to control those elements in society which threaten the routine; if, as in Germany and Italy, the passion drives hard enough, they seek to suppress them. But those elements are precisely the ones which, under a democratic parliamentary system, arise naturally to defend the interests of the working-class—trade unions, socialist parties, even the co-operative movement. With their suppression, of course, the foundations of parliamentary government are undermined. The society is, as it were, in a state of siege. No society in that condition is ever amenable to the claims of reason upon which a parliamentary system depends.

This may be conveniently put in terms of an historical generalization. A democratic political system will always seek, in the long run, to become a democratic society. It will seek, that is, such a distribution of reward as will recognize either equality of claim or such differentiations in the claim as can prove their relevance to a conception of justice framed in terms of an insistent drive to equality. At the outset, its attack will be upon those privileges of status, birth, religion, race, most easily recognizable as unjust in terms of that conception. Formally, at least, it will have little difficulty in securing their surrender. But it will then discover that the real source of privilege remains even when these have been destroyed. It will learn as, very notably, the United States of America is learning, that merely to abolish the privileges of feudalism is in no sense to create an equal society. It will discover that the real source of privilege lies in the private ownership of the means of production, that this compels a system of class-relations incompatible with its notion of justice. It will accept those class-relations just so long as, but only so long as, they directly and measurably satisfy the social demands they encounter. But so soon as those demands no longer appear to them capable of satisfaction at a level they deem adequate, they will seek to abolish that private ownership of the means of production as the direct and essential cause of the dissatisfactions they experience. Because the political system is democratic, they will seek to use its authority to effect this transformation. The alternatives they then pose to the owners of economic power are either abdication from ownership or the forcible destruction of the democratic basis upon which the political system rests. The state then assumes the form, in fact, of a capitalist dictatorship to inhibit the transformation it is sought to effect.

Clearly enough, in formal terms, the British constitution provides all the necessary avenues to achieve this transformation peacefully. But every political democracy that is based upon the principle of inequality in matters of social and economic structure encounters a difficulty here from which Great Britain is no more free than any other country. It is the difficulty that those who benefit by the inequality are so wedded to its righteousness that they tend to prefer to fight for it rather than surrender its advantages. They do not do so, let me insist, from any selfish motives. They do so because long tradition has accustomed them to a conception of justice in which the idea of economic equality has no place. They have the assurance of their achievements behind them. They have the conviction of their right to rule that is born of the age-long exercise of their right. They have the knowledge of the degree to which, even when defeated at the polls, they remain in psychological possession of the governmental apparatus of the country. They are driven by the passionate conviction that the transformation proposed is fatal not only to them, but fatal, also, to those with whose well-being they believe themselves to be charged. They are aware that attempts at such transformation have been defeated, even easily defeated, elsewhere. They have seen the immense cost at which the Russian Revolution has established a socialist system. In this background, it is at least thinkable that they will refuse to abdicate peacefully from their power.

It is important in this context to notice how many and how profound are the doubts of a democratic society in this epoch of crisis. We are warned of its fragility; we are told that of all forms of government it is the most difficult. It is suggested that there is too much interest in politics on the part of the masses; if they were freed from the pressure of this interest, their minds would be set free for higher things like the service of religion. It is argued that the complexity of modern phenomena makes control by experts ever more essential, as though the problems of valuation involved in the co-ordination of governmental problems were matters in which the public judgment was no longer valid. Or we are told of the enormous importance of liberty, which is, somehow, held to be incompatible with increasing government control; and we are informed that we shall all be deprived of our freedom unless a halt is called to this development. That in this view is the implication that government must interfere no further with the rights of private property is rarely openly affirmed; but, on analysis, it always appeals that the safeguarding of private ownership is what the advocates of this attitude have in view. Some critics, such as the Lord Chief Justice of England, emphasize the dangers of bureaucracy; by which, on analysis again, they are found in fact to mean that social reform must work in the leading-strings of those individualist principles evolved by the Common Law.

The temper, in short, that is emerging is one that is sceptical of democratic methods because it dislikes democratic ends. It was prepared for democratic government so long as certain fundamental interests were not touched by its evolving demands. As soon as these were brought into question, it was prepared at once to revise its views of the validity of the democratic hypothesis. That is evident in many ways. It is seen in the very different treatment meted out by British policy to the Soviet Union, on the one hand, and to Hitler and Mussolini on the other. It is seen in the implications of Sir Samuel Hoare's notorious phrase that the struggle between the Spanish constitutional government and General Franco was "a faction fight" in which we as a nation had no interest; it must be rare, since 1815, that a British minister has announced our indifference to the results of a struggle between democracy and privilege. The fact is that since the war our foreign policy is largely unintelligible save as the expression of a determination to discourage all movements abroad which, seeking democratic emancipation, have been driven to recognize that the vested interests of property are the main obstacles in its path; and that discouragement has been enthusiastically welcomed by the propertied class of this country. They show a lack of self-confidence, a tendency to panic, a fear of fundamental examination, like nothing so much as the attitude with which Burke greeted the French Revolution. When a world congress of churchmen urges the need for ecclesiastical bodies to think of the relation of the Christian religion to social problems, it is admonished by the *Times* to remember that the true business of religion is faith and not works. "A world conference," it said, "of Christians might have been better employed in pondering specifically religious subjects, instead of devoting much of its time to political and economic issues." [1] Christianity is held even by its Conservative votaries to be a way of life. There is need, wrote Lord Salisbury, who, as a former leader of the Conservative Party in the House of Lords, can hardly be suspected of unfriendly feelings for private ownership, "for a pledge of loyalty to apply under God's guidance the spirit and principles of Christ to individual conduct, and to every department of social and national and international life." But in the judgment of the *Times* this "pledge of loyalty" is out of place when it deals with "political and economic issues." These, in its judgment, have seemingly no place in a Christian way of life.

We are being prepared, in short, for a break in our habituation

[1] London *Times*, August 2, 1937.

to the idea of political democracy. Its results are not what were expected. Our possessing class is not ready, as Matthew Arnold pleaded with them to be ready, to "choose equality and flee greed." At a time when the need for rational examination of fundamentals is perhaps more necessary than at any time since the Reformation, a temper is developing which gravely threatens the power of reason to maintain its empire. There is growing up a resistence to the idea that a democracy may examine the foundations of property. On the economic field, the owners of property consider sabotage and even resistance justified. On the political field, they consider at least the possibility of refurbishing ancient weapons of constitutional controversy, the power of the Lords, the influence of the Crown, in the hope that this will postpone, and perhaps destroy, the victory of socialist principles. And all this is accompanied by incessant propaganda intended to convince the masses that their own ruin is involved in that victory. That the prophecy may not be falsified, preparation is made for the catastrophe.

There is a vital relevance in all this to the central problems of parliamentary government. For I must insist, once more, that its power to be effective depends not merely upon its methods; it depends also upon agreement upon the objects to which those methods shall be devoted. Disagreement is of minor importance when it is concerned with minor things; it is vital when it moves into the region of foundations. For then men who are led to question what the constitution is doing are led very rapidly to question the validity of the constitution itself. And where the constitution involved is, like that of Great Britain, in itself an infinitely complex thing, a matter of understandings and ideas and sentiments that are always half articulate rather than explicitly expressed, the danger that it may be abused is great. We who have seen what judicial construction can do with a constitution so much simpler than ours, as is the constitution of the United States, can never risk the separation of its underlying theory from its actual functioning. It is a dynamic thing, the instrument of a struggle for power, between opposing parties. As an instrument, it becomes what it can be made to do; and this, in its turn, depends upon what those who operate its principles think it ought to be made to do in the special set of circumstances with which they are confronted. They will have, in those circumstances, an end they wish to serve; and they will normally and naturally assume that the way they make the constitution serve that end is "constitutional." It is from this angle that we must examine the "conventions of the constitution" as the necessary basis for any real understanding of parliamentary government.

3

The conventions of the constitution, Edmund Burke has written, "determine the manner in which the rules of law, which they presuppose, are applied, so that they are, in fact, the motive power of the constitution. In the second place, these conventions are always directed to secure that the constitution works in practice in accordance with the prevailing constitutional theory of the time." But, obviously, the "prevailing constitutional theory of the time" is a very concrete thing. Men work the constitution to make it attain certain ends they deem desirable; the theory is the expression of those ends. "The association of constitutional conventions with law," write the authors of a classic report, "has long been familiar in the history of the British Commonwealth . . . it has permeated both executive and legislative power. It has provided a means of harmonizing relations where a purely legal solution of practical problems was impossible, would have impaired free development, or would have failed to catch the spirit which gives life to institutions. Such conventions take their place among the constitutional principles which are in practice regarded as binding and sacred whatever the powers of Parliaments may in theory be."

But men regard constitutional principles as "binding and sacred" because they accept the ends they are intended to secure.

Will they so regard them if they are doubtful about those ends? It is a convention of the constitution that the standing orders of the House must be so worked as to give full protection in debate to the Opposition. That convention, clearly, depends solely on the will of the majority; in a time of profound crisis nothing would be easier than their suspension. Most of the conventions are vague in form and imprecise in substance. They depend for their life upon the agreement of parties to the way in which they should be worked. Let that agreement be once withdrawn, and no Opposition will doubt that their interpretation by the Government is "unconstitutional." For it is certainly untrue to argue, as Dicey argued, that they must be ultimately obeyed because, otherwise, their violation would produce a breach of the law. The Army Act need not be passed annually in order to compel a summons of Parliament each year. Financial provision for national services could easily be made for two years instead of one. Even a defeated government could remain in office, once it had passed its financial legislation and the bills relating to the discipline of the defence forces, for almost a year. It is because circumstances have continued to make these conventions seem "binding and sacred"—that is, convenient to the objects of the government which observes them—that they are respected.

Consider certain other conventions, more delicate in their nature than those to which I have referred. It is a convention of the constitution that the Cabinet is collectively responsible to Parliament for its acts; that convention was found inconvenient by the National Government in 1931; it was temporarily abrogated, despite the protests of the Opposition, by the "agreement to differ." It is a convention that the King should act only on the advice of his ministers. Does this mean that he must accept whatever advice they proffer, so long as they can persuade the House of Commons to approve that advice? Or does it mean that a King who disapproved of the advice given by one set of ministers could appeal to others to form a government and seek to obtain, by means of a dissolution, electoral approval for his action? There is no agreement upon the point among the authorities. It is certain that a government with an assured majority that was dismissed in such circumstances would regard the King's action as unconstitutional; it is certain, also, that the new ministers would, by the mere implication of accepting office, have taken an antithetic view of constitutionality. The very fact that we do not know the limits of the royal power, that it can remain to be invoked on one side or the other in the twilight zone of crisis, sufficiently indicates the difficulties of the position. For it is certain that the limits of the prerogative would be judged, not on the precedents, which are doubtful by their antiquity, but by the approval or disapproval by citizens of the purpose for which the prerogative was invoked. Let us remember that in 1936 Mr. Baldwin's opposition to the marriage of the Duke of Windsor led a section of opinion to urge on Edward VIII the desirability of a change in government; it was only the self-restraint of the King, and the firm agreement with Mr. Baldwin of the Labour Party, which prevented a constitutional crisis of the first magnitude. Yet that firmness of agreement and that self-restraint may easily be absent on the next occasion when relations between the Crown and its ministers are strained.

Precedents, in short, do not establish conventions unless it is beyond cavil that all persons who may be bound by them will regard themselves as so bound. They are unlikely to regard themselves as bound if they feel really passionately about the purposes to which they become bound as the result of operating the convention. That is, I think, clear from the experience of the controversy over the Parliament Act of 1911; it is clear, also, from the experience of the conflict over Home Rule in 1914. In neither case was the issue pushed to a decisive constitutional choice. But in each case it is clear that we were dwelling within narrow margins which might easily have precipitated disaster. Or, take the crisis of 1936. Suppose that Mr. Attlee had accepted an invitation from Edward VIII to form a new Cabinet and, after a dissolution, proved successful at the polls. Would that have meant that the King was entitled to appeal from his ministers to the country whenever he could find men willing to accept responsibility for his dissent from the policy of their predecessors? Such a view would soon come to mean that the effective pivot of constitutional action was in the hands of those able to shape the mind and will of the King. It would, obviously, be a pivot transcending that party structure which is now the real dynamic of the constitution. It would be bound to receive passionate opposition from those not included in the circle able to influence the royal mind. Sooner or later it would mean that the major political battle would be concentrated upon the limits of the royal power. But that is to discuss the responsibility of the Crown; and its irresponsibility is a dogma of the constitution simply because, as we know it, it is workable only on the assumption that the Crown is neutral in all disputes of a political character.

Or let us take the convention which determines the relation of the two Houses of Parliament. These are now governed by the Parliament Act of 1911; and, within its framework, that statute has rendered obsolete the convention noted by Dicey, "the understanding—a very vague one at best—that in case of a permanent conflict between the will of the House of Commons and the will of the House of Lords, the Peers must at some point give way to the Lower House." That point is now defined by the two years mentioned in the Parliament Act. But that period still leaves great room for conflict. It is not easy to imagine that a Labour government, flushed with success at the polls, would be willing to see its essential measures hamstrung for two years by a chamber which it regards as nothing more than the reserve power of the Conservative Party. Or, let us suppose that a Labour government attains power under conditions of financial urgency akin to those of 1931. Let us suppose that the emergency powers it proposes to take to deal with the situation are not approved by the City of London. It is at least uncertain that it would be able to secure the co-operation of the Peers in obtaining those powers. If it did not, it would be bound—is, indeed, by its programme committed—to ask for the creation of a sufficient number of peers to override any possible opposition in the Upper Chamber. Is it certain that it would obtain the right to their creation? Is it not possible that it would meet a demand, by way, for instance, of a second general election, for an assurance that the will of the country was on its side? And is it not clear that in so strained a situation as this, the exacerbation of party temper would perhaps prohibit, and certainly make difficult, any agreement between the government and the opposition as to what exactly the convention is that governs the relations between the two Houses?

In the usual sense, it is clear enough that the "fundamental liberties" of Englishmen are not in themselves a part of our constitutional conventions. But it is certainly an assumption of parliamentary government upon which, ultimately, all its conventions rest, that the minority must be protected in its rights from outrage by the majority. In that sense, at any rate, the safeguarding of "fundamental liberties" is an important constitutional problem. The issue is twofold. It is, in part, the issue of leaving ideas so free that the government which prevails is a government of opinion; and it is in part the problem of so defining "free" as to secure agreement upon its substance from all parties.

That is a far more difficult matter than it appears to be upon the surface. Legally, we have no fundamental rights in Great Britain; we trust for their protection to the ordinary constitutional machinery of the state. And, in quiet times, we need not doubt that such protection is ample for all necessary purposes. The problem lies in the fact that in periods of rapid social change, the substance of what appears fundamental to one sort of opinion does not appear to be fundamental to another. No one argues that freedom of speech, or meeting, or association is unlimited; for at some point the absence of limitation is incompatible with public order. Freedom of speech, for instance, cannot mean, as Mr. Justice Holmes pointed out, the right to cry "fire" in a crowded theatre. Freedom of association cannot mean the right to form an armed body for the forcible overthrow of the government. There are limits; and those limits are, in fact, defined by the government's view of where these should be drawn. In this country the enjoyment of those rights is the exhibition of one of those paradoxes characteristic of our public life. For, on the one hand, the limitations of the law are severe, while, on the other, there is a tacit understanding that the limitations of the law shall not be enforced. The law, as Dr. Jennings has pointed out, is, for the most part, a legacy from the days "when the country was governed by a small section of the population, and when the 'lower orders' had no function but to obey." It represents the expression by that "small section" of what it thought its needs to be if it was to have power enough to maintain itself against challenge.

In an epoch of tranquillity, the legislation, by common consent, has not been used. Its ambit is extraordinarily wide. "It is sedition," writes Dr. Jennings, "to endeavour to degrade the King in the esteem of his subjects, or to create discontent or disaffection, or to incite the people to tumult, violence, and disorder, or to bring the Government or Constitution into hatred and contempt, or to effect any change in the laws by the recommendation of physical force. . . . A combination of persons to effect this object is a seditious conspiracy; and an assembly at which such statements are made is an unlawful assembly." To all this must be added the immense police control over public speeches and meetings, the power to control processions, even, where the Home Secretary or a Chief Constable thinks it desirable, to forbid them for a stated period in some given district, and the right, under a statute of 1361, to order any person to find sureties not merely for his own good behaviour but also for that of persons who may not be under his control; there is the recent case of Mr. Tom Mann, who was sent to prison for a refusal to find sureties even though the magistrate admitted that he had been guilty of no offence. Trade union action has been deliberately made more difficult by

the Trade Union Law Amendment Act of 1927, the first legislation since 1825 intended to interfere with the freedom of the
workers. The defence forces and the police were thought, before
1934, to be already safeguarded against the danger of disaffection by propaganda; but a statute of that year now contains provisions so wide that it may legitimately be argued that it would
be an offence against the act to make a pacific speech in such a
military area as Aldershot; certainly it would be difficult to say
that a speech which there urged the absolute duty of non-
resistance would not be such an offence. It was long ago admitted by Dicey that, as the law now stands, normal political
controversy is permissible only because the government does not
seek to enforce the law.

It is not, I think, a sufficient answer to its implications to say
either that no government would seek that enforcement unless
it went out of its mind, or that the accused would always have,
if he so wished, the protection of a jury. For the answer to the
first point is, quite simply, that in times of serious strain governments do go out of their minds; and the answer to the second
is that a jury, in such cases, is almost always a collection of very
conventional people asked to judge the conduct of people who
are likely by mere definition to hold unconventional opinions.
The cases, moreover, are likely to be tried by judges whose unconscious assumption is that the holding of extreme opinions in
the political realm is undesirable; the student of *R. v. Pollitt*
will not be tempted to infer that judicial independence is the
same thing as judicial impartiality. Judges, in at least the past
hundred years, have had an enormous influence upon the ver-
dicts of juries. It is certainly difficult not to feel, granted the
nature of the jury-system, that a government sufficiently panic-
stricken to enforce the law will, in all human probability, be able
to obtain the sort of panic-stricken juries it requires.

But even this is not all. For a government, after all, presumably commands a majority in the House of Commons. If
it is stricken with panic, there is at least a likelihood that its

supporters there will show the same sense of panic too. There is no limit to the law-making power of Parliament, and a disturbed government may easily mean legislation without limit against the "fundamental liberties" of Englishmen. A defence of the realm act could control all the usual forms of propaganda upon which the critics of the government rely. The latter, moreover, has in its hands the immense new weapon of broadcasting. Thereby it could create a state of tension without limit in public opinion, without its opponents' being able to command any comparable weapon of response. There is no limit, in short, to the penalties upon opinion a government in a panic may not be capable of imposing; and, when the panic has passed, all the blunders committed by it or its agents are pretty sure to be wiped out, like the blunder of *Ex parte O'Brien,* by an act of indemnity. Certainly there is no occasion on which such an act has been refused these past hundred years.

It is not a satisfactory answer to the prospect of these possibilities to say that they are in a high degree unlikely, that a British cabinet does not lose its head, that the political genius of the nation prevents an abuse of such powers. A British cabinet loses its head just like any other cabinet when it is subjected to unwonted strains. Pitt after 1792, Sidmouth after 1815, both became responsible for reckless suppression; and the political genius of the nation in neither experience prevented the commission of grave injustices. The reactionary temper of those periods was part of a universal movement in which war and economic repression were the outcome of the revolutionary psychological changes induced by the French Revolution. The propertied class was everywhere alarmed, and it used the authority of the state to safeguard itself not merely from violent challenge, but also from any effective discussion of the economic postulates to which it owed its power.

The Russian Revolution has had on our own day a psychological influence at least as great as that of the French Revolution a century and a half ago. Like its predecessors, it has thrown the

propertied class into a panic; its members have become persuaded
that ideas and voluntary associations, which they once regarded
with indifference, now constitute a challenge to their privileges.
They move out to battle against them exactly as in the earlier
time; old-time Jacobin has become new-time Bolshevik and he
is similarly suppressed in the name of law and order. But by
these terms are meant not a framework of principles in application for which there is general agreement. What is meant is the
defence of the old order from the danger of change. There is
even less reason, in so much more interdependent a world, to
suppose that Great Britain will remain free from the pressure of
these ideas. Its insular position, its historic traditions, its great
wealth with its consequential capacity to set the limits of conces-
sion wider than elsewhere, are all of them, of course, important
safeguards against extreme measures. But they are no more final
safeguards here than they have proved elsewhere. They are all
subject to the fundamental condition that men care so much
more for social peace than for the rights of private property,
as the present system views those rights, as to accept without
counter-attack whatever disposition of their content the mass of
the electorate may choose to make.

There is, this is to say, more room for compromise within the
framework of the British system than has been found to be
the case in other countries, though it must be added that room
for compromise is a hope, rather than an assurance, of its successful attainment. The variables in the equation of social peace
are as delicate as they are complex. It is not merely a matter of
wisdom and self-restraint on the part of our governors. At least
as important is the existence of the objective conditions which
make possible their wisdom and self-restraint. They need international peace and economic recovery as the essential postulates
of the conditions of successful compromise. These give men confidence, and where they are confident there is the prospect of
mutual understanding. But there is no certain prospect of peace
in an international situation which visibly deteriorates before

our eyes. There is little prospect of permanent economic recovery when, all over the world, vested interests stand in the way not merely of socialism, but of the very habits of successful intercourse which capitalism itself requires. It has its own inherent and inescapable logic. The world of vested interests cannot continue to deny that logic without paying the price for it. And there can, in the light of the post-war years, be no possibility of mistaking what that price is.

To put it briefly, that price is the war of creeds. Established expectations become armed philosophies, and they go out to do battle with one another. Men whose feet are set on the path of war, whether internal or external, do not speak the same language; how then can they hope to understand one another? To assume, in this kind of atmosphere, that they will accept as "binding and sacred" principles so delicate as those upon which the conventions of the British constitution rest is to go contrary to everything we know from historical experience. In the circumstances we confront, what they do is either to suspend the conventions—a direct challenge to those whose hopes depend upon their continuing operation—or they retain their form while altering the spirit which lies behind that form. In Great Britain, it is the latter danger by which we are threatened. Political parties feel the strain of the pressures to which they are subjected. They seek as best they can the formulæ of peaceful adjustment. They emphasize the special character of our conditions; they urge us to remember that violent solutions are out of accord with the national genius of the people. But the sense of strain is there, and its appeasement depends upon the arrest of that deterioration of the world situation which the wisest of national statesmen are not, of themselves, in a position to secure.

Peace, in fact, depends upon our ability to bring the relations of production into a new harmony with the forces of production. That new harmony means, as in the past it has always meant, a wholesale invasion of the privileges built upon vested interests. They have to be persuaded or coerced into giving way. And, historically, on any large scale and within any brief period of time, they have never, so far, been persuaded. For that persuasion requires a volume of mental adjustment which wholly contradicts the basic *Weltanschauung* of those who have to be persuaded. Their lives have been tempered to the medium in which they live. Their conception of right is limited by the horizon of that medium. The state they built they conceived as an assurance of their purposes. Its apparatus of coercion was intended for nothing so much as to protect those purposes from invasion. They are asked to see that same state, that same apparatus of coercion, used for the denial of those purposes. And they are, more profoundly than any other, the religion by which they live. It is the religion which enshrines all that has made life pleasant for them. They no more doubt its principles than a good Mohammedan can doubt the promises of the Koran. It represents for them all the certainties that give colour and hope to their lives. Are they to admit, if regretfully, yet still freely, that all for which it stands is in fact grave error? Such an admission has not been the previous habit of mankind. Nor do we know of any alterations which should predispose us to believe that a change has taken place in the mental constitution of mankind.

We know, of course, that conflict is more disastrous, by reason of the weapons at its disposal, than in any previous age; but we are still, at least on fundamentals, prepared to fight rather than to give way. We can even, like Japan in the pursuit of its imperialism, lie shamelessly in the language of peace and watch cynically the world refrain from protest out of fear. Little has changed since the Athenians ravaged Melos save the language in which we wrap our excuses for taking our Naboth's vineyard regardless of the price. It may be the pseudo-learned of Germany inventing a fantastic racialism to hide the fact that their leaders have need of the positions held by Jews to reward their followers. It may be the jurists of Italy who prostitute their science to invent a legal philosophy for a non-existent corporative state. It may be the great American industrialists who, as at Ludlow and Herrin and Chicago, shoot down strikers on the pretext that they are fighting to preserve freedom of contract. The sober truth is that those who have power do not propose to abdicate from its possession. They require an ideology to justify their hold to those who do not profit by it, perhaps even to justify it to themselves; and they use their coercive power, which they clothe in the majestic panoply of a state, to impose the acceptance of that ideology upon the masses. The coercion may well wear the appearance of consent so long as the masses do not challenge that possession. Once any considerable section of them does so, their criticism becomes a threat, their organization sedition or treason; and the power of the state is brought into play to crush the challenge to law and order. These are the invariable habits of power, and the greater the inequality they have to maintain, the more savage will be the suppression for which they are responsible.

This is the context, at least, in which the conventions of our constitution are to be understood. Each generation will interpret them in the climate of its predominant opinion. Where that climate is calm, they admit of generous interpretations; where it is stormy, their construction is gradually narrowed until the interpretation put upon them by one side is unintelligible in its spirit to the other. There is no question here of sincerity or good intention. Any class which seeks to maintain its power must adapt the means to the end. As the perspectives of our politics are shaped, the maintenance of capitalist democracy means, in the long run, the transformation of capitalism into socialism by the methods democracy places at the disposal of the masses. That is the way in which the relations of production can be harmonized with the forces of production. But to harmonize them in this way is to contradict the limitations within which capitalism has sought to confine democracy. At the margins, the genius of each is the antithesis of the other. We have moved into one of those marginal periods in which the ultimate assumptions invented by one class for its own advance are sought to be used against that class by another which seeks to replace it. That, in bare outline, is the present disposition of the problem of parliamentary government. The battle has not been joined. We see only, as in the general strike of 1926 or the crisis of 1931, the skirmishes which intimate the likelihood of conflict. But there is no more reason to doubt their meaning than there was to doubt that the attitude of Spanish privilege to the Azaña republic meant that the maintenance of a liberal temper would prove an impossible adventure. If men cannot reconcile the acceptance of a new social system with their consciences, they find it easy to go out on crusade. Once they are in that mood, reason is the instrument of their passions, and the temper in which tolerance is a virtue rapidly disappears.

Nothing in recent years, perhaps, brings out so sharply the growing divergence of temper I have here been noting as the reaction of England to the problems of the Spanish civil war. To the Right, it has either been, as in the phrase of Sir Samuel Hoare, "a faction fight" in which we had no interest in the victory of either side; or, as with Mr. Garvin, it has been a fight of light against darkness in which the victory of General Franco is necessary if civilization is to be preserved. To the Left, sympathy for the Left has been a primary article of faith. The Labour Party was prepared, always with heavy doubt, to acquiesce in non-intervention, provided that it could become real; after the summer of 1937, it threw overboard that acquiescence. The working-classes have provided thousands of volunteers for the Spanish government, and those who have died fighting on its behalf are regarded as martyrs to the cause of democracy. They arouse no such emotion on the Right. Indeed, on the whole issue the two sides seem to have no common premisses between them. At best, the Right would regard the victory of the constitutional Spanish government as full of difficulty, and its defeat as a problem in negotiation not incapable of solution by skilful diplomacy. To the Left, anything short of a complete victory for the government forces would be an irreparable disaster. Their triumph is, as its leaders emphasize, the key to the survival of democratic liberties in Europe. The policy of the British government has therefore aroused its passionate hostility. It has created suspicions deeper than any British action since intervention in Russia at the close of the war.

Why is there this cleavage? At bottom, the answer is that the things for which General Franco stands are approved by the Right, while those against which he is in combat are approved by the Left. The Right prefers to see the defeat of democracy in Spain rather than risk, in its victory, the admission of the authority of an elected popular government to alter the foundations of property. The Left recognizes increasingly that the defeat of the government would be a fatal blow to that authority. It is difficult not to feel that each sees the relevance of its choice in terms of our own problems. Certainly a defeat of the Spanish government would encourage profoundly the forces in this country which feel that the rights of democracy halt at the frontiers of the private ownership of the means of production.

One final remark may be made. A constitutional system, it may be said, exists to promote the rule of law; nothing is less likely than that Englishmen will be willing to abandon a principle which, in some shape or other, goes back to the beginnings of their legal history. But the rule of law means only that the ends of law must pass through the interstices of a defined procedure; that does not define the end of law itself. That end is set by the objects to which the state-power in any society is devoted, and those objects in their turn are set by the class-relations of the society. We are back, in short, at that principle of Saint-Simon which I quoted earlier. In the marriage between capitalism and democracy which has given us our system of parliamentary government, the capitalism is more important than the democracy because the relations of property that it imposes give to the democracy its constitutive principle. The democracy cannot deny that principle without, as it were, dissolving the marriage that has given it birth. It may survive the dissolution, but that will be on the condition only that it is a divorce by consent.

I am arguing, therefore, that the validity of parliamentary government in Great Britain lay in the fact that, for those who made it, it expressed successfully the ends they sought to fulfil when they built society anew upon the basis of capitalism. The British constitution was an instrument for men who were agreed about the way of life the English state should impose. It was nourished by the immense economic success of the system upon which it was founded. The England that became the workshop of the world, the England that could achieve priority over all other nations in access to the world market, could afford to pay the price of all the compromises it involved. That explains the liberty, the tolerance, the social peace that Englishmen have enjoyed. They could, after 1689, afford to make concessions to one another which never implied the reopening of fundamental questions. We must not, indeed, forget that behind the success of the system there lie both the grim struggles of the sixteenth century and the civil war of the seventeenth. We must not forget, either, that both the French Revolution and the Napoleonic wars gravely threatened its ability to remain successful. We must not, either, forget that though its success conferred upon it a prestige which caused it to be imitated all over the world, it has rarely been imitated successfully over any length of time. That is because among most nations in which it has been tried the economic foundations of success were wanting. They rarely had the economic leeway to discover that unity of sentiment which builds the habit of compromise into the foundations of the national political tradition. This is most notably true of Italy and of Germany. In both, there was a longing for the peace which the habit of compromise makes possible. In neither was there ever a sufficiently long epoch of economic well-being for the habit to take root. It was destroyed before it came to maturity because the price of compromise was deemed too high by the owners of economic power.

But the habit of compromise, as I have argued, does not exist in a vacuum. It is always subject to the limitation that it may be destroyed when the conditions that foster its continuance are destroyed. I have argued that they are gravely menaced with ourselves. That menace is reflected by the antithesis between the views of the economic system now taken by the major parties in the state. Their differences inhibit that continuity of policy which, in all large matters of social and economic constitution, has so long been a distinguishing feature of English political history. By inhibiting continuity, they inhibit unity also; and that inhibition, as I have urged, at least raises the question whether the conventions of our system will work in the new phase into which they are passing. I have not, it must be noted, denied the presence of a will to make them work. I have insisted only that the power of this will to be successful depends upon conditions only partly within the control of statesmen. I have also given reasons to suppose that those conditions impose a psychology of their own which pervades, and may easily transcend, even those habits we regard as most firmly rooted in our tradition. We must not forget that the prelude to our historic compromise was war and revolution. Neither came because it was deliberately willed; rather, each came despite strong efforts to oppose its onset. We can make the adjustments our situation requires only in the degree to which we are conscious of the dangers we confront. For it is, above all, in our awareness of peril that we seem to hear the call to act while there is still time.

CHAPTER TWO

The Party System

1

"PARTY government," says Bagehot, "is the vital principle of representative government." That is a generalization which appears obvious to most Englishmen, and, in some form or other, it has been pivotal to the working of our institutions since the civil war of the seventeenth century. It has, indeed, been copied all over the world; and nothing appears to us so definite a proof of dictatorship as when the dictator destroys, as he is logically driven to destroy, all political parties save his own. Yet the existence of these permanent organizations is a more striking thing than we who are accustomed to their operations can readily realize, and it is worth while to begin their examination by reflecting upon this fact.

The real business of a political party in Great Britain is to get a government of its own leaders into office, and, if possible, keep it there. For that purpose, it seeks by every possible means to organize the electorate in the constituencies. It gives parties, dances, receptions. It holds meetings and organizes educational classes. It employs agents, speakers, canvassers. It raises funds for its activities. It seeks to permeate the local and the national press with its propaganda. It tries to discover what is in the electoral mind and, as far as it can, to make the objects it believes to be desired by the public its own objects. Out of the great welter of confused desires by which every electorate is moved, it seeks to discover those which it believes most likely to prove attractive, and to use them as the basis upon which to win power.

So regarded, the functions, and even the methods, of a party are intelligible. But given a party in office as a government, the processes of the party system are surely remarkable. For they have given rise, ever since the eighteenth century, to the idea of His Majesty's Opposition as an essential feature of our constitution. We have, that is to say, a government in office which is, presumably, trying to do its best. It is introducing measures which it believes to be for the good of the country. It is administering the whole machinery of the state as efficiently as it can. Yet we pay a large number of members of the House of Commons to obstruct public business as much as they can, to take the maximum advantage of the government's mistakes, to insist that it is ruining the country, to extract from it, if possible, information by which this can be proved, and to flood the electorate with propaganda intended to show that the government, however good its motives (and even these may be suspected), is in fact doing the worst possible things in the worst possible way. On one set of platforms, as in 1931, Mr. Ramsay Mac-Donald is a brave man who has sacrificed old party allegiances for the higher interest of the nation; on another, he is the lost leader who betrayed his followers for the riband to stick in his coat. To the pre-war Liberals, the Welsh Disestablishment Bill was a necessary incident in the structure of religious toleration; to Mr. F. E. Smith (the late Lord Birkenhead) it was a bill which "had shocked the conscience of every Christian community in Europe." The leaders of parties become the object of affections and dislikes which, in such moments of tension as the Home Rule split of 1886, may make the ordinary social relationships effectively impossible.

The most striking feature of this mimic warfare is that it maintains (or has so far maintained) the peace and does not lead to its infraction. There are drama and incident as one party gives place to the other as the government of the day; but so far no government, on defeat, has attempted to govern in defiance of electoral opinion. This is the more noteworthy because, with growing intensity since the foundation of the National Liberal Federation in 1877, mainly inspired by Chamberlain and directed with genius by Schnadhorst, party organization has grown even more rigid in character. It may be doubted whether, normally, there are a score of constituencies in this country in which a man would be elected to Parliament independently of acceptance of the party label. Roughly, that means that when he gets to the House of Commons, he will be expected, on all major matters, to support the party he represents; if he fails to do so, it is pretty certain that he will not be adopted as its candidate at the next election. The cost of elections, moreover, has tended to make local party organizations increasingly dependent on central control; in the Labour Party it is impossible for a candidate to be adopted without the official endorsement of the National Executive. Roughly speaking, it is accurate to say that every party has now a pretty definite programme, and no person can hope to be one of its candidates who rejects any of its major principles.

This rigidity is, of course, reflected in the House of Commons itself. It has meant that debates and divisions are in all normal cases stereotyped; we do not expect any wide liberty of speech or vote from the private member. Such elaborate cross-currents of opinion as were displayed, for example, on Lord Shaftesbury's Factory Bill of 1844, or in the Don Pacifico debate of 1850, on Palmerston's foreign policy, have now become impossible; they occur only on those rare, and usually minor, occasions when the government permits a free vote in the House. The rigidity, of course, means an increasing control of the House of Commons by the Cabinet; and the secret of that control lies in the fact that the leaders of the government and the opposition alike are in control of the activities of their members through the domination of the party machine. The day of the independent member has gone, and there is no prospect that it is likely to be revived.

The causes of this increased rigidity are not simple. Partly, of course, it is due to the fact that the vast electorate of modern Britain requires a far more elaborate party organization; this,

rally enough, has accreted power to itself. Partly, also, the
at increase in the area of state-intervention has meant a great
rease in government business in Parliament; a more rigid party
ructure is necessary if that business is to be completed within
the necessary limits of time. Partly, too, perhaps, it is possible
that electorates of the modern size tend to accrete about principles in terms of personalities; they return their members less
for their own sakes than for the leaders they are to follow. The
whole system of party has become necessarily professionalized,
and the very width of its tasks has driven it to a discipline not
unlike that of an army. There may be protests against its intensity; there may be "caves" and even revolts. But most members of a party recognize that a break with it is not only a danger
to themselves; it also increases vastly the chance that their opponents will be successful, if the break is of serious proportions.
Any considerable rebellion in a party is, therefore, an occurrence
unlikely save in the gravest circumstances; even in 1931, only
sixteen members of the Labour Party crossed the House with
Mr. Ramsay MacDonald.

It is a feature of the British system, though characteristic
enough of English-speaking countries only, that there should,
broadly speaking, be only two parties in the state which seriously
claim the attention of the electorate. With some writers, indeed,
this position has almost assumed the position of an axiom; and
it is strongly argued that this is the best method of working representative government. I believe this to be true; though it should
be added that the two-party system arises from accident rather
than from design. Certainly the two-party system has the enormous advantages, first, that it enables the electorate directly to
choose its own government, and, secondly, that it brings home
the responsibility for action taken to a determinate group of
persons. In the multi-party systems of the Continent, the choice
of the government is transferred from the people to the elected
chamber; and the voters who have wished to be ruled by M.
Herriot may in fact find themselves governed by M. Poincaré

or M. Laval. The multi-party system, moreover, either makes for coalition government, with its inherent erosion of principle; or for minority government, which is always likely to be weak and, consequently, to lack any effective clarity or purpose. If we assume that parties seek for power that they may translate into action the principles they profess, the more direct and decisive the choice the electorate has to make, the better is the function both of the electorate and of the legislature likely to be performed.

In an interesting analysis, Mr. Ramsay Muir has rejected this conclusion. He argues that multi-party government has the great advantages of avoiding "violent oscillations" from one side to the other. It makes "reasonable compromises and adjustments of view" both possible and necessary. He traces the true development of the two-party system to the evolution of its elaborate organization. This has led to the strict discipline which has involved the "dictatorship of the Cabinet." "It has disturbed the working of our system of government," he writes, "by dividing Parliament into two serried and disciplined armies, a majority whose primary aim is to keep a party government in office, and a minority whose primary aim is to discredit it in order to replace it. This gives unreality to the proceedings in Parliament and has greatly weakened its prestige in the eyes of the nation. Because the Opposition will seize every possible opportunity of discrediting the government, the government party must swallow all its scruples, and support the government in all it does, abdicating the duty of frank and candid criticism except when it is not likely to have any serious result." With ourselves, Mr. Muir believes, "there is a significant and constantly recurring trend towards a three-party system; it is commonly checked by the working of the electoral system, but it continually revives." What he would like to see is a three-party system of the Right, the Centre, and the Left. These would "correspond more or less to the British Conservative, Liberal, and Labour. And this would seem to be the most natural grouping under modern conditions.

In almost all countries, those who take a serious interest in politics may be divided into three types: first, those who do not desire any great changes in the social order; secondly, those who desire great changes, but only in a Socialist or Collectivist direction; thirdly, those who desire great changes, but not in a Socialist direction—rather in the direction of creating the conditions within which individual enterprise can operate with most advantage to itself, and with least restriction of the liberty of others." Mr. Muir points out the fantastic disproportion between seats and votes in the present electoral system, and he advocates the adoption of proportional representation as the best method "of ensuring that every substantial body of political opinion in the country should be represented in proportion to its strength." "It is only," he writes, "on the basis of the security and stability which proportional representation can alone secure that free and responsible criticism can be carried on." [1]

The argument is, obviously, both able and persuasive; I yet believe it to be wholly erroneous. There is no evidence that the prestige of the legislature is higher in countries like France, where the group-system obtains, than it is with ourselves; on the contrary, the deputy's freedom of manœuvre tends to discredit any government by making it uncertain of the steady allegiance upon which alone a great programme can be carried through. The "significant and constantly recurring trend towards a three-party system" in Great Britain has, the abnormality of the Irish Party apart, occurred exactly twice in the last hundred years; it occurred in the thirty years of confusion after 1832 when the modern Liberal and Conservative parties were emerging from the political configuration of the pre-reform epoch; and it occurred again, slowly from 1906 to 1918, and more rapidly afterwards, when the emergence of socialism as a new principle of political action in this country was reshaping fundamentally the whole orientation of our politics. Since approval or disapproval of socialism is now the real issue before the electorate, it is natural

[1] *How Britain Is Governed* (1930), chapters IV and V.

for the division of parties to turn upon their attitude to its principles. A Centre party, such as Mr. Muir desires, naturally disapproves of such an evolution, since, granted our system of voting, it tends to disappear between the two bodies who present the electorate with a definite and decisive choice.

Mr. Muir desires to keep it alive; and he therefore holds the view that Parliament should be a mirror of national opinion; from which he naturally infers the desirability of proportional representation. It is important, first, to note that since Mr. Muir wrote, both Germany and Spain have pretty grimly disproved his contention that proportional representation gives security and stability to a democratic regime; these qualities are, as I sought to show in the preceding chapter, the result of quite different considerations. If we assume, for the sake of convenience in argument, Mr. Muir's three-party system on the basis of revised electoral methods, what is the result? Either we have one party strong enough, as now, to form a government by itself, in which case there is not likely to be any vital change from the present position; or we have a House of Commons in which no party is strong enough to form a government without support from one of its rivals.

The second situation must result either in minority or in coalition government. The weakness of the first hardly needs elaboration in the light of our post-war experience. Its consequence is the substitution of manœuvre for policy. The supporting party is the real master of the situation; and the government postpones those principles in which it believes for others for which it hopes to gain support. Its measures, accordingly, always lack courage and consistency—virtues of the first importance in any governmental system. The second is an intelligible relation under either of two circumstances. It is intelligible during a war, when it is essential to postpone all other differences, supposing that there is agreement about the purposes of the war, to the single object of victory. That is a unity of specific limitation in time which, as the Lloyd George coalition made manifest, is hardly likely to survive the conclusion of peace. It is intelligible, also, where, as with the Blum government of 1936 in France, two parties separated by wide differences are able to unite upon a body of specific objects which they agree to be temporarily more important than those differences. It appears likely, on historic experience, that such coalitions require a dramatic background for their achievement; and it is probable that, like the National Government in 1931, they result either in permanent alliance (in which case there is, in fact, a return to the two-party system) or in a dissolution of the alliance which means a further period of weak government until the electorate makes up its mind about the direction in which it wishes to move.

The real truth is that Mr. Muir forgets the grounds upon which the Victorian party system worked so well. He forgets that the comparatively small electorates of those days were agreed about the objects of the state, and that the volume of legislation was neither big enough nor important enough to require, as it now requires, the initiative for its inceptions to remain in the Cabinet's hands, at least where major matters are concerned. He wants Parliament to govern directly, as it did in the Victorian period, at a time when the circumstances which made this possible have vanished. I shall discuss later in this book his view of the Cabinet as dictator. What is here important is the realization that once we grant the need for legislation on a body of coherent principle, the fragmentization of opinion may easily prove a major disaster. I omit from this survey the less vital arguments against proportional representation—its tendency to multiply groups, the ease with which, as in Germany, it multiplies, instead of diminishes, the power of the party machine. The evils it is sought to cure by this method lie far deeper than any electoral machinery can remedy.

For if we look at parties at all closely, we shall see at once that their dominant principles turn upon those views of economic constitution with which, at any given time, the nation is at all deeply concerned. If, as in the nineteenth century, Great Britain is confidently capitalist in texture, it is about the incidence of policy in promoting different aspects of capitalist ownership that their differences will chiefly turn. Their programmes and their subscribers will be predominantly relevant to those differences. If, as in our own day, the main national debate is either for or against the socialization of the means of production, party organization will mainly, and inevitably, group itself about that debate. Mr. Muir's attempt to find a permanent strand of British opinion, neither Conservative nor Socialist, which desires great changes in the "direction of creating the conditions within which individual enterprise can operate with most advantage to itself, and with least restriction to the liberty of others," breaks down partly because it is a perfectly good description of what most Conservatives would claim as their policy, and partly because, in so far as it seeks translation into measures which neither of the other parties would normally and naturally accept, it is not a basis for effective government. Rather it simply states, quite truly, that whatever the configuration of parties, there will be a corpus of opinion within the state that is unable to contain itself within the measures any government will propose. Such a corpus may be able to influence the policy of parties, but it is highly unlikely that it will be able to control their dominant direction. Its emphasis, in any case, is clearly on the side of Conservatism by the fact that it associates its opinion with the maintenance of private ownership.

Parties, I suggest, are predominantly organizations which seek to determine the economic constitution of the state. I am not, of course, arguing that only economic considerations will determine their policy. The Labour Party will pay large attention to the Roman Catholic vote in matters of education; the Conservative Party will pay large attention to the voting power of Anglicans in the matter of Disestablishment. Every party is, to some degree, a federation of interests to which, as best it can, it will seek to accommodate its policy. But, that granted, the main basis of its operations is the economic basis; the policy of each is unintelligible except in the light of that understanding. It was the Whig acceptance of free trade which won for it the manufacturer's vote; and the Tories clung to protection as long as they could because they were so closely affiliated with the argicultural interest. Anyone who notes the changed attitude of political parties to the Empire after about 1880 will recognize in that change a direct reaction to the perception of new economic opportunities.

Even more striking are the facts connected with their personnel and their funds. Working-men have never played any significant part in the direction of the Conservative Party. An occasional worker has been put on its executive committee; it has found room for a rare candidate for Parliament, usually in a seat where there was no hope; but the highest positions have never been conferred upon them. The great autocrat, the landowner, the financier, the rentier, the business man, these have overwhelmingly predominated in its councils. We do not know with any certainty the sources of its funds. We do know that it mainly depends upon large contributions from wealthy men. We do know, further, that when one of its "safe" constituencies is vacant, the scramble to obtain it is like nothing so much as a private auction in which the ability of the bidder to pay the costs of running the local organization is an important element in his success. We do know, also, that no small part of its funds has been raised by a private sale of honours comparable in character to the method by which James I replenished his treasury by the marketing of baronetcies. We do know, finally, that at each general election an appeal for funds on its behalf goes round in the name of eminent business leaders; and there is no reason to suppose that they are unsuccessful in their effort.

The complexion and habits of the Labour Party are, in these regards, wholly different. The bulk of its membership comes from the trade unions, and its National Executive Committee is mainly composed of working-men. It is rare to find among its representatives more than an occasional rentier or business man; there will be a handful of barristers, doctors, and teachers; there are a dozen members of the House of Lords, about half of whom are peers created by Labour governments to fulfil the statutory requirements of tenure of office. The essential direction of the party, in a word, is in the hands of the working-class, with a small admixture of "intellectuals" and minor business men. Its funds derive largely from the levies voluntarily imposed upon themselves by members of the trade unions; though a considerable part of the local funds is secured by contributions of a penny a week from members of constituency parties, and by such methods as bazaars, dances, and contributions raised at meetings.

We know little more of the sources of Liberal finances than we do of those of the Conservative Party. Certainly until about 1916 they were raised in much the same way as those of its historic rival; the funds of the Lloyd George section from 1917 to 1922 being secured by an almost open sale of honours probably unprecedented in British history. Since 1922, no doubt, the Liberal Party has fallen upon more difficult financial days. But there is nothing to suggest that anything has seriously changed about its method of raising funds except the scale upon which it has access to them. Any party whose hope of becoming a government is small will rarely find it easy to attract rich supporters; and both the decline of Liberal propaganda, on the one hand, and the diminution in the number of its candidates, on the other, suggest that the Liberal Central Office has not been able successfully to cope with the withdrawal of interest in its fortunes by rich men. They have gone to the party from which results might be expected, or, alternatively, they have ceased to concern themselves directly with politics.

It is, I think, impossible to explain this striking contrast except upon the hypothesis that a party is essentially what is implied in the economic interest of its supporters. It is not likely that the Labour Party will consciously adopt a policy which would have the effect of seriously alienating the trade unions, and it is no more likely that the Conservative Party will announce its adherence to measures of which the result would be the alienation of business men's support. Each, at least in its fundamentals, is confined within a framework of principles pricked out for it by the support on which it must rely. Each, outside that framework, is free so to manœuvre as to secure the maximum electoral support that it can. No one, for instance, would expect an announcement from the Labour Party that, after careful consideration, it has come to the conclusion that the trade unions have no cause for quarrel with the Trade Union Law Amendment Act of 1927; any more than one would expect from the Conservative Party an announcement that it is in favour of a compulsory minimum wage of three pounds per week. The area, in fact, within which each is free to manœuvre is drawn fairly rigidly for it by the economic character of the support upon which it relies.

Now the striking thing about the foundations upon which the principles of each party rest is the abyss by which they are separated. Liberal government could succeed Conservative government before 1924 with the assurance to business men that the basic economic structure of our society would be undisturbed. Anyone who examines the "Short Programme" of the Labour Party, issued in the spring of 1937, will see that there is no longer any such assurance. There are promised to the electorate, in the event of a socialist victory, not only wide measures of nationalization, to be completed within a five-year period, but also immense social reforms, which include the abolition of the Means Test for the unemployed, the revision upwards of the insurance rates paid to the latter, and the raising of old-age pensions to one pound per week to a single person, and thirty-five shillings per week to a married couple. The financial implications are clearly immense. More: this kind of legislation is a conscious disruption of the old continuity of policy upon which the parliamentary system previously rested. It is built upon a response to the demands of different interests; it assumes a society motivated quite differently from that of Great Britain at the present time. It is not, I think, too much to say that it is an attempt deliberately to transform the purposes to which the state-power is devoted. It represents one of those "violent oscillations" which Mr. Ramsay Muir has told us it is the purpose of the party system to avoid.

2

Will party warfare over differences so wide as these continue to be "mimic" in character? Can we, in Lord Balfour's phrase, "safely afford to bicker" about fundamentals? The possibilities, clearly, are these. The character of the Labour programme may prevent it from getting a majority over any period it is necessary to consider. In that case, the Conservative Party remains in power, without the possibility of challenge within the framework of the constitution. Or the Labour Party is victorious, and is able peacefully to carry out the changes to which it is committed; this, as I have suggested in the first chapter, would be a unique revolution in history. Or, thirdly, the Labour Party is victorious, but finds that the implementation of its victory is impossible save in terms of crisis, both economic and constitutional. Would it be possible, in this last event, to maintain the classic habits of parliamentary government?

Let us recognize what is involved. A Labour victory would occur at a time when the electorate has been subject to an intense campaign in which it would have been informed that the triumph of socialism meant national ruin. The party would come into office with a programme every item of which was, quite sincerely, anathema to its opponents. They would be gravely alarmed about the future of their capital; they might well, as Viscount Runciman advised them to do, have taken the precaution to export what capital they could in anticipation of possible defeat. There would be a general decline of confidence; the capital market would be weak; the short-term loans would probably be withdrawn from the City of London. Merely to prevent financial crisis, the successful Labour government would obviously have to embark upon heroic measures to stabilize the financial situation. To put through those measures effectively, it would have to count not only upon the support of the House of Lords, but also upon that of exactly those financial institutions whose confidence was most shaken by its policy.

I do not know whether it would get that co-operation; I do not think anyone is entitled to assert that he knows. Clearly enough, it is a crucial test of parliamentary government. It is not easy to be confident that it will meet the test successfully in the light of the events of 1931. For, the delicate questions of constitutionality apart, the whole impact of 1931 was the production in the electorate of a mood of panic. Had the Labour Party been victorious in that contest, its ability to overcome that panic in ways compatible with the normal formulæ would have been slight indeed. In the atmosphere engendered by Mr. Ramsay MacDonald and his colleagues there would have been, almost certainly, a catastrophic flight from the pound; do not let us forget that Viscount Snowden had described the financial proposals of the Labour Party—proposals of which he was substantially the author—as "Bolshevism run mad." Can a party capable of generating that temper turn round on the morrow of the election and explain that nothing said by it during the campaign is to be believed, that the men who yesterday were the would-be authors of the nation's ruin are today worthy of the co-operation of all patriotic citizens —citizens, be it remembered, who believe themselves thereby to be called upon to sacrifice the privileges to which they believe themselves entitled? It is not, let us remember, a situation like that of 1924 or 1929, in which a minority Labour government can be turned out of office the moment it tries to live up to its principles. Our assumption is that its majority has given it control of the whole apparatus of state. The only way in which it can be turned out now lies outside all the normal assumptions of the parliamentary system. How amply will those assumptions work in circumstances of this character?

Faced, it may be said, by the knowledge of these stark possibilities, we are likely to encounter the first of the three possibilities I have mentioned. There will be a long period of Conservative rule, simply because the electorate will not face the dangers implied in any alternative. But this hypothesis is not so simple as it superficially appears. For unless that period is coincident with a fairly continuous development of material well-being, with, as its consequence, advances in social legislation, it will transfer the incidence of Labour's action from the political to the economic field. There will be inevitable industrial dislocation, attempts by strike action to prevent decreases of wage standards on an industrial market, efforts, as by hunger-marchers, to draw attention to the condition of the unemployed. The Labour Party will be compelled to support the struggle by action in Parliament. On past experience, as, notably, after the general strike of 1926, bad trade and its consequences will be blamed on the government; there will start a drift towards Labour victories. Conservatism, in short, will find itself in the dilemma of having, somehow, to meet the demand for an increased standard of life, or paying the penalty at the polls. Within the framework of our system, it has no alternative, at least, over any considerable space of time.

On experience, indeed, it may be doubted whether any modern electorate, under the parliamentary system, is prepared, save in quite special circumstances, to see the same government in office over a long period. That might prove acceptable during the course of a long-drawn-out war; it might be acceptable, also, if the government's period of power coincides with an epoch of continuous prosperity. In Great Britain, since 1832, no government has been in office for more than ten years; in the United States, if we take the first election of Grover Cleveland in 1884 as marking the full re-emergence of the South into the national life, the sixteen years of Republican administration from 1896 until 1912 is the maximum period. In France, in the period since the Dreyfus case, there has been a pretty continuous swing of the pendulum from a chamber dominated by the Right to one dominated by the Left. It is therefore, I think, clear that a Conservative government would have to be quite extraordinarily successful to be capable of any long series of electoral successes. It may be doubted whether either the economic or the international situation—though they cannot legitimately be separated—gives much prospect of that success. When, therefore, the tide turns, that strain on the party system of which I have spoken is bound to be felt.

It may, indeed, be legitimately argued that the longer a party of the Left, like the Labour Party, is excluded from power, the more drastic will be the legislation to which it feels itself committed. For unless its opponent is the author of continual and comprehensive social reforms, it will be bound to take office on the basis of two expectations. There will be the assumption, first, that it must make up for the leeway lost under its predecessor. In matters like housing, education, public health, the treatment of the unemployed, the different standards of legislation envisaged by the major parties are an assurance that this will be the case. There is therefore, from this angle alone, bound to be a pretty steep rise in the level of taxation. There will be the assumption, secondly, that the victory on the political field must be implemented by advances on the industrial. Anyone who examines the history of the trade unions under the administrations of President Roosevelt in America, and of M. Blum in France, will have no difficulty in recognizing this probability. This means, in fact, that a Labour victory would be followed by an attack upon capitalism from three fronts. There would be the move for social amelioration; there would be the drive for better conditions in industry; there would be the legislation intended to socialize the major industries and to take the land into national ownership.

On any showing, it is clear, this subjects the parliamentary system to considerable strain. All of it, I suggest, is clearly implied in the nature of the party struggle we are witnessing. Once the division between parties is set by acceptance or rejection of the capitalist method of production, the logic of the contest turns upon the clash of these purposes. Nor is it, let me add, a contest in which the evolution can be so gradual as slowly to accustom the owners of economic power to the transformation. The announced programme of the Labour Party itself excludes that possibility. It is committed by its terms to a direct parliamentary attack upon the central citadel of capitalism. Once it is given authority by the electorate to fulfil its programme, it would be psychologically impossible for it to attempt its abandonment. To do otherwise is to commit suicide; for to abandon the attempt at the transformation of capitalism would be to surrender the whole ethos of its being.

My argument, therefore, reduces itself to this: a political democracy seeks, by its own inner impulses, to become a social and economic democracy. It finds the road thereto barred by the capitalist foundations upon which the political democracy is built. The validity of those foundations therefore becomes the central issue in politics. The party of the Right seeks to prove the validity of capitalism by making it work successfully upon the basis on which all economic systems are judged in a society where there is universal suffrage; that is, by offering a constantly increasing standard of life to the masses. It will remain in office so long as the masses are satisfied with its performance. Once they are dissatisfied, they will return the Left to power; and the Left will begin, or attempt to begin, the task of transforming capitalist foundations.

The party system, then, operates in an atmosphere different from anything known in the two and a half centuries of its history. So far, its function has been the settlement of what may be termed quantitative differences; now it is called to settle differences that are qualitative in character. What it is vital for us to understand is that the constitution within which it works has been built upon the presumption of quantitative difference. The principles of Gladstone always started from the same premises as those of Disraeli; so did those of Mr. Asquith and Mr. Lloyd George start from premises which, in broad substance, Lord Balfour or Lord Baldwin would have been willing to accept. The one issue of fundamental difference in the hundred years of modern parliamentary history before the war was the exclusion of Ulster from the Home Rule Act of 1914. That was an issue on which Ulster was prepared to fight rather than to give way; effectively, the Liberal government of 1914 abdicated before the threat of conflict. In those hundred years, the nature of the disputes between political parties tended, therefore, to conceal their unity of essential purpose and emphasize their inessential differences. Broadly, they were never debating the foundations of the state. They were discussing—always, until 1928, in terms of a franchise which, for nearly sixty years from 1832, was a narrowly limited franchise—the precise manner in which the capitalist system should be run; they were never debating whether it should be run at all. Each put its immediate emphasis on one point rather than another; neither ever laid its emphasis upon those points which might bring the system itself into question. It is this unity of essential purpose which made possible continuity of policy. Whether in the realm of empire, or foreign affairs, of social principle, or of economic method, Liberals and Conservatives alike could accept without repining the results of each other's governments because the policy of neither touched the basic question of the ultimate constitution of property. They conducted the affairs of the nation upon the agreed principle that this could not be brought into debate.

They were, of course, perfectly sincere in this, for they believed that as a basic question it was not seriously open to discussion. The complexion of politics, moreover, hardly gave them any reason to suppose it was. Until 1874 there were no workingmen members of the House of Commons at all; until 1906 they were hardly more than a significant handful; until 1922 they were never the official Opposition, in a position to influence the fate of a government. In all those years, moreover, they had never had an integral part in the formation of policy from within either of the older, historic parties. Neither thought seriously of them as possible candidates for the House of Commons; an illuminating letter of Mr. Ramsay MacDonald makes it plain that inability to secure a Liberal candidature as late as the 1890's was the real reason why he joined forces with Mr. Keir Hardie. It is evident from contemporary discussion that the formation of the Labour Representation Committee in 1900 was not felt by either Conservatives or Liberals to be a matter of any outstanding importance; if anything, Liberals tended to resent Labour candidatures on the ground that they divided the vote against the common enemy, the Conservative Party. Even during the long years of Liberal supremacy from 1906 to 1914, it may be doubted whether the significance of the Labour Party was grasped on either front bench. Their occupants might pick and choose possible concessions from among the items in the Labour programme of those years—the Trades Disputes Act of 1906 for example. They would deal with sweated industries, as in the Trade Boards Acts; or with unemployment, as with the establishment, in 1908, of the Labour Exchanges; or with the grim problems of old age by the granting, in the same year, of five shillings per week to persons above the age of seventy. It is yet certainly true, I think, to affirm that there was nothing seriously to differentiate this legislation in principle from efforts like those of Lord Shaftesbury or Viscount Cross. These are simply the necessary "concessions" of which Bagehot spoke, enlarged, it may well be, by the pressure of an electorate far more literate and, through its trade unions, immensely more organized for pressure than it had been in his day.

After the war, there is an immediate and dramatic change in the perspective of the political scene. The Russian Revolution, the large extensions of the franchise, the new consciousness of power in the trade unions, the widespread sense that the war was itself an expression of the breakdown of capitalism, all these brought a new tempo into politics. Their impact was emphasized by long-continued depression, by the high cost of living, by the technological revolution in industry, by the psychological changes in habits and social relations produced by the war. The Labour

Party became the official Opposition. For the first time, it became a great national organization, comparable in character to the older parties. It put itself upon a frankly socialist basis. It did not, indeed, either in its government of 1924 or in that of 1929, have the courage to experiment with its principles. But at least it showed in 1931 that it was not prepared to abandon them; and, rightly or wrongly, the history of Europe and America in the years since then has persuaded it that it was not mistaken in refusing that betrayal. The result of this evolution, accordingly, has been to make the economic constitution of society the pivot of party difference. It is upon that axis that, granted the parliamentary system, all future discussion is to revolve.

But the startling result of this evolution is its effect upon the older parties. This may best be put briefly by saying that it has, for all major purposes, compelled their consolidation. The formation of the National Government in 1931 was a real turning-point in the history of British political parties. Announced as a purely temporary alliance—its Prime Minister spoke of it as likely to last only a few weeks—it has developed into a permanent coalition. There is nothing to distinguish the partners from one another, and the real basis of their unity is their common front against the implications of a socialist programme. That hostility, indeed, they even share with the Opposition Liberals who, free trade apart, would find no major principles of differentiation separating them from the National Government. The effective choice for the British voter today depends, on any realistic view, upon whether he is for or against the socialist transformation of the economic basis of our society.

The true inference from this is implicit both in Bagehot's analysis, and in Lord Balfour's comment upon its implications. It is that, since 1689, we have had, for all effective purposes, a single party in control of the state. It has been divided, no doubt, into two wings. It has differed within itself upon matters like the pace of change and the direction of change; it has never seriously differed upon the fundamental principles of change. It has been able to quarrel without repining upon the extent of the suffrage, the limits of religious toleration, free trade or protection, the character of social legislation, the amount of self-government to be conferred upon the colonies, the details of foreign policy. Its quarrels upon these have always, so to say, been family quarrels in which there has been ample room for compromise. The one issue on which this has not been the case has been Ireland, and it is important that, when the Irish problem was solved, the solution accepted was applied by force and was the outcome of an agreement upon its terms between the two wings. Neither has ever moved so far from the other upon any vital question as to bring an ultimate disharmony into view. Each has always remained convinced that the private ownership of the means of production could not legitimately be called into question. The men who directed the destinies of both circles came, broadly, from the same social environments; they spoke the same language; they moved in much the same circles; they depended upon the same common stock of ideas. They thought in the same way because they lived in the same way. Members of either wing could cross to the other without any alteration of fundamental doctrine. A Tory democrat like Disraeli could be more advanced in matters of social legislation than a Liberal like Gladstone or a Radical like John Bright. A Conservative aristocrat like Lord Cecil could have more cosmopolitan conceptions of foreign policy than a Radical "man of the people" like Mr. Lloyd George. A Liberal, like Sir Herbert Samuel, could take the same view of the problems of Indian self-government as a high Tory like Sir Samuel Hoare. A Conservative like Lord Baldwin, with a high sense of *noblesse oblige,* had a much higher conception of the responsibilities of capital than a Liberal business man like Viscount Runciman.

The explanation surely is that they all agreed about the framework within which they were to operate, and the society of which that framework was the expression was rich enough and elastic enough to permit ample margins within which discussion of differences could be at once permitted and lead to acceptable compromises. For, invariably, the framework itself was not brought into discussion. It had never been so brought since the success of the parliamentary forces in the Civil War had settled the lines of its construction. Nor was there, until the other day, any need for its discussion. The nation as a whole felt that it had made its bargain with fate. Odd individuals like Robert Owen, small groups like the Fabian Society, might arise to point out that the bargain would have to be reopened. In the confidence of a society the success of which hardly appeared seriously capable of challenge, there seemed no good reason to take such scepticism at its announced value. That is why, throughout this period, the doubters, Carlyle, Arnold, William Morris, Ruskin, were never really taken seriously. They were "unpractical" people—poets, critics, prophets; in any case Cassandras whose predictions could be discounted by the magnificence of the trade returns. The rulers of Great Britain never doubted the solidity of their achievement. Why should they, who drew tribute from the whole world, who, America apart, had built a higher standard of life for their subjects than had ever been secured in any other country or time?

The power of the conquerors to confine the debate has ended. They are now compelled to discuss the framework they had assumed to be unalterable. Between them and their opponents there now lie differences hardly to be bridged upon the old terms, or in the old way. Herein is the central problem that the party system confronts. For the constitution that it operates had translated its unity upon assumptions into institutions habituated to that unity. Freedom of speech, freedom of association, these were the outcome of the assurance, the self-confidence, bred of unity. Their power to preserve them lay in the fact that they chose the issues to be discussed, and it was difficult for issues other than those they decided to choose to be discussed at all. The Irish learned this; the genius of Parnell forged the weapon of obstruction to compel attention to the wrongs of Ireland. Until his advent, British policy on its problems had been a typically

English mixture of cajolery and repression. It is not unfair to argue that this was also their method with the Labour problem until the new status of the Labour Party decisively altered the contours of debate. The handling of that alteration lies at the heart of the future of parliamentary government.

Let us note that these are not characteristics of Great Britain only; they are universal in capitalist democracies. We can see the same forces compelling the consolidation of Republican and Democrat in the United States as a party of property seeking to resist the invasion of its hitherto uncontrolled empire. Rather more slowly, the same evolution occurs in Canada; and it is already setting the frame of events in Australia and New Zealand. In South Africa, its arrival has been retarded by the intensity of the colour question; what has occurred there is the consolidation of the White peoples in a joint exploitation of the Black. The same is true of France and Holland and Belgium, if in different degrees. The party system can operate capitalist democracy so long as the masses remain satisfied with the results of capitalism. It is able, then, so to guide and shape the course of public opinion that no questions reach the status of legislative possibility which may injure the essence of capitalist security. But the narrowing horizons of capitalist success have brought such questions exactly to that status. The ability to find a new basis for unity then becomes the condition for the survival of parliamentary government.

3

I have dwelt in this chapter on what I conceive to be the essence of the party function in the modern state. I have argued that, in real substance, the absence of legal recognition for the existence of parties does not mean that they are not effectively a part of the machinery of government itself. Officially, no doubt, the Cabinet is merely a body of His Majesty's ministers charged, under parliamentary supervision, with carrying on the business of administration. But the point is that they are His Majesty's ministers because their party supplies them with a majority in the House of Commons, and there is no way in which they can otherwise continue in their posts save through a constitutional revolution. What keeps the party together? In part, no doubt, the momentum of organization itself, in part the power of leadership to attract followers. But, above all, the cohesiveness of a party is the outcome of the decision of its members to promote, as Burke said, "particular principles in which they are all agreed." I have argued here that, at bottom, those "particular principles" will be found to be economic in character. Often enough, no doubt, that character may be obscured by the complex crosscurrents of the intricate thing that society is. But two facts go to show that the economic foundation provides the durable texture of party composition.

The first is the fact that all political parties which endure for any considerable length of time are founded in economic discontents. This is true of Whig and Tory in England, of Republican and Democrat in the United States. Where third parties arise, like the Labour Party in England, or the agrarian party in America, the same is true. Parties which have been built around religions have rarely been able to maintain themselves for long; or, if they have done so, they have been compelled to adopt an economic programme only casually relevant to their religious origin in any direct way. And the same rule holds for nationalist parties, like the Irish in Great Britain, or the Flemish party in Belgium. The claim for national autonomy is a protest, in the last resort, against economic opportunities withheld, as the nationalist deems, by the superior power. That is why one of the first expressions of nationalism, after independence has been secured, usually takes the form of a protective tariff. It is desired to secure the home market for the home producer out of considerations in which the interest of the consumer may easily take a very secondary place. All this, of course, is natural enough. Since the most important thing to any individual is the way in which he gets his living, it is inevitable, as Madison said, that "the only durable source of faction" should be property. The party is a mechanism to control public opinion about property in the particular way its members deem desirable.

The system, of course, engenders its pathological results upon which observers, like Ostrogorski and Michels, have written well-known treatises. Ostrogorski, indeed, after an exhaustive examination of parties in Great Britain and the United States was driven to propose their abolition as the only way to prevent the monstrous perversities for which he believed them to be responsible; he felt, like Halifax at the time of their origin, "that the best kind of party is in some sort a conspiracy against the nation." But all he could propose in their place was voluntary associations for the promotion of particular objects, and it is evident enough that his scheme would be fatal to the necessary coherence which government requires. An electorate requires to know what its candidate feels about foreign policy not less than his sentiments about anti-vivisection; and examination usually makes it pretty obvious that his views on foreign policy are close-linked with views on economic matters so as to form, however imperfectly and unconsciously, a philosophy or way of life which he is prepared to recommend.

The truth is that there is no alternative to party government save dictatorship in any state of the modern size. Government requires leaders; leaders require not an incoherent mob behind them, but an organized following able to canalize the issues for an electorate with a free choice. The case for party as the necessary condition of representative government was made as long ago as Burke, and there has since been no answer to his argument. The imperfections which result are simply due to the fact that, because we live in an imperfect world, because, also, we are not wholly rational creatures, politics is a philosophy of the second-best. And because behind the activity of parties is the strongest interest man has—his interest in getting a living upon the terms this experience teaches him to be just—parties will exhaust all the artifices of which human nature is capable to secure victory each for its own side. The "whispering campaign" against President Roosevelt, the legend of Chinese slavery, the slogan of "Hang the Kaiser"—these are not the most generous of techniques by which to win. But when the interests in the result of the struggle are so intense and, let it be added, so unequal, they are not techniques which any party will put on one side. Granted that man is a pugnacious animal, that thought is difficult, that, especially in an unequal society, there are conflicting ambitions, and envy and hate, it could hardly be otherwise. Washington's "alternate despotism of one faction over another," which "has perpetrated the most horrid enormities," and "is itself a frightful despotism," is yet, on balance, better than the despotism which suppresses the party system altogether. The price of the one, after all, is exclusion from office. But the price of the other, as we have grimly seen in our time, is the concentration camp and exile, organized violence by the government tempered only by assassination of its leaders.

Quantula sapientia nos regamur; the lament of Oxenstierna is perennial in human history. We can mitigate that unwisdom in large degree by the mechanism of parties, so long as we may presume the good faith and fair play of those who operate it. But the condition of these qualities is a fragile one. It is, said Mr. Gladstone, "bound up with the growth of mutual confidence between the great parties in the State, transcending the political differences of the hour." But that "mutual confidence" has, historically, always depended upon the fact that political parties are agreed on the fundamentals. Those fundamentals, broadly speaking, are set by what Burke called prescription, and the greatest part of prescription is the established expectations of property. My point has been that we simply do not know what will happen to the party system, with the political democracy it makes possible, when a major party in the state denies the title of prescription to its privileges. We here, on all the evidence, enter the realm where the research of reason reaches but a little way. Most people would agree that a confiscatory denial would be followed by instant conflict. Would denial accompanied by some measure of compensation preserve the understandings of the system? Again, we do not know. In Italy and Germany, men had begun to suspend the formulæ of constitutional democracy even before there was legislation to deal with property; the debate, merely, was sufficient to throw property into a panic and achieve the Fascist state. The optimist argues that our traditions are so different as to make foreign experience irrelevant to our problems. I have given reasons in this chapter for the view that the basis for this optimism is more fragile than it appears to be on the surface.

For we must remember that party leaders, however anxious for an accommodation, have, in fact, an authority which reaches but a little way. They have to persuade their followers; they cannot coerce them. A party leader therefore tends to be, as Bagehot said, an uncommon man of common opinions. His power lies, very considerably, in the identity of his views with those of his supporters. The combined influence of Peel and Wellington forced Catholic emancipation upon the Tories; but Peel broke his party when he accepted the necessity for the repeal of the Corn Laws. So, too, not even the unique authority of Mr. Gladstone could persuade the Liberals of the eighties to the acceptance of Irish Home Rule without a split which cost him about one-third of his followers. Mr. Ramsay MacDonald was in agreement with his Cabinet colleagues over almost all the economics proposed in the financial crisis of 1931, but the overwhelming majority of his party broke with him on the question of a ten per cent cut in unemployment pay.

A party leader, in short, must never be so much in advance of his party that its members cannot willingly follow him in the divergence he makes from its normal highroad. In the kind of situation we confront, the leader of the Conservative Party has two obligations, if Mr. Gladstone's "mutual confidence" is to be preserved, not easily reconcilable with each other. On the one hand, he has to tell his followers that the economic programme of the Labour Party would be disastrous to the nation; a view, quite certainly, that they accept with passionate sincerity. On the other hand, he would have to tell them that if the mass of the electorate prefers the programme of disaster, they must reconcile themselves to its acceptance. On any showing, that is a hard task. It is particularly hard because the means through which, as bankers and investors and business men, they can register their antagonism to its operation are only partly within his power to influence. How many Conservative investors would refuse to change English securities into foreign because their political leader informed them that a newly elected Labour government ought to have a fair chance; that government which, as it were the day before, he was warning the electorate would, by its triumph, jeopardize the security of the nation?

The converse, of course, is just as true of the Labour Party. As a government without a majority, its followers, not very happily, permitted it to legislate within the framework of capitalism. It is at best highly dubious whether a Labour Prime Minister in command of a majority would be permitted the luxury of refusing to put his principles to the test. The second MacDonald government produced the defection of the Independent Labour Party from among its supporters by the degree of its indulgence in that luxury. It is, I think, as certain as anything can be certain in politics that a third experiment in such indulgence would split the Labour Party from top to bottom, with immense defections from its ranks to the Communists. That, quite inevitably, would produce a grave crisis in our affairs. And in the degree that the opponents of a Labour government, in and out of Parliament, strove to put obstacles in the path of carrying out the programme for which it believed itself to have a mandate, I believe the main result of their effort would be the heightening of the strain and not its diminution. It would arouse tempers on both sides; passions would run high; and the consequent atmosphere would not easily permit the possibility of accommodation.

The fact is that the intellectual abyss between parties requires a strategy almost too heroic for human beings to adopt. On the one hand, it seems to require from the Conservative Party some such philosophy as this: "Socialists," its leaders must say, "will ruin the country if they obtain a majority; and your ruin will be involved therein. We must therefore strain every nerve to prevent their victory as an unthinkable disaster. But you must remember that, if they are victorious, we must do nothing that will jeopardize the peaceful application of their victory. That peace is a higher good than your property. The British constitution is unworkable unless we assume the right of a government, which the House of Commons supports and behind which the electoral verdict clearly is, to implement in legislation the programme upon which it won its victory."

That would, I say, be an heroic strategy for Conservative leaders to adopt. It might persuade the supporters of the capitalist regime to recognize that, however justified their fears of the consequences of socialism, they would not, if defeated at the polls, be entitled to act upon their fears. On the other hand, it might have the effect of persuading them that counsel of this kind indicated a lack of virility in the men who gave it, that if their leaders are sincerely persuaded that socialism means national ruin, they ought not tamely to accept defeat because of a snatch victory at the polls which a more fortunate campaign, with an electorate always uncertain of its own mind, might easily be persuaded to reverse.

But let us look, for a moment, at the same position from the other side. Can we imagine a Labour Prime Minister, on the morrow of a victory at the general election, addressing his followers on these lines: "We have at length got our majority for socialism. We intended to use our power to lay the foundations of the socialist state for, as we have urged for so long, it is impossible to patch up any longer the decaying structure of capitalism. Unfortunately, our victory and its consequences have produced such panic on the other side as to make it doubtful whether the implementation of our victory can be carried through peace-fully. We ought not to jeopardize peace, which is more impor-tant than socialism. The British constitution is unworkable unless the minority is prepared to abide by the verdict of the polls. Clearly, it is not prepared so to abide. My colleagues and I there-fore propose, in the interest of peace, to postpone the introduction of the measures we promised, and for which we have the neces-sary support in the House of Commons, until it is clear that their introduction is unlikely to provoke conflict."

Such an attitude is the negation of government; a leader who adopted it would not remain a leader for twenty-four hours. And it is no more a possible attitude if the Labour Party were to say today that they would undertake not to begin their experiment in socialist transformation until they were assured that its begin-ning would not outrage their opponents. For, first of all, no one can give them such an assurance, least of all those who live by the conviction that socialism means disaster. And, secondly, to announce that they would act only on these terms is deliberately to invite the creation of that sense of outrage in order to compel the postponement of the experiment. It is, as it were, to invite every industry it is proposed to socialize to become an Ulster in order to prevent socialization.

The only possible tactic, in fact, the socialists can pursue is, as a democratic party, to assume that "mutual confidence" be-tween parties of which Mr. Gladstone spoke. So long, that is, as the law permits them to make propaganda for socialist ideas, their obligation is to inform the electorate as clearly and incisively as they can of the principles upon which they propose to act if they are elected to office. The only constitutional right of their opponents is to persuade the voters, if they can, not to accept so-cialist principles. But there is literally no meaning in our constitu-tion if a socialist victory, after long years of propaganda in which its consequences have been fully explained, is to be followed by the withdrawal of that "mutual confidence" on which its opera-tion depends. That is the announcement that one party only is

entitled to define the ends of parliamentary government; and
this is certainly not a hypothesis of possible action that the other
party is likely to accept. Certainly, if it did, it would cease to be
a party by so doing.

The strategy I have been discussing explains from another
angle what I meant by arguing earlier that until our own day
we have been governed in all fundamental matters by a single
party in the state since 1689. For though that party has given the
appearance, by its technique of division into two main wings, of
bifurcation, the fact always has been until now that both wings
did define in common the ends of parliamentary government.
Those ends, broadly speaking, may be described by saying that,
always within the framework of the private ownership of the
means of production, whatever government is in office must respond, within the limits of the possible, to the will of the electorate; the electorate being, at the next general election, the
judge of the adequacy with which the commission had been fulfilled. That was what Dicey meant by saying that our system
made the electorate the political sovereign of the country. It decided what party should form the government and, in broad outline, what it should form the government for. There is not, and
there has never been, in our system any body of fundamental
rights, either explicit or implied, that are safe from change by
the direct will of Parliament; and, both legally and constitutionally, there is no limit to the power of Parliament to effect those
changes it chooses to approve.

It must, we are told, have a "mandate" to do so; or it must
not "outrage" the feelings of the minority; or it must act, in the
use of its authority, with the wisdom and discretion upon which
successful government depends. The first of these arguments is
in a different category from the others, and it requires a brief examination. Relatively, it is a new doctrine, which may be said to
date from the Newcastle Programme of the National Liberal
Federation in 1891. Its rough substance is that a party will not,
as a government, submit measures to Parliament without an-

nouncing beforehand that it proposes to carry them if it can. Clearly, as a doctrine, the theory of the mandate is subject to a broad construction; for in the period of any government's office contingencies will occur, the threat of war, for example, upon which, in the nature of things, a government is bound to act without seeking the approval of the electorate for its decision; the declaration of war in 1914, the prolongation of the life of Parliament in 1916 beyond the term set by the Parliament Act of 1911 are examples of this necessarily wide construction. So, also, is the National Government's "Doctor's Mandate" of 1931. On that occasion the question of whether the nation should adopt a tariff system was deliberately left open for future inquiry. A few months after the election, a Cabinet committee, with the approval of the majority of the Cabinet but with strong dissent from Lord Snowden and some of his Liberal colleagues, decided that a tariff was desirable. There was no collective Cabinet responsibility for the decision, and it is surely obvious that a theory capable of so broad an interpretation is not a restriction of a serious kind.

In any case, in its usual form, the doctrine of a mandate would not apply to a Labour government, for its programme of announced measures is already before the country. If the doctrine is clothed with the very different meaning that a government ought not to introduce fundamental changes, above all in so delicate a realm as the constitution of property, without a substantial majority, we move at once into the region of the third of the limitations I have listed above. The government, it is there said, must use its majority "with wisdom and discretion." Obviously, all this raises questions which cannot be reduced to constitutional form. What is a "substantial" majority? Is it to be set in terms of seats won or of votes cast? The thing to which a government will attach attention is its possession of a working majority in the House of Commons. In 1924, for example, the Conservative Party was in a minority of votes (forty-seven per cent of the total poll) but had 415 seats out of 615 in the Commons. After the general strike, it used that majority to pass the Trade Union Law Amendment Act of 1927, though, on the theory of the mandate that I have just discussed, it had no authority to do so, and although, at the time, the results of the by-elections were already beginning to foreshadow the Labour victory of 1929. Was that the use of a majority with "wisdom and discretion"? The same considerations apply to the Hoare-Laval incident of 1935; and Lord Baldwin has recently admitted that in the general election of 1935 he deliberately misled the electorate about the scale of rearmament which he had made up his mind to be necessary. Were these also "wisdom and discretion"?

The truth, of course, is that we tend to think a government has acted with wisdom and discretion when we approve of its policy; and conversely. So long as it is able to maintain its majority, there is no constitutional test of the validity of its acts except the judgment of the voters at the next general election. To argue otherwise is to take one of two positions. It is either to say that when people strongly object to what a government is doing they may take action against it; this is an extra-legal remedy clearly outside the conventions of the party system. Or it is to say that, in a special sense, the King is the guardian of the constitution, and if he considers that the government no longer possesses the confidence of the country, he should dismiss it even though it still commands a majority in the House of Commons. I shall deal fully with the implications of this view later. Here it is probably sufficient to say that the King's judgment in such a case cannot possibly have any objective validity about it, and that the only result of his intervention must be to make the royal prerogative the subject of a passionate political controversy in which the very existence of the monarchy would be hazarded.

The argument that a government must not "outrage" the feelings of a minority is, of course, not a constitutional argument at all. It is simply an indication, which there is no reason to doubt, that at some point, never capable of precise definition, a minority will not submit to the power of the majority. But this is merely to say in other words what I have been arguing in this chapter, that the party system depends for its success on the fulfilment by each side of certain understandings which they must not violate if the system itself is to endure. The question is whether a programme like that of the Labour Party would be such a violation, and the answer to that question cannot be given on any *a priori* grounds. For, once again, there is no objective test of "outrageous" legislation. Its impact as "outrageous" depends upon what is in the minds of those who receive it. If they decide to regard it as "outrageous," pretty certainly all the conventions of parliamentary government will break down. But it is not, I think, possible for a government to decide not to introduce legislation to which it is pledged and for the right to introduce which it has, as an opposition, struggled for long years, because the other party announces that it will regard the "mutual confidence" of the party system suspended in that event. For that is to say that, majority or no majority, the anti-socialist party is entitled to permanent tenure of political power. That is not, of course, a tenable view in a political democracy.

But it is held in fact, and that it should be held illustrates the truth of my emphasis that the conventions of our constitution are, at best, fragile things, that it is a matter of great delicacy to uphold them. The great success of the party system was that it enabled them to function, with only rare moments of strain, for two hundred and fifty years. It did so, I have urged, because the terms on which it operated enabled the essential questions of economic constitution to be excluded from the subject-matter upon which parliamentary decisions had to be made. Circumstances have made this exclusion no longer possible. We are brought face to face with the foundations of our society, and we cannot avoid the necessity of deciding upon their future form. Epochs in which such decisions have to be made are always epochs of critical strain. It will at least be interesting to see whether the long habitation to peace which the party system has secured us will survive the experiences it is certain to encounter in the next generation.

CHAPTER THREE

The House of Lords

1

THERE have been fairly continuous efforts to reform the House of Lords for something like forty years. That is a tribute at once to the pivotal position it occupies in our constitutional system and to the delicacy of the problems raised by its very existence. For as the second chamber of a political democracy, it is, by almost universal consent, an indefensible anachronism. That a body consisting of some 750 peers all of them, save the bishops and the law lords hereditary, responsible to no one but themselves, should have the power to delay the enactment of any non-financial legislation for as much as two years is a startling thing. It has endured only because in each of the conflicts of the last generation the House of Lords has preferred to abdicate rather than to fight, and because it has thus far proved impossible to discover among parties any common agreement to the principles upon which it should be reformed.

To grasp the nature of the House of Lords something of its present characteristics must be understood. It is no longer, in the old sense, a small body of representatives of the old landed aristocracy who are accepted as the natural leaders of our society and perform great public services in return for the privileges they possess. No doubt there is still a small number of families, the Cecils, for instance, and the Stanleys, who have for nearly a century past played a conspicuous and worthy part in the political life of the nation. But half the membership of the House of Lords dates from the last fifty years, and the vast majority of recent creations have been no more than a tribute to plutocracy as such. In the eight years of his premiership Mr. Asquith recommended the creation of 108 peers; in six years, Mr. Lloyd George created 115. Motor-car manufacturers, newspaper proprietors, brewers, distillers, and bankers vie with elderly statesmen, retired soldiers and sailors, an occasional physician or scientist of eminence, a handful of civil servants and ex-ambassadors, for access to the chamber. It has become the body to which men are appointed whose distinction or wealth is too great for the offer of a knighthood to appear sufficiently flattering.

It has become, also, what Mr. Ramsay Muir has happily termed the "common fortress of wealth." More directors of public companies have seats in the House of Lords than even in the Commons. The old prejudice against trade—so long as it is on an ample enough scale—disappeared slowly after 1870, and rapidly after 1900. There is now no great national industry whose leadership, so far as its capitalist side is concerned, does not find its appropriate representation in the House of Lords. It is still necessarily represented also in the Cabinet; for by law two Secretaries of State must sit in the Upper Chamber, and it has been an unbroken custom since the Revolution of 1688 to confer a peerage upon the Lord Chancellor. Since Lord Salisbury, indeed, no Prime Minister has sat in the Lords during his tenure of office; and the deliberate choice by George V (said to have been made on the advice of all living ex-Prime Ministers) of Mr. Baldwin, who was then comparatively unknown, over Lord Curzon on the ground that it was almost essential that a Prime Minister should sit in the Commons, makes it at least highly unlikely that in the future he will be chosen from among the members of the Upper Chamber.

The House of Lords consists of some 750 members; but it is a very different body in its working aspect. Its normal attendance is about 35; and there are only thirteen occasions since 1919 when more than 200 members have been present at a debate. In the same period, the average attendance at a division has been just under 100, and the number of peers whose speeches average more than one in each year is 98. Nearly half the members of the House have never contributed to the debates by speeches; and there are more than 100 peers (excluding minors) who have not yet taken part in its proceedings because they have not taken the oath. We do not know with any precision the party affiliations of members from the usual books. But it appears that 12 peers belong to the Labour Party, about 80 to the two branches of the Liberals, three or four to Mr. Ramsay MacDonald's National Labour group; while the rest either avow no political allegiance or are members of the Conservative Party. I have been able to find some 400 members who announce themselves as Conservatives.

For normal purposes, therefore, the House of Lords is a body of less than 50 members. There is no doubt that, as such a body, and in quiet times, it possesses great merit. Its main debates are likely to be conducted, on either side, by statesmen of standing and experience, with occasional interjections from representative churchmen or an eminent law lord. It is a leisurely chamber; and, in quiet times again, it can scrutinize with a leisured efficiency the bills sent up to it from the House of Commons. It can raise, also, large public questions which the government of the day does not yet believe to be ripe for legislation; and, from that angle, like an important correspondence in the *Times*, it provides a useful sounding-board through which public opinion can be formed. In the Great War, for example, an occasional speech from Lord Morley or Lord Courtney did admirable service in allaying excessive passions, or in reminding the public that there would be the problems of international peace when hostilities had been concluded. The Lords, moreover, do admirable work in the examination of private bills.

If there is to be a second chamber at all in a democratic state, the House of Lords, when a Conservative government is in office, is perhaps as good a second chamber as there is in the world. Its debates reach a high standard; it does not have to consider any temporary gusts of passion by which an electorate may be swept; it has time to discuss all kinds of issues which require ventilation and can hardly hope for discussion in the overburdened House of Commons. The real problems to which it gives rise occur only in periods of deep controversy when a progressive government is in power. For it is then that there sweeps into view its character as the "common fortress of wealth." It becomes the reserve power of the Conservative Party, determined to correct the consequences of a progressive victory at the polls, so far as lies in its power. And, even after the limitations on that power introduced by the Parliament Act of 1911, its authority remains impressive. It cannot, indeed, any longer defeat financial measures; and a financial measure is now legally defined as one certified by the Speaker of the House of Commons to be such. But it can amend or reject any other measures so that their passage to the statute-book depends upon the ability of the government which introduces them to pass them through the House of Commons in three separate sessions within a period of not less than two years, should the Lords persist in opposition to their passage.

It is true that the Parliament Act has reduced the House of Lords to a definitely subordinate position in the state. It can no longer touch finance; and on all other matters, so long as the government of the day retains its majority, and with it the will to go on with any legislation to which the Lords take objection, it can only attempt revision or delay. But this is, in fact, a much greater power than appears on the surface for social reasons. In the first place, the Lords use their power of rejection very unequally. It is inoperative when a Conservative government is in office; it comes into action only when Liberals or Labour is in power. It means, secondly, that the Lords can, in their own discretion, hamstring the legislation, say, of a socialist government at any rate for the first two years of its existence; and it can thus, in effect, compel the Commons to waste much time over legislation for no reason other than purely partisan hostility to it. The fact that, as Lord Lansdowne said, it will be careful to pick the best fighting ground for its action, only makes things worse; for that means that the decisions of the Lords look only to the possible effect on the next general election. Moreover, as the government moves into the last years of its period of office, the power to delay is, in fact, the power contingently, at least, to postpone indefinitely. Suppose, for example, that the House of Commons, in the fourth year of a Labour government, passed a measure for the naturalization of the drink trade which was rejected by the House of Lords; if the government was defeated at the next general election, that would mean that the bill would be postponed, not for the two years envisaged by the Parliament Act, but until such a time as the Labour Party was able to secure a fresh lease of authority from the electorate. And the power to delay is more significant because it may well be exercised on a critical occasion when a government to which the House of Lords is hostile is seeking for emergency powers. In that event, recalcitrance from the Peers either involves an immense creation of socialist peers to flood out the opposition in the second chamber, with the need, as a result, to postpone all other issues to its reform; or its means, alternatively, should the Crown refuse the right to create peers, a penal dissolution compelled by an irresponsible chamber in the interests of the Conservative Party.

It is said that the power to delay is justified because great changes ought not to be introduced until the country has really made up its mind that it wants them; the House of Lords offers assurance that only the persistent will of the electorate is given legislative expression. But upon this there are two things to be said. First of all, the House of Lords offers that assurance only when the Conservative Party is out of office; it permits great changes without any delay when the Conservative Party is a government. And, secondly, no one can look at the history of British legislation in the past hundred years and argue that great changes have in fact been introduced in any spirit of reckless haste. The process of political enfranchisement took from 1832 until 1928. The establishment of a national system of primary education took from 1813 until 1870; a similar system of secondary education was begun in 1902, continued in 1921 and 1936, and is still incomplete. Home Rule for Ireland was debated at regular intervals from the sixties of the nineteenth century until 1886; it was embodied in a bill in that year and again in 1893; after a series of abortive half-measures, a Home Rule Bill was introduced once more in 1912, and went to the statute-book, under the Parliament Act in 1914. The issue of employers' liability was raised by *Priestley v. Fowler* in 1837; it was not established as a legal principle until 1880. A long campaign resulted in the appointment of a Royal Commission to advise upon the reform of the divorce laws; it reported in 1912; but it was not until 1937 that a minor part of its recommendations was translated into statute. The preamble to the Parliament Act itself says that the reform of the House of Lords is "an urgent question which brooks no delay"; but in the quarter of a century which has passed since an act of Parliament noted that urgency, no bill upon the matter has gone to the statute-book. On the average, in our system, it takes nineteen years for the recommendations of a unanimous report of a Royal Commission to assume statutory form; and if the Commission is divided in its opinion, it takes, again on the average, about thirty years for some of its recommendations to become statutes. If we take the famous programme of 1918 of the Labour Party as the date when it put the issue of socialism squarely before the electorate, over twenty years will have passed before there is any prospect of its principles' being given even the prospect of statutory action. In the light of these examples, which it is possible to multiply indefinitely, I do not think it can be seriously argued that political parties in this country persuade the electorate to embark upon great changes without due consideration.

The argument, acccordingly, that the action of the House of Lords in preventing "rashness" is desirable, fails on two grounds. It fails, in the first place, because the prevention is applied to one political side only; and it fails, secondly, because in this situation the argument of "rashness" really means that by rejection of some given measure the House of Lords is assisting the Conservative Party in the Commons in its work of partisan opposition to the completion of its task by a progressive government. That partisan opposition is justified in the House of Commons, for in these circumstances that is what Conservative members were sent there for by the electorate. In the House of Lords, opposition of this character is unjustified simply because it is built upon the assumption that the Conservative Party can always pick the legislation it will allow its opponents to enact. For no theory of a "mandate" underlies the action of the House of Lords. The need for the Parliament Act of 1911 had been recently affirmed by a general election; but the Lords were only with difficulty persuaded to pass it under threat of a creation of peers. The Baldwin government had no "mandate" for the Trade Union Law Amendment Act of 1927, and it was bitterly opposed by the Labour Party; but the House of Lords saw no evidence of haste in a bill torn to pieces in debate in the House of Commons, and they passed it without a trace of difficulty. Obviously enough, a power to delay which operates only as a barrier against legislation in one direction will prove as intolerable to a Labour government in the future as it did to a Liberal government between 1906 and 1914.

2

It is, indeed, recognized that this is so, for no one now defends the present composition of the Upper Chamber. The Left wants either no second chamber at all, or one which, on some adaptation of the Norwegian model, will effectively confine its functions to those of a technical revising body in the narrowest sense of that term. The parties of the Right want a real second chamber, which is in effect to say that they want one so reformed that it will have the necessary authority to delay the proposals of the Left if the latter should become a government. Lord Salisbury, indeed, in introducing his proposals for its reform in 1932 was honest enough openly to avow the purpose he had in view. There was, he said in effect, a danger that there would one day be a socialist government; he regarded socialism as disastrous; and he therefore desired a second chamber powerful enough to delay as long as possible the coming of socialism.

His proposals proved inacceptable; for it is agreed between parties at present that any reform of the powers and composition of the Lords should command some general assent, and, so far, no proposals of this character have been forthcoming. But it is worth while to examine the principle of Lord Salisbury's proposals in order to grasp the meaning of the motives which lie behind them. He envisaged a chamber of some three hundred members. Half of them were to be elected for twelve years by the hereditary peerage, and the remaining half nominated by the government for the same period, vacancies being filled as they arose. The powers of the chamber were to remain the same as now, save that the definition of a finance bill was to be, not in the hands of the Speaker, but of a joint committee of both Houses under his chairmanship. In order to prevent the swamping of the hereditary electorate in an emergency, the prerogative of the Crown was to be limited so that not more than twelve new peerages could be created in a single year; and the provisions of the Parliament Act were not to apply to the new second chamber. Its reform was to be effected only with its own consent.

Quite obviously such a scheme, if its first composition were determined by a Conservative government, would necessarily contain an overwhelmingly Conservative majority. At the maximum, only twelve of the peers elected by the hereditary element would be members of the Labour Party; and there would be no means of redressing that balance unless practically the whole of the nominated element represented Labour. The limitation of the prerogative right to create peers, moreover, would normally mean that something like a generation would have to pass (supposing that in that generation the Labour Party was continuously

in power) before the majority of the hereditary electors were
Labour; and even this involves the assumption that the sons of
all peers created by the Labour governments accepted, when they
succeeded to their titles, the views held by their fathers. It involved putting the definition of a finance bill, not into the hands
of a person, like the Speaker, vowed to impartiality, but into the
hands of a committee chosen on strict party lines, in which it is
almost inconceivable that there should not be a permanent Conservative majority also. It involved, as well, the idea that so long
as this second chamber was satisfactory to itself, there was to be
no constitutional method whereby its character was to be changed.

It is not really very surprising that the proposals were rejected,
that, indeed, there was strong opposition to them from among
Lord Salisbury's own colleagues on the Conservative side. They
were, frankly, a method of keeping the Conservative Party in
permanent office by indirect means. But, if less openly, that is the
result reached by almost any method of reform, direct election
apart, which is advocated from the Conservative side. The purely
nominated senate of all the talents, chosen either for life or for
a term of years, would be a necessarily Conservative body, at
least as to its majority, unless it were admitted that a practical
equality of view should obtain from the outset; retired soldiers
and sailors, ex-civil servants and ambassadors of the administrative division, presidents of the British Federation of Industries,
even Presidents of the British Academy and the Royal Society,
are not very likely to hold socialist opinions. But it is pretty certain that no Conservative government could obtain approval
from its supporters for equality of view. No doubt it would
agree to nominate a handful of trade-union officials, a few of
the old Labour ex-ministers, and perhaps some of the better-
known members of the National Executive Committee of the
Labour Party; but almost certainly its generosity in nomination
would be forcibly restrained by its own rank and file somewhere
about that point.

Nor is a mixed second chamber, in part elective and in part

nominated, any more satisfactory. That, again, almost certainly involves a permanent Conservative majority; and it is probable that the peers would insist upon some element chosen by the hereditary peers. The Labour Party would, quite certainly, reject these principles; and they would not, further, as their own programme makes clear, be persuaded to accept any principle of delay which gave the Upper House a two-years' control over the authority of the popular chamber, or put barriers in the way of a rapid compulsion upon the Upper House to accept the will of the elected assembly. None of these proposals, or such variants upon them as would involve an element of indirect election (as from the County Councils for instance), is likely to meet anything but determined socialist opposition.

Nor can anything be said for an elected second chamber, whether chosen on the principle of territoriality or of function. The difficulties of the first principle are manifold. There is the difficulty of the area of the constituencies; there is the difficulty of the date at which the chamber is to be chosen; and there is the difficulty—once it is based, as it would be difficult not to base it, upon universal suffrage—of the powers, especially in relation to finance, that it is to exercise. In all modern states where there are two elected Houses, it has always been found that effective power gravitates to one of them. In the United States, it is the Senate; in France, it is the Chamber of Deputies. And, a federal state apart, there is no point in a second elected chamber unless either its constituency unit or its date of election is different from that of the first. But the inherent weakness of making either different is the certainty of an ultimate collision between the two bodies. Out of that collision, there always emerges the necessity of constitutional change, since the result of a two-chamber scheme on the electoral principle is to leave unresolved the question of where the actual will of the voters is to be found.

Nor is functional representation more adequate for this purpose. There is the insoluble difficulty of the proportions in which capital and labour are to be represented. There is the at least delicate and, I believe, impossible issue of where the boundary-line of the units of representation is to be drawn; effectively, that was found impossible even in a purely advisory body like the German Economic Council. There is also the difficulty of women. If they are to be represented as a function in proportion to their numbers, then the profession of the married housewife is the most numerous, as it is certainly not the least responsible, in the country. Unless they are given representation in proportion to their numbers, there is no intelligible principle upon which the size of their representation can be calculated. And all this is apart from the question of why exactly a function, like that of medicine for instance, is properly relevant to the purpose of a legislative assembly. There is not a medical view of foreign policy, or of the nationalization of mines, or of free trade. If doctors voted for a candidate because of his views on these matters, they would not, in fact, be voting as doctors at all; while if they voted for some of their numbers on grounds strictly relevant to their professional interests, these would not be entitled to speak in their name on subjects not of medical concern. There is, in fact, no effective relevance between professional representation as a principle, and an omnicompetent legislative assembly. There is, indeed, no such relevance even where the functions of a body so chosen are limited to advice. That is why the German Economic Council was so useless as a general body, and why, also, in some of its sub-committees its experts were able to give such valuable advice. For they were then, by the careful delimitation of the subject-matter referred to them, really dealing with matters about which they had expert knowledge.

There is, then, no conservative principle for the reform of the House of Lords that can hope for the assent of the Labour Party. It should be added that no Labour proposal, either, is likely to secure the co-operation of Conservatives. The formal policy of the party is still in favour of single-chamber government, and there is reason to suppose that this still commands a considerable body of support. The old view of the Abbé Sieyès that if the second chamber agrees with the first it is superfluous, while if it disagrees, it is obnoxious, still seems to many common sense. Postwar experience of the parliamentary system, moreover, has tended to strengthen this view. It has shown that a second chamber either tends to be part of the technique of reaction against a progressive government, and that in any case its main result is to slow down the rate of change at a period when the facts call for a rapid adjustment of social principles. The Labour Party has not been impressed by the view that, since most modern states have a second chamber, its existence may almost be taken as an axiom of political experience. For many of its members, that judgment simply confuses the ancient with the essential; and socialist writers have pointed out that on the side of the principle of a second chamber are thinkers of the quality of Bentham, Franklin, Condorcet, and Jefferson.

But the problem has not been considered in general principle since the war. If it should be, it is possible that the party would accept the idea of a small revising chamber on the condition that it had no power effectively to delay the passage of legislation approved by the House of Commons. The new body is envisaged as perhaps a hundred members in number, and it would be elected by each newly elected House of Commons from lists prepared by its constituent parties in proportion each to its own strength. The composition of the body would therefore reproduce that of the House of Commons; and its membership would be renewed after each dissolution of that House. A government with a majority in the popular chamber would therefore find its majority ready-made in the new revising body. It would have no reason to fear there the destruction or the delay of its programme. All the functions now usefully performed by the House of Lords could be performed also by the new body. It could contain men not less eminent on either side, if they were prepared to stand for election in the name of their party. It could serve as a useful place of retirement for elder statesmen who no longer felt equal to the heat and stress of popular election and the tiring work of the Commons. It could ventilate great subjects in a general way, as the House of Lords is accustomed to do. It would be able, to adapt a classic formula, to advise and encourage and warn. The one vital power of which it would be deprived would be the power to interfere with the effective passage of the government programme to the statute-book.

But, of course, that power is precisely the vital power of the House of Lords. It is certain that its abrogation, whether by reason of the establishment of a single-chamber system, or by this alternative method, would be passionately resisted by Conservatives. For a simple reason: once that power disappeared, nothing would stand between capitalism and the will of the electorate within the framework of the constitution. An essential intermediate defence of the present system would be torn down, and property, once there was a socialist majority, would on this scheme have no means of interposing a technique of postponement to the will of the popular assembly. That is well understood on the Conservative side; hence the urgent demands of almost every annual conference of the party that the task of reform be undertaken while its own government is in office. The weakening of a chamber still able to resist any strong attack upon the present system of property seems to an overwhelming majority of Conservatives a maxim of elementary prudence. This, certainly, is a constitutional issue in which there is not even an approximation to common ground between the parties. That is why, often as the need for reform is invoked, often as Conservative leaders admit the desirability of reform, they tend always to leave the present position undisturbed. They are aware that almost any principle of change which they could persuade their supporters to adopt would be regarded by their opponents as a deliberate and dangerous weighting of the constitution against them.

"The House of Lords," said Lord Rosebery, "will pass in a storm." The more carefully its nature and place in the constitution are scrutinized, the more does the truth of this aphorism appear. The real significance of the House of Lords simply lies in its position as the "common fortress of wealth," and its anxiety to use its powers in defence of the rights of that wealth. Take away from it that character, and the problem of its reform becomes simple at once. But take away from it that character, also, and on the constitutional plane the power of wealth is at once submitted to the power of numbers. It will not tamely accept that submission. For so long as even the curtailed powers left to it by the Parliament Act remain, its ability to work mischief to a Labour government is immense. It can, as I have pointed out, strike a fatal blow at emergency measures; it can hamstring the programme of a government by delaying their passage for the first two years and postponing it, in the last two, for a period that the hazards of public opinion at the polls may well render indefinite. Concealed in this ability is, in effect, the power also, as was shown in 1910–11, to compel what is nothing less than a penal dissolution. And this ability, it must be remembered, is a weapon exercised only against one party in the state.

How real this power is can best be seen by considering the kind of occasion on which it might be used. Let us suppose a Labour victory at the polls, the formation of a Labour government, and the introduction of the measures to which it is committed, and, for the moment, let us assume that it takes over the reins of office without encountering any serious initial difficulties. Its measures are broadly divisible into two categories— measures of immediate social amelioration, the treatment of the unemployed, for instance, and measures like the nationalization of the mines of which the advantage, if any, can be reaped only over a considerable period. It is clear enough that from the angle of political strategy, while a Labour government might be willing to use the machinery of the Parliament Act for the second category, it could not use it for the first, since its hold on the electorate would largely depend upon its ability to satisfy the demand for an improved standard of life. Interference with this category by the Peers would therefore have to be followed by the threat to swamp their opposition by new creations; authority from the Crown to effect these creations would necessarily have been a pivotal part of Labour's electoral programme, as it was in both 1931 and 1935.

That would bring the destruction of the House of Lords immediately into view. For, first, if it gave way before the threat, it would be necessary for the Labour government to move at once to its reconstruction to prevent the repetition of the threat, while if its members decided to "die in the last ditch," the number of the House of Lords as enlarged by the new creations would be so great as to render it an absurd body which it would be imperative to reform forthwith. On either hypothesis, therefore, the Lords would disappear, and with them an essential bulwark in the defence of wealth against socialism.

But this is to assume that on these considerations the Crown would grant the right to create peers. We have no certainty that this is the case. In what was relatively the minor dispute of 1911, the opposition of the Peers resulted in a demand by the Crown for two general elections before the grant was conceded. We may be confident that all possible pressure would be brought to bear on the monarch to repeat this strategy. The doubt whether the country has really made up its mind; the duty of the King to facilitate a consultation with public opinion; the insistence that so great a change ought to receive the special stamp of electoral approval; the monarchical obligation to save the constitution from "outrage"—all these would be exploited to the full. It would be insisted that the Opposition would, in the event of his refusal to take his Minister's advice, be prepared to accept office and dissolve; an electoral defeat of the Labour Party would confirm his action. Who is there who cannot see the character of such an election, with the voter persistently informed that a Labour victory endangers the very existence of the throne?

Clearly enough, we move here in troubled waters, and no one can predict what would happen if the ship of state were launched upon them. The difficulty of the position may be put by saying that (1) if the House of Lords is left as it is, a conflict, sooner or later, with a socialist government is inevitable; (2) that if it is reformed by the Conservative Party, a chamber would result entirely inacceptable to the Left; and (3) that if it is reformed by the Labour Party, the character of the new chamber would be entirely inacceptable to the Right.

Why is this the case? The answer, I think, is the important one that the question of the reform of the House of Lords is one of those issues of constitutional structure the roots of which go down into the economic foundations of the state. That has been the case on every occasion of serious conflict between the two Houses. It was so in 1831–32 in the controversy over the Reform Bill; it was so in 1909 in the conflict over the Budget of that year; it was so, again, in 1910–11 in the conflict over the Parliament Act in which the real issue was Conservative dislike of Liberal legislation. And each of these conflicts, it must be remembered, is of relatively minor proportions alongside the possible conflicts which now begin to come into view. For whereas the older issues touched only upon quantitative differences of opinion capable, as the events showed, of compromise, the differences which now emerge are of an entirely distinct character. They are not differences of more or less; they are questions which by their decision wholly alter the class-structure of our society. Since the House of Lords is a pivotal institution to the making of that decision, it is not easy to imagine its giving way without a passionate effort to retain its powers.

It may be said that after all it is entirely reasonable for the House of Lords to ask for an assurance that the great changes for which the Labour Party asks are supported by the permanent will of the people. It has always given way in the past so soon as the popular will has shown itself determined; and to require a second general election in proof of that determination can hardly, in view of the magnitude of the issue, be regarded as excessive. But the answer to this attitude is plain. The House of

Lords is not an impartial and objective body which takes an independent and detached view of the public opinion it encounters. Its composition makes it, and is intended to make it, a fundamental part of the institutional strategy of the Right. It is intended to see that, as Lord Balfour once put it, in office or out of it the Conservative Party is permanently in power. Any dissolution compelled by its action is always against one side. It appears, therefore, as a penal dissolution; and a dissolution of that character is bound to seem a violation of the constitution to the party against which it operates.

But this is to argue, it may be said, that the Labour Party fears to secure a reconfirmation of its policy from the people in whom, as a democratic party, it declares itself to have confidence. This is a mechanical view that has no substance behind it. A political party mainly dependent upon the poor is bound to suspect an instrument which lies so largely in the hands of its rich opponents. It is natural that it should oppose the claim that its activities, as a government, are subject to hazards from which the Right is free. It comes into office, on its own view, upon the basis of a known programme for which it has secured the approval of the electorate. The principles on which it will legislate are known; the methods it will use are also known. Why should it jeopardize its victory by submission to the power of a non-elected assembly whose urgent will to prevent its success is known, further, before ever it came to office? Conservative governments do not seek electoral authority for their interpretation of their mandate under such a compulsion. The Baldwin government did not after 1926, nor did it, again, in 1936, even though on the Prime Minister's own admission its rearmament policy was a direct contradiction of the assumptions upon which it had secured re-election in 1935. No constitution can long remain successful if its basic assumptions are to operate unequally as between parties.

It is not, therefore, very accurate to say, as Mr. Ramsay Muir has argued, that the House of Lords is "only a revising and delaying body; and not very effective even for that purpose." For what is important is the point at which it has the power to delay. It is, as he remarks, definitely in a subordinate position to the House of Commons; the Parliament Act has given the effective initiatory authority to the elected chamber. But it has preserved to the House of Lords a crucial power at exactly the moment where it needs that power to fight, not on abstract grounds of reason, but on very concrete grounds of privilege. Its delaying power is simply an instrument of wealth, devised as a bulwark against the will of the masses. That power is, in his own words, "an anachronism in a democratic state." For while, in form, the veto-power of the Lords is gone, in fact much of its substance remains. It may even be argued that indirectly its power over finance remains. For every great measure of social reconstruction is in essence a bill for the redistribution of income, and the authority to postpone its enactment is financial authority of a very considerable kind.

3

It is sometimes urged that the way out of these grave difficulties lies in a quite different field. There are many Conservatives who recognize the unequal operation of the Lords' authority, and they admit the unsatisfactory character of a penal dissolution. They therefore argue that the way out of the dilemma lies in allowing the rejection of a measure regarded by the government as vital to be consultation of the electorate not by means of a general election but by way of a popular referendum. It is, they point out, democratic; it separates out the issue upon which the voter is to decide; and this confinement of the decision to a single issue preserves the government from the necessity of a penal dissolution.

Superficially, there is something both plausible and attractive about this scheme. But it breaks down pretty obviously upon close examination. For, in the first place, it still leaves the issue

of whether a referendum should be held in the hands of the
Upper House, that is to say, in the hands of the Conservative
Party. Our quarrel is with the discrimination between Right and
Left which is inherent in the composition of the House of Lords;
this proposed remedy does not alter the fact of that discrimination. But there are even graver objections. Few people can seriously suppose that complicated questions are susceptible of being
dealt with efficiently by the method of mass voting; no one
would have suggested, for instance, the submission of the Derating Act of 1929 to a referendum. The principles of a measure,
abstracted from all the details which give it point, become utterly
unreal. "Are you in favour of the nationalization of the mines?"
is a very different question in reality from the clauses of a bill,
and its scrutiny requires an atmosphere of consideration which is
not possible to an electorate of millions. Nor is it possible to
divorce consideration of a particular measure from the general
record of which it is a part. There may be hundreds of thousands
who vote against the government on a mines bill not because they
have any view upon that measure but because they dislike the
government's foreign policy; separation of issues is simply not
a possible technique. The background in which a referendum
would be taken, in fact, would be the same as that of an ordinary
general election. Everyone would know that rejection of the bill
would be a resounding challenge to the prestige of the government, and its opponents would be certain to use the occasion for
ends far beyond the narrow limits to which the theory of the
referendum seeks to confine the voter's judgment. And in any
case the experience of the referendum abroad, above all in
Switzerland and the United States, does not suggest that it is
a very helpful addition to the armoury of democracy. If it is
confined to obtaining answers to questions of principle, then, in
the absence of concrete details, the questions are devoid of real
meaning. If it is enlarged to consider the full amplitude of a
complicated statute, then it is useless to pretend that a mass
judgment upon its clauses is in any way a valid one.

That can be shown quite simply, I think, by taking one of the most dramatic political incidents of 1935. I do not suppose that anyone would argue that the submission of the question: "Are you in favour of the Hoare-Laval proposals?" to the electorate would have produced an answer capable of any effective interpretation. To have asked for a judgment upon the full proposals, moreover, would have been to ask for a decision many of the details of which were unknown to members of Parliament before their publication, even, it may be said, to many ministers themselves. Long and close scrutiny, no doubt, would enable the serious-minded elector to reach a decision; but a referendum does not create the conditions under which a long and close scrutiny is possible.

The fact is that the whole theory of a referendum misconceives what an electorate is for. It forms a view upon a general web of political tendency; it returns men to vote for or against the large pattern of that web. Political parties organize that pattern for decision as best they can. To select out of it a single strand and ask the voters to separate it from the general web is to call them to a function for which, as a mass, they are unsuited. Direct government, in short, is not the same thing as self-government; it may, indeed, as the experience of Fascist countries has shown, be the exact antithesis of it. The business of an electorate is to choose a party to be a government and, at the end of its term, pronounce judgment upon its record as a whole. Particular measures within that record throw the whole judgment out of perspective if they are selected as objects of popular decision. They do so not least because, as soon as they are so selected, they cease to be particular objects. They become confused with the general judgment which a democracy feels able pretty effectively to pronounce.

4

"The order of nobility is of great use," wrote Bagehot, "not only in what it creates but in what it prevents. It prevents the rule of wealth—the religion of gold." We need not admit his emphasis that the "religion of gold" was the "obvious and natural idol of the Anglo-Saxon" as more true of one country than of another. What is certainly no longer the case is that there is an "order of nobility" in this country in the sense in which Bagehot used the term. Our society is what Mr. Tawney has termed an acquisitive society, and the modern House of Lords expresses all that is implied in that term. Effectively, it represents material success, whether gained in the past or in the present, on the principles by which success of this kind can be achieved in a society like our own. How completely it represents this ideal can be put quite simply by saying that we naturally expect a very rich man to end up in the House of Lords, and that we are invariably surprised when a man eminent for something other than wealth finds his way there.

So long as the underlying principles of our society were not called into question, there was no special reason to question the claim of the House of Lords to a share in the business of government. I have already alluded to the important merits it possesses; beyond these, it had what is for Great Britain one further quality of great importance: it was venerable. It had existed as a part of the English constitution for as long as we had possessed a constitution. Many of the members who played an eminent part there were themselves almost a living embodiment of the history of England. The House of Lords was never rationally defensible after about 1867; but, until 1906, there was never an urgent need to defend it, and it had become one of those significant institutions which, like the Albert Memorial, we take for granted. It was not, as it were, out of tune with its times, because its times did not seem to be out of tune with itself. For the greater part of the nineteenth century reverence for the aristocracy, as distinct from reverence for wealth, was still a significant element in the Englishman's outlook. Men might on occasion sneer at it, as both Dickens and Thackeray were prepared to do. But the reader of Trollope's novels—a supreme index to the best mind of the average Englishman in the sixties and seventies of the last century—will not discover in them any suggestion that the right of the aristocracy to rule may be called into question.

It was, indeed, already apparent to Bagehot that this was because the inferiority of the House of Lords to the House of Commons was an established constitutional principle. He approved of the view that in any conflict between them the Lords must, in the long run, give way. What he did not see was that the result of the fusion between aristocracy and wealth would altogether, in a society built upon universal suffrage, transform the place of that chamber in the state. Many factors contributed to this end. In part, it was the result of the invention of limited liability; the peers became directors of companies and ceased, in large measure, to have a separate interest from those of finance and industry. In part, it was the declining ability of the peers to achieve the highest places in politics; it is significant that after 1870 Lord Rosebery is the only peer in our politics whose reputation was made in the House of Lords. Partly, again, it was the consequence of the chamber's great increase in size; nobody can pretend to the exclusiveness which is of the essence of aristocracy, if it doubles its numbers in fifty years.

But the real reason for the rise of a rational attitude to the House of Lords' claim to an effective share in political power is the fact that it is so deeply committed upon the fundamental questions it has to decide. It is neither more nor less than a chamber in which, in the last resort, the interests of property are defended from attack. In that defence, the House of Lords is a massive unit set over against what, tomorrow, may be a majority of the nation. As soon as that perspective of its character comes into view, the critic is bound to feel what Bagehot's critic felt—that the "only cure for admiring the House of Lords is to go and look at it." *Then,* the argument from antiquity counts for nothing; it is so much the more proof that the institution is an anachronism. Then, also, the very solid merits of the chamber are seen in a different light, for it becomes readily perceptible, at least to the critics, that all those merits can in fact be obtained from a chamber which is not subject to the defects from which the House of Lords patently suffers.

The truth is that an undemocratic institution cannot survive in a democratic society unless it is able constantly and rapidly to adjust its behaviour to the demands of the democracy. The fact, indeed, that the House of Lords is old does not mean that it is incapable of adjustment; until now, at least, the Crown has shown, so far as its public behaviour is concerned, that capacity to adjust is not necessarily incompatible with antiquity. What has made the House of Lords an impossible body is the fact that where it is tempted to be active in defence is just where the democracy is tempted to be active in offence. The House of Lords, in short, by its very constitution dramatizes the conflict between wealth and numbers whenever numbers decide to embark upon that conflict. It becomes of necessity a major symbol, because it ceases to have meaning unless it is willing to arrest the movement of change. The logic of its own composition impels it to that arrest, and, as it does so, embraces all the irrationalities in its constitutional position.

For the irony of that position is that a chamber acutely aware of its own defectiveness is unable to find the means for its reform. As soon as the question is asked: What is it to be reformed for? it emerges that no answer can be given upon which party differences admit of an agreed answer. Conservatives want to reform it in order, at bottom, to postpone reforms that threaten a change they deem too drastic in the present class-structure of society; socialists, precisely to prevent that postponement. The kind of reform that would emerge on the one view is incompatible with the kind of reform that would emerge on the other. The longer the debate continues, moreover, the more honestly, indeed, it is conducted, the less room does there appear for compromise. We are in the curious position that each party seeks to avoid the issue—the Conservative Party was pledged to reform in 1925—because it knows that any proposals it puts forward will be regarded by the other side as a decisive challenge. But that delay does not mitigate differences; rather, it tends to exacerbate them. For its result is merely to bring nearer, on the assumption that constitutional government is preserved, the day when, from the necessities of its position, a Labour government will be compelled to remove the House of Lords from its path; and it is certain that both the method and purpose of that removal will provoke passionate antagonism from the opponents of Labour.

It is curious to note how different the position seemed to Bagehot when he surveyed it seventy years ago. The House of Lords, he thought, "is quite safe from rough destruction but it is not safe against inward decay. . . . Its danger is not in assassination but atrophy; not abolition but decline." He saw the weakness of a body in which "most of its members neglect their duties . . . all of its members continue to be of one class, and that not quite the best." He prophesied that, like the Crown, it might lose its veto. Yet there has been no inward decay in the House of Lords. The functions it performed in Bagehot's day it performs as well, if not better, in our own. Its real danger is, in fact, the assassination he deemed impossible. By reforming it from the Conservative side, we may well destroy the safety-valve of the constitution—the power to override its decisions. By reconstructing it on principles satisfactory to Labour, we run at least the risk of provoking in the owners of property the determination to be done with a democratic system that endangers their power. The statesman who is able to find his way amid these grave dilemmas will indeed be entitled to the gratitude of the commonwealth.

CHAPTER FOUR

The House of Commons

1

NO honest spectator could, I think, observe with any care and continuity the habits and procedure of the House of Commons without a real admiration for its qualities. It is, after all, a rare and remarkable thing that a body of miscellaneous amateurs will go on, for sesson after session, hearing dull men put arguments before them at great length in favour of purposes in which they believe; more, that we should raise to one of the most supreme dignities in the Kingdom that Speaker whose business it is to see that the right of these dull men to be heard is protected by perhaps the most elaborate procedure human nature has so far devised.

We tend to take government by discussion for granted, and to assume that, when the division has been taken, it is a moral obligation to abide without repining by the result. We ought rather to remember that government by discussion is probably the rarest of all arts, so difficult, indeed, that there are only two or three countries in the world where it has endured for any space of time. To let your opponent say his say, even when you are convinced that he is wrong; to leave him the opportunity to convince those who are either dubious or indifferent that, despite your attitude, he is probably in the right; to see the cause you believe to be urgent defeated, and yet to accept the results of that defeat as part of the normal day's work; all this would be almost incredible if it had not actually occurred. Englishmen are said to be a complacent people, given to the luxury of self-congratulation upon their own achievements. I am inclined to believe that the more fully the working of the House of Commons is considered, the more reason they will be found to have cause for their sense of achievement.

It is, after all, a big thing to have built an institution the operations of which have maintained social peace for two and a half centuries. The House of Commons has not only been able to secure as high a talent as there is in the nation consistently in the nation's service; through its mechanisms, the men possessed of the effective power of the state have been persuaded to surrender that power as soon as it was clear that they would not secure a majority in the House of Commons. Not this alone. The debates of the assembly, whatever their defects, have had two enormous merits about them the significance of which it would be very difficult to overestimate. They have, broadly speaking, been an assurance that, when great issues are being discussed, whatever it is worth while to say upon any theme will by someone be said; and it has, as a rule, been well enough said so as to catch the ear of the nation and to educate it. A really important debate in the House of Commons is an occasion at which we can be sure that, without compulsion, most of what is best in the nation will assist as listeners. They will canvass eagerly the arguments used, the quality of the speeches. The chief press-organs of the country will comment upon them. A host of voluntary associations will pass resolutions upon them. Whatever the weakness of the House of Commons, it has made the British a more consciously political people than any other in the world.

That is an achievement, no doubt, effected slowly over the course of some two hundred years; in a more or less conscious way, its evolution may perhaps be dated from the controversy over Wilkes's election. That event demonstrated that the public opinion of the common man had to be taken into account in the making of government decisions. No doubt the common man, in a social system like ours, was slow in awakening to a sense of his own power; not until after 1867 did he begin, with rare exceptions (known in the history-books as notorious agitators), to be aware that he need not approach his rulers cap in hand. But that awareness has consistently grown. It has been one, and not the least important, of the reasons for the long British tradition of free government. My point is the simple one that the House of Commons was the central instrument which made this process of awareness possible. It made a relationship between member and constituency which compelled the House of Commons to realize that its life depended upon attentiveness to the public opinion it encountered. The business of the House was so to govern itself that it made the maximum response it deemed possible to the demands it encountered. The sanction for this attitude was the knowledge that without a satisfactory response there was always the danger that a constituency would exact remissness for defect in this regard.

It is, moreover, a relation into which all the elements of the population now enter; no one could now truthfully say, what Bagehot was able to say, that the "common order of work-people" is a section which need not be taken into account in estimating the influences that determine public opinion. Universal suffrage has meant that there is no stratum in the population whose view may be regarded by political parties as insignificant. To produce from the great welter of interests that thereby have influence, a policy which is adequate to the maintenance of efficient government is, of course, a very difficult task. That it has so far been successfully performed is very largely due to the place the House of Commons holds in the esteem of the nation.

What is the House of Commons for? Until we are clear about its purposes, we cannot really understand its significance. After all, to give supreme legislative power to a miscellaneous body of 615 men and women, mostly amateurs in politics, would not produce a successful legislative assembly. The secret lies in the way in which the House of Commons is organized and the ends for which that organization is applied. Above all, it is important to realize that the House of Commons is not an exact mirror of the interests and opinions of the nation. If it were, it could not possibly perform its work. For those opinions and interests are so various in their formidable complexity that any House which sought to find any effective place for a considerable number of them would be too atomic in character to be capable of coherent policy. The life of the House of Commons depends upon its representation of only such predominant strands of general public opinion as will, normally, enable a government to be formed behind which there is an effective majority. Thereby that government is able to inject a stream of continuous tendency into affairs. The business of making a government and providing it, or refusing to provide it, with the formal authority for carrying on the public business is the pivotal function of the House of Commons upon which all other functions turn.

It means, of course, that the life of the House of Commons is necessarily lived in terms of the party system. Parties are the basis upon which the organization of the House for coherency is made possible; and the member of the House of Commons must, with very few exceptions, be a good party man if it is to do its work adequately. The philosopher in his study may repine at this necessity. He may insist that this involves the sacrifice of individual conscience to party allegiance. He may argue that it leads members blindly into the division-lobbies on matters about which they have not even heard the debate in the chamber. He may write angrily, for reasons I shall discuss later, about Cabinet dictation in the House. The facts are quite different from these closet abstractions. The number of times when an average member feels inclined to vote against his party, especially when it is in office, is pretty small; and the evidence seems to show that when the impulse so to vote is an urgent one, he obeys it. It is foolish to imagine that in matters of debate a member must make up his mind upon each separate item the House decides. The House is a body for getting business done; the member's task is to be aware of large tendencies and to be on hand to support those the general direction of which he broadly approves. If he has so nice a conscience that a scrupulous examination of mostly technical minutiæ is the necessary preamble to his vote, the proper comment upon his attitude is that he is not by temperament suited to be a member of a legislative assembly.

The question of Cabinet dictatorship is a more complicated one, and I shall postpone its discussion until a later part of this chapter. To grasp the nature of the chamber in general, the first thing to realize is that the initiative in legislation does not, and ought not to, belong to the House as a whole. Its business, primarily, is to make a government to whom, so long as it gives that government its confidence, it is prepared to entrust that initiative. The alternative is, as in the American system, that every member has his private rostrum that he thinks of special importance. Masses of bills then would get introduced, most of them would be ill-considered; a few of them would be compromised (and most of them badly), and those few, without any necessary relation of coherence, would find their way to the statute-book. By leaving the initiative in legislation to the government, the House assures itself of the capacity to consider a programme. The government, indeed, is nothing so much as a committee of the House created to put before it measures for its acceptance. That relation secures that the measures involved are likely to be those about which significant public opinion is concerned. And this is more especially the case when a crowd of great problems presses upon the House for treatment. Unless it was able to confide to some few of its number the task of settling with which of those problems it should deal, and how it should deal with them, it would find itself helplessly inefficient for its work.

To make a government, then, with the initiative in legislation is the first task of the House. How it performs that task I shall discuss when I come to deal with the problem of Cabinet-making. If we assume that a government is in being, what are the functions the House must perform? There is the ventilation of grievance. There is the extraction of information. There is the business of debate, with the attempt through debate to sustain public interest and to educate it in the significance of what is being done. There is what we usually term the selective function of the House—which means that subtle psychological process whereby one member makes a reputation and another fails to make one, with its consequential repercussions on the personnel of governments. There is, lastly, the question of what place, if any, the private member as such is to occupy in the direction of the Commons' business. Each of these matters requires separate consideration.

It will be noted that I have assumed here that the examination and control of finance are not separate and special functions of the House of Commons; properly regarded, I believe that to be the case. Finance is not something apart from policy, but an expression of it. By deciding what to do in other spheres, the House largely decides by inference what it is to do in the financial sphere. Of course the Chancellor of the Exchequer must cut a big figure in the House—after the Prime Minister, perhaps the biggest figure. But most of what he does is, in fact, less subject to or, indeed, capable of scrutiny than what is done by most of his colleagues. A big body like the House of Commons cannot discuss estimates; it can concern itself only with the general policy which lies behind estimates. Members can say: "We wish more were being spent on secondary education"; they cannot usefully say in debate, save by way of general illustration, that more money ought to have been provided for nursery schools in Essex. That will interest, whether by attraction or repulsion, the members for Essex constituencies; but the members for Lancashire or Glamorgan will soon begin to protest that the House does not exist to spend its precious hours upon the particular grievances of one part of the country. If the House of Commons is ever to look at estimates seriously, from the sheer aspect of financial adequacy, it will have to develop organs for their examination quite different from any it now possesses.

The same applies to the problem of ways and means. A dis-

cussion of the Budget can never, in the whole House, be much
more than a close application of the general principles of taxation to the Chancellor's proposals. He can be urged to recognize
that he has set the income tax high, or that he is not taxing
millionaires enough. He can be warned, with graphic illustration,
that he is placing too large a burden on the food of the people.
It can be insisted that his duties on motor-cars discourage the
production of the kind of vehicle likely to penetrate the foreign
market. He can be urged to remember that he has a fruitful
source of neglected revenue in the taxation of urban land values.
Members can be eloquent upon his characteristic tenderness to
the farming interest. He can be warned that he is depending
too much on raising money by way of loan, and not enough, in
proportion, by way of taxes. But however skilful and knowledge-
able the criticism he receives, its real impact, in a miscellaneous
assembly, is bound to be general and not specific in character.
He has to retain the control of major outlines in his own hands.
The alternative is legislation by the chamber itself, and the experience of both France and the United States suggests comprehensively that this will mean bad legislation. The responsibility
of a committee for the construction of a Budget is too diffuse to
give it either the unity or the coherence that are requisite. Again,
it is possible that, with different organs of control from any it
now possesses, the House of Commons might be able to assert
its primacy over the Chancellor. We may doubt whether, if it
did, that would mean a better financial system. But it does not
possess them; and their absence means that either the Budget
must be his budget, in whatever form he is ultimately willing
to accept responsibility for it, or it must obtain another chancellor
and, in all probability, another government. It is normally unwilling to take this step; and this, in effect, means both that its
dislike of his general financial methods must be part of any case
it makes, through the Opposition, against the government; and
that the real verdict will subsequently be delivered by the electorate at the polls.

After forming a government, the most essential function of the House of Commons in our system is the ventilation of grievance. No government can satisfy everybody, and some governments fail to satisfy some interests, important or unimportant, very badly indeed. It is inherent in the nature of a democratic system that any man, or group of men, who can persuade a member of the House to raise his grievance, should have the opportunity of getting it discussed. It may be Mr. O'Brien, who is arrested without due process of law at the instance of the Home Secretary. It may be Miss Savidge who is severely questioned by the police after being acquitted in a court of law for the offence charged against her by the police. The co-operative movement may feel strongly about the taxation of their profits by a Chancellor of the Exchequer who, as an eminent advocate, had advised them that, as they do not make profits, they cannot be liable for taxation. It may be Mr. Plimsoll heroically struggling against the government's refusal to impose adequate human standards upon the owners of merchant ships. It may be the official Opposition, either moving a general vote of censure upon the government or claiming a day to insist upon what it believes to be some obvious inadequacy in the conduct of foreign affairs. The subject is unimportant. The method may be as humble as a simple question to ministers, or as dramatic as a motion to adjourn the House on a question of urgency. The essential point is that the grievance, real or unreal, may be ventilated and that the government, as best it can, must seek to produce a satisfactory answer to the claim of grievance.

Of the value of this right, no one who has watched it in operation can have any doubt at all. No better method has ever been devised for keeping administration up to the mark. It assures that what a government does will, overwhelmingly, have to be done in the light of day and answered for in the light of day also. I do not say that it gives an assurance that justice will be done; it does give an assurance that there will be a careful examination into the accusation of injustice. The minister against whose department the accusation is made knows that he is on trial. He is eager, if he possibly can, to convince the House; he is even anxious, if he can, to persuade his critic to accept his explanation. There are many cases in which the private member, with a serious grievance to protest, has been able to secure a prompt movement to redress. In the Savidge case, for example, the whole House, indifferently to party competition, was on the side of the member who moved the adjournment of the House; and the temper of the assembly was such that the House Secretary had to concede the setting-up of a Royal Commission on Police Powers and Procedure which led to a significant revision of the powers assumed by police-authorities.

Naturally enough, of course, the method has its limitations. Its power to alter the action of the government depends fairly precisely upon the degree to which it embodies a party attitude. Few votes of censure are likely to be carried. A Chancellor embarrassed by the legal opinion he rendered as a private advocate will take refuge in Conservative enthusiasm for any new burden laid upon the co-operative movement. In a recent case where industrial workers in Admiralty dockyards were dismissed without knowing their accusers or the charges brought against them —a wholly un-English procedure—the Minister concerned contented himself simply with asking for trust from his party and dismissing the unanswered charges of unfairness by applying the party majority to the question. In the Palestine disturbances of 1936–37, the government manœuvred itself out of a difficult attack by promising a Royal Commission on the question, and then appointing it with such terms of reference that the real roots of the grievance with which it was asked to deal were beyond the scope of the Commission's inquiry; so that public opinion conveniently forgot the grievance involved in its contemplation of remedies suggested for quite different ills. Or a Minister may simply refuse information where grievance is suggested on the ground that it is not in the public interest to answer the question. Or he may deny the existence of a grievance which, though real in fact, is not susceptible of the kind of proof that endangers his position in the House of Commons.

All these are important limitations, yet, even when they are weighted at their utmost, the value of the right is profound. How right may be seen from a simple example. It is certainly true of the parliamentary system that, after such an exhibition as General Göring gave in the Dimitrov trial, he would not have been able to remain a member of a British government for twenty-four hours. A British Prime Minister would have been aware that he would be questioned in the House about the habits of such a colleague; and he would have rushed to obtain his resignation before the House met in order to be able to assure its members that he shared their indignation at them. The power to ventilate grievance means the power to compel attention to grievance. A government that is compelled to explain itself under cross-examination will do its best to avoid the grounds of complaint. Nothing makes responsible government so sure. Where this power is absent, the room for tyranny is always wide; for nothing so develops inertia in a people as the inability to formulate grievance and to see that its redress is pressed upon the central source of power. This, at least, the House of Commons secures, and upon big occasions it secures it in a background of dramatic emphasis which concentrates wide attention upon the issue involved. The Savidge case was what the journalists call front-page news until the government had given assurance of remedy for the complaint. Can anyone imagine a Berlin stenographer's receiving similar treatment if she had complained to a Reichstag deputy about the unwelcome attentions of the German Gestapo?

Hardly less vital than the power to ventilate grievance is the power to extract information. Parliamentary government lives and dies by the publicity it can secure not only on governmental operations but on all the knowledge it can obtain on the working of social processes. I take, as a purely random instance, July 21, 1937. Mr. Eden answers questions about foreign policy in Spain and China, on the importation of slaves into Saudi Arabia, on the impact of the Palestine Report on Anglo-American relations, on Hungarian propaganda against Czechoslovakia in England, on the relevance of the League Covenant to Sino-Japanese relations, on a speech made in Berlin by the British Ambassador, and on the reform of the League of Nations. Mr. Duff Cooper explains how it is proposed to protect British shipping from attack by General Franco, the conditions of employment in naval dockyards, the allowances to seamen at Singapore, the regulations about vaccination at Sheerness, an alleged incident during submarine exercises near Portland Bill. Mr. Ormsby-Gore answers questions about an advisory committee on colonial labour, on industrial disturbances in Trinidad, on slavery in the Aden protectorate, on the partition of Nigeria, on the system of land-tenure under the Alake of Abeokuta, on the clove industry in Zanzibar, and so on. Sir Thomas Inskip explains his policy on munition factories, on the supply of aeroplanes, and the general problems of defence co-ordination. There are questions on aviation, transport, road accidents, the supply of railway cars, delays in electrification, the extraction of oil from coal, the dangers of siliceous abrasives in sandblasting, the adequacy of the staff of the Chief Inspector of Factories in watching for the illegal employment of boys between the ages of fourteen and seventeen. To put it summarily, it may fairly be said that there is an almost inexhaustible appetite for information, and a remarkable willingness to satisfy the appetite.

The process of questioning has important results. It brings the work of the departments of state into the public view. It makes them realize that they are functioning under a close public scrutiny which will continuously test their efficiency and honesty. It mitigates, even if it cannot wholly prevent, the danger that bureaucratic habits will develop in the civil service; men who have to answer day by day for their decisions will tend so to act that they can give a good account of themselves. No one can read the question-period over any length of time without the

clear impression that whatever the light of day can do to make
intelligible the business of administration this process is in a
high degree likely to do. But its merit, great as this is, does not
end there. Some questions will reveal a defective state of affairs.
The Minister is made aware that his answers have proved unsatisfactory. He feels that he must go further than the answer
his department is able to render. He is eager to placate a special
or general public opinion which continues to insist that more
should be known. He appoints a select committee, a departmental committee, or a Royal Commission to report upon the
problem. Or he thinks that some question ought to come into
the public view upon which there is inadequate knowledge, or
confused or irritated public sentiment. A committee will discover
the facts and trace the outlines of a policy upon which, at a later
stage, action may become possible.

Investigation by committees has been one of the most vital
techniques contributed by the parliamentary system to the meth-
odology of representative government, and it has been made
possible only by the fact that the parliamentary system exists.
Not a few of the reports these bodies have issued have been
landmarks in the history of their subjects. In education, in the
improvement of factory conditions, on poor-law reform, on the
machinery of government, on the reorganization of the army, on
the limits of ministers' powers, on the principles of local taxation, we have reports that have profoundly affected the contours
of policy. When the Budget leakages of 1936 provoked an angry
feeling in public opinion, the work of the Porter Committee did
one of the most cleansing pieces of work the public life of any
modern state has known—a piece of work, it should be added,
that would have been possible only under a democratic form of
government; and the same is true of the remarkable inquiry by
the Fisher Committee which resulted in the dismissal of a permanent secretary of a department from the public service. In a
sense, the Fisher report is even more remarkable than that of
Mr. Justice Porter. The latter applied to an alleged scandal

which was the theme of universal discussion. But the former tackled, rigorously and thoroughly, one which, at most, was known to hardly more than half a dozen persons and could easily have been met by private action which would have successfully screened the facts from the public view. It was interesting evidence of the way in which the technique of parliamentary government has developed a tradition of self-criticism in the civil service which is the supreme safeguard against the vices of bureaucracy.

The method, of course, like that of the ventilation of grievance, has its limits. The value of investigation by committees depends very largely on the personnel of committees, and this raises interesting problems upon which it is worth while to say a word. Our system in this regard suffers from a number of dangers. A Treasury zest for economy may provide it with inadequate secretarial assistance. Its members may be appointed less for the knowledge they possess than because the Minister desires to confer a distinction upon a friend. There is a tendency, in appointments, to specialize in retired statesmen and, on the Labour side, on trade-union officials whose "moderation" can be trusted. There is a straining towards unanimity in the reports —a belief that the strength of the conclusions lies not in the power of the analysis but in the arrival at conclusions least calculated to disturb existing interests. The report of the Royal Commission on Local Government is an illuminating example of these dangers. After all its monumental labours, it timidly refuses to face any of the problems it was invited to examine. Its value consists almost wholly in the evidence tendered to it by the witnesses, especially officials, who appeared before it. The evidence is of great significance; but it is not merely to receive evidence that a Royal Commission is appointed.

Yet even when all this is taken into account, the importance of the technique is very great. Without it, and without the mass of information daily made available in government publications, there would be hardly anything of the factual basis we possess for carving out principles from the raw material of life. After all, we must remember that Karl Marx's massive indictment of capitalist civilization was largely built on facts made available to him by investigations undertaken through parliamentary pressure. On any showing, that is a remarkable fact. Once again, if we compare these habits with the limited and dubious publicity of Fascist countries, the contrast is all to the advantage of the parliamentary system. There is no Fascist country in the world today which makes available to its public opinion truthful statistics about wages and prices, the number of unemployed and their treatment, the operation of the judicial system. There is none, either, that permits discussion even of the results of the half-truths it makes available. To make the facts known and to work out principles of politics which display the meaning of those facts are achievements it would not be easy to overestimate.

The House of Commons is, also, a debating assembly. There has been a tendency in the post-war years to underestimate the significance of this function. We are all of us, in some degree, *laudatores temporis acti;* we fall, easily, into the temper which insists that the great age of Parliament is the one we just fail to remember. Politicians of the Baldwin epoch say that the House is not what it was when Mr. Asquith was Prime Minister, and in Mr. Asquith's day they looked back with regret to the greater days of Gladstone and Disraeli; no doubt some old member of those days used to sigh for the epoch when Pitt and Fox crossed swords with each other. The debates, it is said, are not of the old standard; they are too dominated by the leaders of the House; they are empty and mechanical performances because, in ninety-nine cases out of a hundred, everyone knows what the result is going to be. It has become almost the proof of political sophistication to sneer at the House. The "talking-shop" leads many people to sigh, like Carlyle, for Colonel Pride and his little platoon.

On all this, there are many things to be said: not least of them that the alternative to the "talking-shop" is the concentration camp. A society that is able to discuss does not need to fight; and the greater the capacity to maintain interest in discussion, the less danger there is of an inability to effect the compromises that maintain social peace. I do not think there is any reason to assume a decline in the quality of debate. The habits of the House have altered as its composition has altered; the composition of the assembly no longer reflects the upper class and little else. Members are differently educated; they have different subject-matter to discuss; and the style of the debate naturally adapts itself to the new circumstances it encounters. Anyone who turns over the Hansard of sixty or seventy years ago will find all save the supreme historic speeches unreadable; it is only now and again that one can catch the historic voices coming through, a little faint, perhaps, with the years. One will find the same repetition, the same verbosity, the same domination of leaders. The House empties when Mr. Gladstone has replied just as it emptied when Mr. Baldwin sat down. Speeches no more altered opinions in the House of a generation or two generations ago than they alter opinions today. It is tempting to argue that not even the critic of parliamentarism expects that they should. There is no more reason to suppose that they will than there is to expect that a multitude of sermons will produce a community of Christians. The process of debate is not an effort in sudden conversion; and those who attack the House because its speeches seem to reach but a little way are in fact guilty of one of the simplest of intellectualist fallacies.

A parliamentary debate is only a part of a long, cumulative process no single piece of which is likely in itself to be important. Most of it, after all, must be sober and undramatic work. A House of Commons that is in a continuous frenzy of excitement is a House that is in a succession of crises; that is usually the index to a government in office that is on its way to the grave. What matters is less the occasional great debate than the impact produced on electoral opinion by the pattern of the whole Parliament. In this sense, certainly, the debates have an enormous importance. What they are in themselves and, hardly less, what is written and said about them in a thousand articles and a thousand speeches are the living material out of which the voters' choice is made. It was in the debates that Mr. Baldwin won that curious place in the affection of the British people that no one has been able quite to explain. It is in the debates that Mr. Attlee establishes his claim to be a national leader. What Mr. Eden has to say in defence of his foreign policy is dissected and analysed until every word is made to yield its possible, or impossible, implications. A democracy lives by the spoken word and what is said in print about that spoken word. Not unnaturally, the big occasion is the vital thread of the pattern; we can be sure that Mr. Baldwin's speech in the debate on the abdication of Edward VIII will be one of the foundations of the future judgment about him. But the big occasion is only one thread. Parliament could not endure upon a diet of great occasions.

Nor is it, I think, important that, in all normal circumstances, the result of a debate is known before the division is taken. That, after all, is what the party system is for; the convictions of members would be fragile indeed if government and opposition alike could not normally count upon their votes. The trends of policy must have some coherency of direction; if members are to turn the government out each time, for instance, they think that Mr. Attlee has had the best of Mr. Chamberlain, we should be in a sorry plight. Members are not, as the legend runs, voting against their convictions. They are saying what, on balance, we all say, that though they do not like this particular clause in this particular bill, or are uncomfortable about this special item of policy, they would rather have the government they support in power than an alternative against which they would, in all probability, desire to vote far more frequently.

And it must not be forgotten that the theory of mechanized voting is, as a matter of proportion, a travesty of the facts. There are limits beyond which a government dare not push its majority for fear of losing its majority. Mr. Baldwin had to sacrifice Sir

Samuel Hoare; Mr. Chamberlain had to abandon the original form of his National Defence Contribution. In 1923, after Mr. Bridgeman's blunder over *Ex parte O'Brien*, it was proposed to pass a bill of indemnity in which the arrested men were deprived of their legal right to compensation. The whole House protested against a principle which, it was urged on all sides, was a violation of "fair play"; and the government had to yield to the opinion of the House. The argument of a mechanical debate devoid of reality is, in short, nonsense. It fails to take account of the long negotiations which usually precede the formation of policy by parties, the weighing of the facts, the eliciting of opinions, the consultation of interests known to be affected. It misses the point that parties are unresting in their efforts to keep in touch with the opinions and sentiments of their supporters, that a vital test of good leadership in the House of Commons is the ability to gauge just how far the leader can take his followers. Debates do not normally overturn governments just because the main art of a government is to produce for its supporters what they expect. When a leader fails to do this at the point where he produces a sense of outrage, he finds, like Peel in 1846, or Mr. MacDonald in 1931, that his party throws him over. The secret of the division-lobby is not, as Mr. Ramsay Muir seems to think, the fact that the government has the threat of dissolution in its hands. A government which could not live save by the constant invocation of that threat would very rapidly cease to be a government.

The selective function of the House of Commons is the most mysterious of all its habits; it is far easier to describe the mysterious alchemy it expresses than to explain it. The making of a reputation in the House is not a direct function of ability; many men of first-rate intelligence—Sir George Jessel, for instance— were failures in the House of Commons. It is not accessible to oratorical talent or debating power merely; it was never, for instance, moved by Brougham, whose importance was almost wholly derived from outside the House of Commons. A reputation for character may give a member great standing in the chamber even when it is not allied to any exceptional mental power; Lord Althorp and Mr. Walter Long are both examples of this prestige. The House will admire without respect, and no one can watch the interplay of its proceedings without observing how carefully it draws a distinction between these. It will listen with far greater attention to a bad speaker who, in a halting way, is trying to say something he feels deeply, or to convey information which it believes to be significant, than to a facile debater who is obviously speaking, however well, merely to bring his name before the public. It tends to distrust the clever man who tries to score points. It dislikes the pontifical type who appears to be instructing members for their own good. It is a very difficult assembly to bully, even from the front benches. It will accord little but suspicion to a reputation brought into the chamber from outside unless its possessor assumes that he must, *ab initio*, win the goodwill of members. It hates the member who uses invective as a speciality, yet there is nobody so sympathetic to one the intensity of whose attack is measured by some deeply felt experience which lies behind it.

The easy thing, of course, to say of all this is that the House of Commons is an attractive club, with all the habits that pertain to this special institution. There is no doubt a real truth in this; men who have to live together and work together for years on end can hardly, even amid the conditions of modern party warfare, help developing between one another the habits of good fellowship; these, moreover, are important and valuable, because they tend, within limits, to create the atmosphere necessary to that art of successful compromise which is of the essence of parliamentary government. If the government side stood to the opposition in the posture of gladiators determined to draw blood, it is clear that debate would be at least difficult and understanding impossible.

But, in fact, these habits serve another purpose of immense importance. The impact of a member upon the House is a very good way (though it is not the only way) of testing his availability for ministerial position. A man who is to rule a department well must have the qualities which enable him to be acceptable to the House of Commons. That he is so acceptable does not mean that he will be a good minister; but not to be so acceptable does probably mean that he is not likely to be an effective one. It is not merely true, as the old Greek proverb has it, that office shows the man; it is still more true that ability to win the attention of the House is a proof of fitness, at least in some degree, for power. It is a part of that art of managing men which is the pivot of leadership. It brings out qualities by tests which go to the root of character. A government that is not subject to criticism may pick its members as it will; any fool, as Napoleon said, can govern in a state of siege. But a government the members of which are constantly under the fire of criticism, who have, before it, to maintain the appearance of reasonableness, to refrain from losing their tempers, to show courtesy and restraint as their normal temper, who have to recognize that there is a point at which neither rhetoric nor reiteration is an answer to argument, a government schooled to this discipline is at least likely to keep its head in any but the gravest times.

Broadly, I think it is true to say that the House enables this kind of quality to be made available for office through the kind of reputation it gives to its members. No doubt it makes mistakes, but it does not often make bad mistakes. Those whom it finds interesting or persuasive are very likely to be interesting or persuasive, and such men are moved to make the effort to display these qualities because the rewards of their recognition in our system are so obviously great. The House, in a word, is able by its atmosphere to draw out from a man the best of the qualities that are important for ruling in a party system. That has been remarkably demonstrated in our own time by Lord Baldwin. The qualities that gave him his peculiar hold over the House were the qualities that, a little later, gave him his peculiar hold over the nation. It is, I think, certain that so delicate an affair as the abdication of Edward VIII could not have been carried out so successfully without that hold. It is impossible to do more than hint at its secret; but I believe that the centre of its mystery lies in the power to evoke a sense of trust which transcends the division of parties. That is the quality Lord Althorp had; it is the quality, also, that explains why, without any very notable intelligence, Sir Edward Grey exercised so remarkable an authority over members. And it should, I think, be added that the trust, in its turn, depends upon the intuitive sense of the House that the minister concerned respects it and, through it, the great, if impalpable, assumptions upon which it rests. The Parliament of 1918–22 was a bad Parliament because there was lacking any abiding sense of that trust and, similarly, the Parliament of 1931 was a bad Parliament because the circumstances in which the election that preceded it had been fought rendered it impossible for that trust to be asked for and given.

To the operation of this trust two things are necessary of quite pivotal importance. The first is a relatively great stability in the membership of the House. Members who are not accustomed to one another for fairly long periods cannot take one another for granted; they cannot know one another's personality in a way that builds a tradition, an *esprit de corps*, a sense, despite differences, of a mutual adventure in search of great ends. The rapid change of membership in the House of Representatives is not the least significant of the reasons why the power of the American Senate has proved so much more influential than the theoretically equal power of the House of Representatives. But anyone who remembers that Mr. Gladstone was in the House of Commons for more than sixty years, and Mr. Disraeli for more than forty; that Mr. Asquith was a member for a little less than fifty years, and that Mr. Lloyd George has passed more than half his life there; that though Mr. Baldwin slipped into great place, as it were, by accident, he had been a member of Parliament, at the time of his first Premiership, for fifteen years, and that, with a brief interlude, Mr. MacDonald at the same period had been a member for eighteen years; will realize, from these among many instances, their import. Few people can live long periods of their lives amid great events without getting something of their "feel." They are introduced to the environment of successful administration. They learn the team-work, the discretion, the vital habit of action after reflection, that it involves. They learn, too, what is fundamental, that the business of direction in a system of government means not merely the issue of orders, but the issue which will have to be defended against public criticism. On the whole, the earlier they are accustomed to this environment, the greater is the chance that they will become successful in mastering it. That is why, in general, a young aristocrat is likely to be a better minister than a business man who enters the House of Commons for the first time in middle age. That is why, also, on the Labour side, an elderly trade-union official will rarely— there are notable exceptions—make a successful House of Commons man. As a rule, to have served a long apprenticeship to an alternative vocation breeds habituations too different from those required by the service of politics.

To the operation of this trust, also, it is, I think, generally true to say that the parliamentary Opposition must be strong enough, both in numbers and in quality, to put the government on its mettle. Strong enough in numbers for several reasons. A House in which the Opposition is small tends to become slack in its habits. Attendance becomes irregular. The disproportion of strength is so great that men do not take pains. There is an insufficient incentive to mutual understanding. The burden on the representative speakers against the government is too great for them to do their work well. The Opposition must be strong enough in quality for several reasons also. For without skilful generalship, the Opposition case goes by default. The effective work of criticizing the government fails to be done. Because it so fails, the ears of the country do not listen to the proceedings of the House, and the educative force of its debates is lost. More than this: a weak Opposition begins to lose confidence in itself. It loses its integration and becomes not merely self-critical but publicly self-critical. The result is to transfer public interest from its function as an Opposition to the inferior problems of the personalities involved in its internal differences. It becomes defeatist and even irresponsible; it loses what in a parliamentary system it is fatal to lose, the ability to take the offensive when the opportunity presents itself. For every Opposition has to pass through two phases if it is to transform itself into a government. There is the phase where it seeks to make the case against the Cabinet of the day; after a period, it is rare for such a case not to offer itself on solid grounds. But there is the second and more difficult phase in which the negation of the first is transformed into the ability to convince the electorate positively not only that the government is a bad government, but also that for the sake of the country the Opposition ought to take its place as soon as possible. No Opposition can produce that conviction unless its front bench has quality enough not only to take the offensive, but also to seem to take it on comprehensive and adequate grounds.

I shall deal later with some of the implications of this view, when I come to discuss the character of political parties in the contemporary House of Commons. Here it is sufficient to say that the conception of the offensive is central to the whole strategy of parliamentary government. For because that government depends upon the party system, the warfare of parties in the House is the predominant political means whereby the battle sways from the one side to the other. It is not, of course, the only means: profound industrial events, like the general strike of 1926, may produce an immense and independent impact on electoral opinion. But, even so, they will culminate in a decision, whether negative or positive, taken by the government of the day. That decision will present an issue to the opposing party, and its ability to use the issue for the purpose of making known its central philosophy is the real test of its quality, the proof of its power to take the offensive in party warfare. That was the great art, to take two modern examples, of Mr. Gladstone and

Mr. Lloyd George. The Midlothian campaign of the one, the Limehouse speeches of the other were exactly such a seizure of the offensive as I have discussed. Each was able, by skilful leadership, to focus the whole mind of the electorate upon issues he wished to have discussed from the platform from which he chose to discuss them. Each prevented his critics from staging the debate from the angle that would have suited them. Each, accordingly, made a majority of the electorate feel that their possession of power was vital to a victory for the side he represented. It is the selective function of the House to bring to party leadership men who can render this service to their parties. Certainly, up to the close of the war, it was a function remarkably fulfilled. Certainly, also, I think, since the war it has been better fulfilled on the Right than on the Left. When we come to deal with the party structure of the House of Commons, we shall see why this has necessarily been the case.

The last of the general questions which I must here discuss is the place of the private member in the organization of the House. It is fashionable for critics of the present position to lament almost with tears over the decline of his status. He is bound hand and foot, we are told, to the party machine. He can ask questions, he can debate, he can introduce his little bills and his private members' motions, so long as it is understood that no consequence will follow from them. But party has made the Cabinet the master; if he does not obey the party whip he will soon find himself cast into the outer darkness. A Conservative constituency will not adopt again as candidate a member who repeatedly votes against his party; and the control of the Labour machine is, it is pointed out, even more rigorous. Its standing orders permit a member to refrain from voting where his conscience is engaged, but he may not go into the division-lobby against a party decision without risking his right to continue as a member of the party. For all serious purposes, therefore, we are asked to regard the private member as a mere unit in a division-list, with no effective sphere of independent action of his own.

The lament, I suggest, is wholly misconceived. It mistakes the functions the modern House of Commons has to perform; it mistakes the purposes of parties in the modern state; it is an anachronistic legacy of a dead period in our history when politics was a gentleman's amusement, and the sphere of governmental activity was so small that an atomistic House of Commons was possible. The only way to restore to the private member the kind of position he occupied eighty, or even fifty, years ago is to go back to the historic conditions which made that position possible. History does not permit us to indulge in such luxuries.

The problem of modern government is a problem of time; this is the basic reason why the initiative in legislation has passed from the private member. In general, if a matter is important enough to be embodied in a bill, it is desirable that the responsibility for its passage should rest with the government. It cannot, in any case, hope for time unless the government approves of it; and if it is a matter upon which it does not feel keenly enough to introduce it, the chances are strongly against its being worth while spending the time of the House on its passage. I do not think this conclusion is invalidated by the fact that a private member, Mr. A. P. Herbert, has by his zeal and energy secured a small instalment of divorce-law reform. For, because his bill was not a government bill, he was compelled to accept drastic amendments which narrowed its scope in a high degree, and the truncated measure which resulted will probably prevent the serious rationalization of the marriage laws for many years to come. If anything, Mr. Herbert's experience shows plainly that when any big theme requires legislative action, only the government has the requisite authority to deal with it on an ample scale.

If, therefore, we assume that the general function of legislation ought essentially to be initiated by government, what remains for the private member? The ventilation of grievance; the extraction of information; the criticism of the administrative process; what contribution he can make to debate. In addition to these, he can raise, in private members' motions, the discussion of large principles that test the movement of public opinion. He can serve on committees of inquiry. I do not myself think that this can be regarded as a small field of action. But I should agree that, especially for members on the government side of the House, it is not an adequate field for an active-minded man. The problem, I therefore suggest, is to enlarge that field without treading on the essential right of government to initiate legislation. This can, I believe, be done without any such invasion, if we once assume that the real function of the House is to watch the process of administration as the safeguard of the private citizen. In the proper scrutiny of delegated legislation, in the improvement by analysis, by criticism, by suggestion, of departmental work, in the enlargement of the place of the select committee of inquiry, in one system, there is a wide range of service awaiting the private member of which we do not, in the present organization of the House, take anything like full advantage. I shall try later to discuss the methods by which this might be done.

But it must be emphasized that such an enlargement ought not to interfere with the Cabinet's control of the main stream of parliamentary activity. Coherence of policy would at once be lost, and with it the ability to place responsibility where it truly should lie. Indeed, it may be fairly said that the real success of one system lies precisely in the definite allocation of responsibility that it makes possible. It is an immense advantage always to know who is to blame when something goes wrong. Anyone who compares the American system with ours can see at once that this is the case. It is usually unfair to blame the President, for he could not get just the bill he wanted; he had to placate this interest and that, not seldom in a secret way that public opinion cannot adequately explore. It is not always fair to blame Congress; it ceases, under the separation of powers, to remain a legislature if it accepts the position of the President's creature. Once the power of the Cabinet over the private member was relaxed, we should have what is in fact government by public meeting.

It is only because party leadership is vested in the Cabinet that the House does not present the spectacle of a mass of vested interests each struggling to see that it is maintained and protected by the governmental process. Those who ask for the abrogation of any considerable measure of Cabinet control are actually asking for what would be bound to develop into the destruction of ministerial responsibility.

I cannot believe that our system would benefit thereby. The resultant legislation would not be built upon principle; it would be much more like the "pork barrel" legislation of Congress. Ministers would be continually sacrificing this and that to one well-organized interest after another; they have, as it is, to sacrifice enough. It is, moreover, a bad thing to make any government put forward and, later, administer measures in which it does not really believe but which it has accepted under threat of defeat. Mr. Ramsay Muir has argued that the result would be "moderate" measures, because the diminution of Cabinet control would leave the private member free to be inventive in the general interest.

That is, I think, an excessively simple view. It wholly misconceives the nature of the House of Commons. For beneath the formal fact of territorial representation—for which no convenient substitute has so far been discovered—the House is essentially a vocational body. Members, no doubt, are elected for Devonport and Dover, London and Manningtree. But that does not conceal the fact that they are lawyers, business men, retired soldiers and sailors, bankers, railway directors, trade-union officials, and the like. Each of them cannot help watching the process of legislation in terms of the vocation to which he belongs. We all know that an owner of coal royalties would take a very different view of the purchase price in a scheme of nationalization to which he was entitled than a miner or even a cotton broker. We know that miners in the House will take a very different view of miners' hours of labour and their reasonable limits, than, say, the members for the dockyard constituencies. The weaker Cabinet control is, the more we drift back to the system of which the private enclosure acts of the eighteenth and nineteenth century are the supreme example. The American Senator is independent of the executive power in the way some critics in this country think desirable. It is not, I think, unfair to say that it is exactly that independence which constitutes the power of those vocational lobbies which are such a vicious feature of the American system.

I do not, of course, mean to say that we do not have our lobbies in England. The power of the agricultural interests and of industries like shipping, iron and steel, textiles, and so on is unquestionable. On the other side, there is the immense influence of the Trades Union Congress over the Labour Party. But, given Cabinet control, the ability of the lobby in this country to dominate the private member is mitigated by two important factors. It is mitigated by the ability of the civil service to give advice to the Minister against the lobby's urgency, and it is mitigated by the fact that the member is subject to party control just because the Cabinet is identical with the party leadership in office. The one, on each particular instance, means an independent examination of the lobby's plea for assistance. The other means that a member who surrenders to the lobby may jeopardize his seat, and a group of members who by that surrender threaten the stability of the government may find themselves staring dissolution in the face.

"Efficiency in an assembly," wrote Bagehot, "requires a solid mass of steady votes"; we may add that this "solid mass" is also the main safeguard against the worst forms of corruption. That "solid mass" is provided by party control and there is nothing we know of to take its place. The alternative is government by interests so articulated that the problem of making governmental responsibility clear is never adequately solved. No doubt the power to dissolve is a very great power. We see the alternative in its absence in the United States and France. In the one, the President gets his way, in so far as he gets his way, very largely by the use of patronage—about as undesirable a method of persuasion as the imagination can conceive. In the other, because members know that a dissolution is unthinkable, their sense of responsibility for what is done is tragically small. More than that: the power to upset a government without paying the penalty therefor means that many of the great decisions are made without reference to electoral will. The country votes for M. Herriot, but the chamber yields to pressure from outside (and dubious pressure at that) and it gets the government of M. Poincaré, or M. Doumergue, or M. Laval. At least we are saved by Cabinet control of the private member from monstrous perversions of this sort.

One final remark may be made in this context. The Cabinet minister in our system, has, with all his defects, served as a rule a long apprenticeship which breeds a very real sense of responsibility; the selective function of the House provides, in this regard, at least some safeguards of importance. The methods by which a candidate is chosen give us no such assurance of responsibility. A young aristocrat, a business man who hopes by his wealth to find a seat in the House the avenue to social distinction, the barrister who knows that, given some competence, he may hope for a place on the Bench if he serves his party well—these are types in which the Right seems to specialize without repining. On the other, the big trade unions are able to put many of their officials directly into the House without the need too carefully to inquire into their fitness for the place. The more one considers our method of choosing candidates, the more their control as members by the Cabinet or party to which they owe allegiance seems a wise innovation. It puts the onus of responsibility for action squarely where it ought to be; that enables it to be judged when the Cabinet's term of office is over. At the same time it provides a debating assembly which reflects pretty accurately the dominant composition of the electorate. Party control is an assurance that, normally, the private member will do what he is sent to Westminster to do; and even if he is kept in his place by his masters, he is fully able to make his views known. The result is a system which, with all its defects, makes for the clear direction of affairs and the full discussion of that direction. These are merits the greatness of which men feel only when a change of system prevents the possibility of their operation.

2

The Cabinet is a committee of that party or parties which command a majority in the House of Commons. I shall discuss in a later chapter the methods of its organization and functioning. Here I shall be concerned with the consequences of the view urged above that the secret of parliamentary efficiency is the control of the House by the Cabinet. What, in effect, is the purpose of that control? Above all, clearly, to put a coherent programme into operation, and to secure for it the formal legal consent that the constitution requires. Parliament is the organ of registration for the Cabinet. On the ability of the Cabinet to secure that registration depends the success of our whole system of government.

Now the essence of the method lies in the terms upon which the control is conducted. The Cabinet has to elicit consent; it cannot exact it. The difference is fundamental to our system. The Cabinet has to conduct its operations in the public view. It is subject to a constant stream of criticism, both within the House and without. Its problem is to be able to maintain the loyalty of its supporters despite the impact of this criticism upon them. That is not so easy as it appears. A Cabinet has to learn the direction of its supporters' minds. It has to recognize that in the making of every policy there are limits beyond which it may not go. A bad blunder may easily disturb the very foundations of its majority. A clear drift of electoral opinion away from its support may sow a spirit of rebellion in the House before which even a government with a vast majority is impotent. Maintaining a majority is never a simple and straightforward matter, for the discipline of followers is not the obedience of private soldiers to their commanders. There enter into its making a host of subtle psychological considerations the accurate measurement of which is vital to the Cabinet's life. It is dangerous to run the House on too tight a rein. Excessive secrecy, grave discourtesy, continual threat of resignation or dissolution, inability to quell an angry public opinion outside always breed revolt. A Cabinet maintains control in the degree that it is successful in not going too far beyond what the House approves. It must know when to yield, and it is important to yield gracefully. A Cabinet that tries to carry off its policy with too high a hand is almost always riding for a fall.

Cabinet control, this is to say, is subject to its ability to be sensitive to public opinion; and even a great majority will fail it if it is supremely insensitive. With a great majority, Mr. MacDonald had to give way on the Unemployment Assistance Regulations in 1934; with a great majority, also, Mr. Baldwin had to sacrifice Sir Samuel Hoare in the Abyssinian crisis of 1935; with a great majority, again, Mr. Chamberlain had to give way on his National Defence Contribution of 1937. Since an unpopular policy always creates the fear that it may lead to defeat at the next general election, members are unwilling to serve under a Cabinet which does not recognize that it is leading them to defeat. "There is the hard, ineluctable fact," said Sir Samuel Hoare when he resigned, "that I have not got the confidence of the great body of opinion in the country, and I feel that it is essential for the Foreign Secretary, more than any other Minister in the country, to have behind him the general approval of his fellow-countrymen." Had Mr. Baldwin refused to withdraw the Cabinet's proposals on Abyssinia, it is certain that a considerable part of his followers would have voted against him, and resignation or dissolution would have followed. The retirement of Sir Samuel Hoare was the propitiatory sacrifice he had to make.

This necessity of sensitiveness is, of course, greatly increased when the Cabinet is in a minority in the House. The temptation, in any third party, is always to force it to concessions in order to enhance its own prestige. It wants the country to be aware that the Cabinet lives of its grace. That is why minority governments are always both weak and short-lived. At some point, they cannot go on making concessions without seeming to be devoid of the authority to govern, and they spend a considerable part of their time trying to discover a good pretext for dissolution. The third party, no doubt, like the Liberal Party in the 1924 Parliament, considers that it has given the Cabinet what Mr. Asquith called a "discriminating support." But what appears to it an attempt to keep the Cabinet on the right lines always appears to the Cabinet a sword of Damocles wielded so as to injure government prestige; and the Cabinet inevitably seeks to escape from that position as soon as it conveniently can.

The more normal position, nowadays, is the majority position; since 1868 we have had only two real minority governments and both of them were failures. In the normal position the Cabinet, as I have said, lives by its ability to maintain the confidence of the House. That does not mean its ability to avoid defeat. Sir Robert Peel was defeated in 1834 on an amendment to the Address. In six years from 1834 the Melbourne government was defeated fifty-eight times. The Aberdeen government was defeated three times in a single week in 1853. Mr. Balfour was beaten in Committee of Supply in 1903. Mr. MacDonald's government was beaten ten times between January and August of 1924. Every defeat, no doubt, is in some degree a diminution of the government's prestige; the critical appetite grows by what it feeds on. But the Cabinet is the judge of what defeat it will accept as fatal enough to involve resignation or dissolution. A direct vote of censure would, no doubt, always be accepted as fatal; so, too, would a defeat upon some major measure pivotal to the Cabinet's policy. But it is of the essence of parliamentary strategy that, these two exceptions apart, the government alone decides when it cannot go on.

What is central to the position I am describing is that, broadly, the whole process is so conceived as to be in effect a gigantic preparation for the next general election. In normal circumstances, the Opposition cannot defeat the Cabinet in the House unless, as in 1886, the policy of the Cabinet produces a split in the ranks of its own supporters. And such a split will as a rule be the reflection of a split within the Cabinet itself. This may, as over Home Rule or the financial crisis of 1931, be a difference over matters which are regarded as fundamental; or it may be, as with the Rosebery Cabinet of 1894–95, that temperamental incompatibilities within itself have failed to produce the team-spirit which is essential to its effective functioning. The normal position is that, granted a majority, a Cabinet will live out its life until it deems that the moment has come when it may hope successfully to face the constituencies. No small part of its power depends upon its ability to judge the successful moment of such choice.

Mr. Baldwin, with an ample majority, risked such a choice in 1923; the result was his defeat. But he chose such a moment again in 1935 when the Opposition was clearly uncertain about the differences between its own policy and that of the government; the electorate then gave him an overwhelming renewal of confidence. It is in the exercise of the decision to dissolve that the importance of the function of the Opposition becomes manifest. Its life is, above everything, an attempt to break the confidence of the electorate in the government. It therefore seeks to capitalize every mistake the government makes, to minimize the effect of every success the government can claim. It is, in short, trying to use the parliamentary process to persuade the electorate how much more fitted it is to govern than its rival. It is notable that to achieve this result it requires almost exactly the qualities a government itself requires. Private members of the Opposition must give full support to their leaders; divisions on policy within the Opposition, if they are on points of major importance, so weaken its striking power as to prevent it from seizing the initiative when the moment comes for its seizure. A bad government not only can live for a long time when the ranks of its opponents are divided; it may even win an election by default. For if the Opposition is not agreed upon the positive policy it presents to the electorate, the chances are overwhelming that the country will not understand the case it is trying to make. A government, in these circumstances, may well be returned to power because the electorate cannot be persuaded that the victory of its rivals implies the ability to use their majority successfully.

Party history since 1832 suggests that a change of importance is taking place in this connexion to which attention should be drawn. The life of a party under the parliamentary system has normally depended very largely on its ability within a reasonable period to win an electoral majority. No party since 1832 has held office for more than ten years. This has been important because it has meant that parties, being relatively sure of proximity to power within a brief range of time, have been able to attract able men, eager for place, to their ranks and to hold them there. The party was able to gratify their ambitions by the knowledge that loyalty would naturally bring its reward. The basis of the success of the system lay in this proximity to office. It is doubtful if a party which had no prospects of this kind to offer would be able to hold its ground. Men naturally gravitate to the places and professions that give the prospect of a successful career.

I think it is fairly certain that this aspect of the party system was made possible by the fact that both parties in the state were built on the same broad foundation, revolved, as it were, on the same axis of property-concepts. Each could become a Cabinet without unduly disturbing the other, since it was expected that, within one or two elections at most, the other would take its place. Each could succeed to the other, since, revolving round the same axis, the range of oscillation of policy was limited. It was even possible, as the career of Mr. Churchill makes evident, for a man to cross from one side to the other and back again without really changing his intellectual principles; he sat as normally and naturally in Liberal as in Conservative Cabinets.

Only once since 1832 has the implication of Cabinet control been challenged from within the House; that was by the Conservative Party in 1912–14 over Ulster.

Cabinet control is the reward of a successful party; it is accepted because, so far, its consequences do not greatly disturb the Opposition. Broadly speaking, it does not outrage their established expectations, for they know that the basis on which Ministers make good their electoral promises does not seriously differ from their own basis. The electorate, in a word, was until quite recently choosing between two wings of the same party rather than between two different parties. The line of demarcation between them was, to use the terms I suggested earlier, quantitative rather than qualitative in character.

It is interesting to note how, in the pre-war history of Socialism, that character was preserved. British Socialism was Fabian in its outlook; and though Fabians drew different conclusions than either Liberals or Conservatives about the future of our economic system, they accepted without any difficulty the premisses of that system. They agreed that the economics of marginal utility—the real foundation of capitalism—was unanswerable. They repudiated the Marxian doctrine of the class-war. In their famous manifesto during the South African conflict they accepted all the assumptions of imperialism as valid. They believed that there was no way to power save through the ballot-box; they sought the permeation of existing political parties rather than the creation of a separate political party of their own. Even if their principles were to win a majority in the House of Commons, they were convinced that they could not be put into action without the consent of the other side. Fabians entered the pre-war Liberal and Conservative Parties in the same way that some of them attached themselves to the pre-war Labour Party.

The significance of this philosophy can be seen in the position of that pre-war Labour Party. It was founded in 1900 by the trade unions not on the basis of any general doctrine but simply to secure more adequate trade union representation in the House of Commons; it owed its first great victories again not to any general doctrine, but to the threat to the safety of the trade-union movement implied in the Taff Vale decision of 1901. From 1906–14 it was a radical branch of the Liberal Party, asking, indeed, wider concessions from capitalism than the older parties were prepared to give but not differing in ultimate principle from radicals like Mr. Lloyd George. It is known, indeed, that as late as 1911 the latter was thinking of a reconstructed Liberal government in which members of the Labour Party would take their place; and Mr. Ramsay MacDonald was in favour of negotiating with him to that end. Some sentences of Sir Austen Chamberlain, moreover, suggest that in that year a government of all parties was at least a possibility, partly to deal with the menace of German militarism and partly to solve certain difficult questions, like the House of Lords and Ulster, which no single party was believed to be capable of handling alone.

The point I want to make is the simple one that parliamentary government, built upon the assumption that the Cabinet controlled the House of Commons, worked because all parties accepted the premisses of the economic system of which it was the expression. Men might drift to one side or to the other; they were not permanently exiling themselves from power by the opinions they held. Party warfare could be conducted in the confidence that sooner or later each side would win a victory, and that its defeated opponent would honourably abide by the result. It would do so because the use of that victory by its successful rival would never so gravely disturb it as to suggest that the victory was being intolerably abused.

"Our English system," wrote Bagehot, ". . . makes party government permanent and possible in the sole way in which it can be so, by making it mild." By mildness, as he explains, he means two things. First, that parties do not push their principles to their logical conclusions; and, second, that Ministers, when they get into office, always devise a middle course "which *looks* as much as possible like what was suggested in opposition, but which *is* as much as possible what patent facts—facts which seem to live in the office, so teasing and unceasing are they—prove ought to be done." But by "mild government" Bagehot really means a policy which the owning classes accept. This he makes clear by his insistence that parliamentary government is incompatible with what he calls the "ultra-democratic" theory. Universal suffrage, he argued, meant that "the rich and wise are not to have, by explicit law, more votes than the poor and stupid," and this, he was convinced, meant the ruin of the parliamentary system. "If it be true," he wrote, "that a parliamentary government is possible only when the overwhelming majority of the representatives are men essentially moderate, of no marked varieties, free from class-prejudices, this ultra-democratic Parliament could not maintain that government . . . each class would speak a language of its own; each would be unintelligible to the other; and the only thriving class would be the immoral representatives, who were chosen by corrupt machination, and who would probably get a good profit on the capital they laid out in that corruption."

Bagehot is here in effect saying three things. Members of Parliament, whatever their party views, must ultimately hold the same type of opinion because, otherwise, they could not compromise with one another. With universal suffrage, they will cease to hold the same type of opinion. Compromise will then be impossible, and the parliamentary system will break down. The conditions he postulated as essential lasted, broadly, until 1918. Until that year there was no adult male suffrage; and women's suffrage of the same kind did not come until ten years later. Until that year, also, the Labour Party had never possessed more than a twentieth part of the membership of the House of Commons. The overwhelming bulk of the membership of both the older parties came from much the same groups of men. There were aristocrats, business men, lawyers, in each. They spoke, in Bagehot's phrase, the same language; they were able to understand one another. Because this was so, they used the power of the state for the same ends. Whichever party was in power, the same interests were in power; for they were represented with no great dissimilarity in both. They could therefore accept control by the Cabinet because the direction it gave to affairs was not one from which either side violently dissented. It secured what Bagehot called "the deference" of its constituents. Its common assumptions were taken to be the "best opinion" of the nation. What we have to consider is the effect upon these conceptions of the changed situation after the war.

3

The whole underlying conception of parliamentary government is based upon the view that the state is a neutral factor in society. In the ceaseless interplay of party warfare now one party, now another, becomes the government and so becomes entitled to the operation of its authority. Since each party aims at the common welfare, its opponent can accept its victory since the results of that operation are directed to purposes which they jointly share. Certainly before the war, there would have been few to dissent from this analysis. The substance of the common welfare might be differently defined by each; it was never so differently defined that either was compelled to deny the validity of the other's formula to such a degree as to be forced to action upon its denial of a non-constitutional kind. Liberals might insist that a Conservative government was ruining the country; Conservatives might feel of Mr. Gladstone what Queen Victoria thought, that somehow the "terrible old man" must be got rid of; everyone knew that these were, so to say, the steps in an elegant minuet never to be taken too seriously. Whatever could be done for the common welfare by either party was, it was assumed by both of them, done to the best of its ability. And when the Labour Party became an independent group in the House of Commons, for reasons I have explained it accepted the assumption upon which the system was founded.

The framework within which this assumption operated, the subconscious major premiss of the whole system, is contained in the idea of Bagehot's "middle course." It is the idea of a policy which, whatever its substance, does not disturb the private ownership of the means of production. Parties may quarrel about the emphasis to be given to this or that element in the rights of property; they do not regard it as possible to quarrel about the rights of property themselves. All the habits of parliamentary government, all the characteristics of the House of Commons of which I have spoken, depend upon *that* quarrel's being excluded from the field of reference. The confidence of members in their parties, the confidence of their supporters outside were always based upon the assumption that questions regarding the ultimate economic constitution of society could not be reopened. The nation was a going concern which, upon this matter, had made its final bargain with fate.

That is what Bagehot meant by saying that the "mass of a Parliament ought to be men of moderate sentiments, or they will elect an immoderate ministry and enact violent laws." By "moderate" and "violent" he means laws that in the judgment of a liberal-minded and cool-headed political economist of the sixties can reasonably be approved by his "best opinion" of the nation; that is, as he explains, the opinion of the "rich and wise" as against the opinion of the "poor and stupid"; the coincidence of the adjectives is itself a significant index to the basis upon which his views were founded. Certainly he would have conceived it to be wholly contrary to the "best opinion" for one of the parties in the state, itself the alternative government, to call into question the foundations of a capitalist society. The ministry which did that, he would have argued, must by its very nature be composed of "immoderate" men; the proposals for which they are prepared to make themselves responsible are "violent" proposals. He would, no doubt, have traced them to the conference of the franchise upon the "poor and stupid" section of the population. He would have argued, as Macaulay argued to the House of

Commons in the debate on the Charter, that there is no possible compatibility between universal suffrage and the rights of private property. That road, he would have felt, leads straight to the destruction of parliamentary government.

It is on that road that we have set our feet; and it is, clearly, important to discuss the change in the principles of parties in the effect they may have upon the working of the House of Commons. Those changes are, in their fundamentals, two in number. The first is the virtual fusion of the Liberal Party with its Conservative rival to form what is now substantially a party for the defence of the private ownership of the means of production. The second is the open espousal by the Labour Party, now the alternative government in the state, of the principle of the public ownership of the means of production. What is likely to be the effect of this change upon the working of those characteristics of parliamentary government which are, as I have here argued, the secret of its success?

It is, of course, clear that the Conservative Party has moved widely from the moorings Bagehot would have regarded as a safe harbour in his own day. For good or ill, we live in a collectivist society; and, granted a parliamentary system based on universal suffrage—the assumption is of primary importance—even a party which exists to defend capitalism must use the power of the state to mitigate the consequences of social and economic inequality. The margins of the "concessions," to use Bagehot's own terms, which a party of property conceives itself bound to yield are ampler by far than any he could have imagined. What the "best opinion" of the "rich and wise" thought possible in 1867 is very different from what is deemed possible by the same element of society in 1937.

But it still stops far short of the frontiers within which the Labour Party dwells. Those frontiers are defined by the purpose of attaining the public ownership of the means of production by the use of a parliamentary majority. The shift in the axis of Labour thought since the war has been remarkable. "We of the

Labour Party," said the programme of 1918, ". . . recognize in the present world catastrophe, if not the death, in Europe, of civilization itself, at any rate the culmination and collapse of a distinctive industrial civilization, which the workers will not seek to reconstruct." That recognition has haunted the margins of Labour thought ever since the close of the war. It was not, indeed, the basis upon which the party sought the outlines of a new philosophy suitable to the implications of the recognition. Few of its leaders ever doubted the recuperative power of capitalism; few, either, saw any necessary connexion between capitalism and war. Fewer still, least of all those in Parliament, saw the coming of Fascism as capitalism's way of relief from the pressure of political democracy. Only a rare figure arose to suspect that a refusal to "reconstruct" capitalist society might involve a challenge to the foundations of the parliamentary system. They believed firmly in what Mr. and Mrs. Webb called the "inevitability of gradualness." The Labour Party, in their view, would move to the position of a government with a majority in the House of Commons. It would then, by stages, introduce socialist legislation. Since this would represent the will of the people, it would, they were convinced, be accepted by the other side. The possibility that the assumptions of parliamentary government were unworkable for these purposes only vaguely crossed their minds.

Between the frontiers of Conservative thought and those of the Labour Party in Great Britain there is, in fact, a doctrinal abyss now unbridgeable in terms of the old continuity of policy. The width of that abyss has so far been concealed for two reasons. It was concealed, first, because neither of the two Labour governments, while it was in office, sought to put socialist measures into operation. It was concealed, secondly, because the revolt of the Labour Party against the capitalist system was really a simple revolt of moral indignation, unaccompanied by an economic philosophy different from that of capitalists themselves—I have already pointed out that the Fabians accepted the principles of orthodox economics—or by any reconsideration of the nature of the state. Their argument was largely the argument that, under capitalism, men did not get a "square deal," and that socialism would make this "square deal" possible. They could demonstrate the patent inadequacies of capitalism in operation. They believed that as the mass of the workers came to realize in daily experience the burden of these inadequacies, they would demand their transformation. They would then, at the polls, confer upon the Labour Party the right to effect this transformation and, under its ægis, Parliament would gradually induct us into the socialist state.

The underlying assumption of this view was the naïve one that capitalism, the decline of which the Labour Party itself proclaimed, would remain unchanged in its habits during the period of its decline. The whole mind of the party was so concentrated on the parliamentary process as to produce the impression that it really believed that political democracy operated in a vacuum independently of the economic framework within which it was contained. It did not see that there was a dynamic in capitalism which compelled it to adjust the political philosophy of business men to its necessities. Capitalism lived by profit. It organized the functioning and habits of society by its ability to make profit. It used the state-power to build the conditions in which the making of profit was possible as a continuing adventure. The level of wages, the hours of labour, the standard of the social services had all to be adjusted to the fundamental requirement of capitalism that profit should be made. It was the natural and logical habit of a capitalist society to use the state-power to remove from the path of the capitalist the obstacles that stood in the way of making profit. That was the purpose of the state, and the capitalist thought of good and bad, wise and unwise, policies in terms of their relationships to that central purpose of the state. To free private enterprise from obstacles which endanger the right to profit is the inherent logic of capitalist society; and that same logic compels it to regard the state-power as an instrument to that end.

All this has been largely concealed from the Labour Party because it has accepted traditional economics and the traditional theory of the state. Above all, it regarded the latter as a neutral factor in society available to those who won a majority in Parliament. It had seen the state as neutral, as equally responsive, to Conservative and Liberal governments; it saw no reason to suppose that, as a government also, it would not have the same experience. What it wholly failed to understand is that the neutrality of the state between Liberals and Conservatives was due to the fact that both had the same fundamental ends in view. Both believed in the validity of a capitalist society. Both proposed so to work the parliamentary system in that society as to make possible its continued functioning. But those ends and that validity were denied by the Labour Party. It proposed to work the parliamentary system not for capitalist ends but for ends incompatible with these. The result of this antithesis of purpose is one that the Conservative Party has faced. But it cannot be said that the Labour Party has begun to do so.

Capitalism in a period of crisis, I have said, is bound to readjust social standards to the conditions in which it can resume the making of profit. It cannot have confidence in any other conditions. It has habituated not merely its votaries but also a large mass of the population to the belief that social wisdom is the creation of those conditions. Its conceptions of law and order are wholly adjusted to them. Bad trade has meant a decline, good trade a rise, in wages, quite independently of the complexion of the government in power. Periods of industrial crisis—witness the great depression of 1929—have necessarily been periods in which business men, on their premisses quite logically, have called for a halt in social amelioration by government action. The thesis of the Labour Party proceeds independently on these assumptions. Its programme calls for the acceptance of principles which business men have always declared to be unworkable; and by its insistence on the right to operate its own principles within the framework of parliamentary government it in fact invites capitalists to co-operate in their own abdication. Put from the capitalists' angle, this may be summarized by saying that the Labour Party invites the capitalists to co-operate in achieving the economic ruin of the country.

And the ground for this invitation is the inherent right, in a parliamentary democracy, of the majority to rule. It is expected that the Labour Party will be allowed to form a government exactly as though it proposed to carry on the work of its predecessor instead of undoing that work. Its opponents will be allowed to ventilate their grievances in the usual way; the country will, in the usual way, also, be educated by the process of parliamentary debate; and, at the end of a five-year period, the country will be asked once more to choose between the Labour Party and its rival. Anything else, argues Mr. Attlee, is unlikely because mature political peoples, "who have had years of experience of personal freedom and political democracy" are unlikely to find either Communism or Fascism to their liking. Mr. Attlee rests his faith on our national character and the long tradition of peace which the success of our economic system, until quite recently, conferred upon us.

But working to a socialist society through the parliamentary system does not mean merely that the standing orders and the conventions of the Constitution are observed. It means also that business men who have no confidence in the new order will yet so restrain themselves as to act as though they have. It means that the atmosphere of consent necessary to the transformation will be forthcoming from men who have been using all the resources at their disposal to prevent its coming. It means that they will respect the Constitution when each item of policy for which it is operated under a Labour government is a move towards a society they believe to be capable neither of efficiency nor of success. That kind of self-restraint has not been their habit in the past. "It is the secret of our governing class," Mr. Shaw has written, "who, though perfectly prepared to be generous, humane, cultured, philanthropic, public-spirited, and personally charming,

in the second instance, are unalterably resolved in the first to
have money enough for a handsome and delicate life, and will,
in pursuit of that money, batter in the doors of their fellow-men,
sell them up, sweat them in fetid dens, shoot, stab, hang, im-
prison, sink, burn, and destroy them in the name of law and
order."

The language is forceful; it is not more forceful than the facts.
All the habits of the House of Commons are built on the theory
that in the last analysis the differences between parties are so
small that men can reason about them, and compromise about
them, instead of fighting about them. Political power has, since
1689, been for all effective purposes in the hands of a single
class, the owners of the instruments of production. The whole
purpose of the law has been directed to enforcing the consequences of that ownership. Every category of law is permeated
by notions which derive from that end and no other end. One
can see that purpose at work in the Combination Act of 1799 in
one century, and in the Trade Union Law Amendment Act of
1927 in another. It explains the condemnation of Loveless and
his colleagues in 1835, and the condemnation of Michael Kane
and his fellows in 1937. Because the one case is a hundred years
away, the governing class can share our resentment at the harsh-
ness of Lord Melbourne and his colleagues; it no more shared it
then than the governing class of today shares the resentment of
the trade unions at the imprisonment of Michael Kane. The governing class reads the principles of constitutional morality in the
circumstances of the situation it occupies; if it finds them a threat
to its safety, it is prepared without regret to throw them overboard.

The truth surely is that it is one thing to respect the normal
functioning of the parliamentary system when the Labour Party
is in opposition; it is quite a different thing to respect it when it
has the right to function as the government of the country. The
one entails no disturbance in the wonted order of things; the
other entails—it has no point unless it does entail—a fundamen-

tal disturbance. The Labour Party's philosophy assumes that this difference is unimportant. It assumes that "fair play," the "rules of the game," and the rest will come naturally to men who made revolution and civil war to win the power they now enjoy. It assumes that concepts like justice and right transcend the limitations of the society in which they are applied; that men can agree about their meaning even when, to use Bagehot's phrase, they have ceased to talk the same language. Anyone who knows the history of our Empire, the long list, for example, of deliberately broken pledges about land-settlement in East Africa, or the massive legislation used in India to repress even nascent trade unionism and the Congress movement, will realize that men who think their privileges at bay will fight to defend them. The Labour Party can realize that the use of Parliament to deprive Roman Catholics of the right freely to exercise their religion would be met with conflict, and that even though Parliament had a majority of the electors behind it. But it cannot bring itself to believe that this decision could be made by men to whom the religion of property is a faith so intense that it has moved, is, indeed, moving them all over the world, to bend every form of social institution to its service.

From one angle this is the safeguard of the existing order of things. The Labour Party, like the trade unions, has grown up within its framework. Its power is so great that it tends by the very possibilities its transformation calls into being to permeate them with its own view of the limits of possible political action. In all the great crises of the post-war period, their principles of strategy seem to have been based upon the belief that it is better to compromise with capitalist power than to threaten it. Neither Labour government dared to be responsible for a single socialist measure; it preferred to depend on the possibilities of social reform. The argument that it had no right to attempt socialist measures, being a minority government, omits the fact that even as such it was at least entitled to introduce them, and, if defeated in the House of Commons, to ask for electoral ratification of its effort. The trade unions embarked upon the general strike—which had no meaning if it was not a challenge to the government—without any preparation at all; and the lesson they drew from that magnificent display of working-class solidarity was the significant one that it is an impotent technique. In the Mond-Turner conferences they made an attempt to share with the employers the position of the residuary legatees of profit; they did not draw from their failure the inference that the capitalist is not prepared to abdicate from his position as the final authority in society. "Everywhere," Mr. Strachey comments on the post-war epoch, "the workers' leaders abstained from using the workers' strength in return for promises which, the moment the danger-point was passed, the ruling capitalists wholly repudiated." Of this habit, Mr. Lloyd George's notorious repudiation of the Sankey Report on the nationalization of the mines, which he had promised to carry out "in the letter and in the spirit," is only the supreme example. And as an index to the temper of Labour, we must not forget the contrast between the militant repudiation of British intervention in Russia in 1920 and the tame and timid resistance to non-intervention in Spain in 1936–37.

The years of depression have produced in the Labour Party a dual attitude of great significance to any study of the parliamentary system. They have been years in which Labour proclamations have been sharply contrasted with Labour action. On the one side has been the announcement, first, of a decisive rejection of the capitalist basis of society and, second, a programme intended to give concrete form to the consequences of that rejection; on the other, there has been an increasing search, in practice, to find terms of accommodation with capitalism. Only in this way can we understand, especially in the light of the menace of Fascism, the constant rejection of unity with the Communists by the party, its refusal, even, to allow its members to appear on platforms with members of the Communist Party. Only in this way can we understand, also, such action as that of the Transport and General Workers' Union in expelling from membership, in

1937, some of its own leaders for what can only be regarded as exceptional devotion during a strike which was actually officially approved and led by the executive of that union. Symptoms like the "Black Circular," the refusal of some unions to allow Communists to be delegates to the national conferences of their organizations, the refusal, even, to participate in organizations for the relief of the victims of Fascism, if Communists belong to these organizations, the use of all the influence at the disposal of the party machine to damp down discussion of the strategy of power, are of great importance.

For their basis is the belief in the existence of a democratic "community" in Great Britain capable of being separated in practice from the capitalist society within which it lives. From this, it seems to the leaders of the Labour Party to follow that so long as they maintain their belief in this democratic community, they can detach enough capitalist support from their opponents to persuade them that conflict will not be worth while. "We are," they seem to say, "inherently reasonable people. On the political side, we refuse to have in our party men who, though they are Socialists, like ourselves, are doubtful whether socialism can be accomplished peacefully; and though we propose the nationalization of the means of production, we propose adequate compensation for existing owners. On the industrial side, we strive with all our might for accommodation. We discourage unofficial strikes. We penalize militant trade unionists in every organization we can influence. Our political and industrial leaders have even combined to damp down all working-class agitation against British Fascism. We are wholly on the side of law and order. We assume that our opponents, equally with ourselves, are interested in the full maintenance of the democratic process. We shall continue to think so until their actions show us that we are mistaken."

That is, I think, a fair statement of the orthodox Labour position. Its central weakness is, of course, obvious. It is simply untrue that the opponents of Labour have, equally with itself, the same interest in the maintenance of democracy. On the contrary, if democracy becomes the instrument of socialist policy in action, then the interest of Labour's opponents in its maintenance becomes minimal in character. This central weakness is due to the refusal of the Labour Party to recognize that the state is the instrument of that class in society which owns the instruments of production, and that it cannot utilize that state for its own purposes so long as that class remains in possession of those instruments. It is arguing that its own moral condemnation of capitalism will be convincing to its opponents as soon as it has an electoral majority. It refuses to see that the moral principles of men are, in the mass, not intellectual abstractions of this character. In the mass, the convictions of men are born of their class-interest, and the ability of the society, as it functions, to satisfy the established expectations which are built upon their class-position. We do not change our fundamental ideas because the result of a general election has gone against us unless that result proves one of two things: either it must prove to us that there was no foundation for the fears we predicted, or we must find a definite improvement in our expectations. Sir Edward Carson and his friends did not conclude, from the two general elections of 1910, that they ought to accept the steady will of the electorate. Rather they believed that they could prevent its fulfilment by fighting against its application. The event proved them right.

Now, Bagehot was justified in saying that men in office take a very different view of their responsibilities from that which they take when they are in opposition. The genius of the parliamentary system is, undoubtedly, to persuade the majority to avoid, so far as it can, what will be represented as an abuse of the power of victory. That was true of the crisis attendant on the Parliament Act of 1911; the Liberal Party could have used its authority to abolish the House of Lords. That was true, also, of the Home Rule controversy. But any government that is threatened with the prospect of civil war as the consequence of going on to the end of the road is bound to think of all possible accommodation before it makes up its mind in any final way. There are a hundred psychological factors in the whole framework of the House of Commons to assure us of this. The two front benches do not, any more than their supporters behind, wage a *bellum omnium contra omnes*. Largely they are personal friends, and extremisms are profoundly mitigated by their friendships. They have grown accustomed to the idea that the mere arrival at power is an achievement in itself; Mr. Ramsay MacDonald, perhaps more truly than he knew, called the Labour government of 1924 an "insane miracle." Are politicians, to whom office is the supreme prize, to jeopardize its possession on the very morrow of victory? That, at least in general, has not been their nature.

It does not take any special insight to see how immense would be all the forces deployed to persuade a Labour government to be cautious in the use of its victory. The immense authority of the Crown would be exercised, as it has been used in the past, to mitigate the acerbities of party difference. So would the power of the press and of the churches. The departments would emphasize the gravity of error, the need for time, the explosive nature of a false step. The Cabinet would have to remember the possible consequences of panic in the City, the result of a determination in the House of Lords to fight, the danger that crisis at home might produce grave international complications. Hesitation would be natural enough in men who cannot fail to understand that they are playing with fire. Once they begin to implement their victory, there can be no going back. They cannot but be aware that they will invoke furious opposition. They cannot but remember, either, the possibility of the same panic confusion that wrecked their predecessors in 1931. They must recognize that if they are not equal to the occasion they confront they run the risk of ruining the party they lead. This is even more likely to be the case if they take office, as they may well take office, in a period of falling trade. The temptation, at least, to play for time in these circumstances is an overwhelming one.

My point is the simple one that unless a Labour government

is prepared to meet a crisis of the first magnitude, the forces it will encounter will persuade it rather to operate the capitalist system than to move to its transformation. There is so much in the realm of social reform that it can attempt without the provocation of its socialist programme that the temptation to rely on social reform will be profound. "Let us," the moderate members of the Cabinet will say, "let us consolidate the ground we have won. Let us get behind us a strong public opinion determined to support us from the knowledge that our first measures have been for their relief. There are the unemployed; we can better their treatment. There are the aged and the infirm; we can endow them more adequately. We can improve education and housing, public health and recreation facilities. We can reverse the engines of foreign policy by the conscious revivification of the League. There is workmen's compensation, the repeal of the Trade Union Law Amendment Act of 1927. The people expect these things from us; they will welcome them. With the support we have won by measures of this kind, we can proceed far more effectively to the task of socialization." Mr. Faintheart can even whisper that all this, with an acceleration of the time-table of the House, can be achieved in the first two years of power. All of them can go to the statute-book under the Parliament Act. Then, with the new support they will have gathered, the new experience Ministers will have gained in running their departments, the Cabinet can proceed to its graver tasks.

It is to this attitude, certainly, that the nature of party conflict will push the Labour Party; and its own theory of the state will reinforce the suspicion that it is a wise procedure. It might even be accompanied, for window-dressing purposes, by that nationalization of the Bank of England which would not, as Mr. Keynes has warned us, cause a single capitalist to lose a night's sleep. What would be the result of adopting it?

That it would be greeted, in the first instance, with relief, even with applause, by the opponents of the Labour Party almost goes without saying. The Cabinet would be congratulated on its real-

ism, on its ability to take a broad view of things; and that mood
would last, as it lasts with most governments, during the "honeymoon" period of the government. But it would begin to dissipate
early for two reasons. In the first place, it would soon begin to
arouse the inevitable opposition in the House of Commons, as
the Conservative Party began to measure the dangers of its success. Its implication, if successful, would be their defeat at the
next general election, and they would be compelled, sooner or
later, to insist on its extravagance, its heavy burden on trade and
industry, and so forth. And, indeed, unless it was attempted in a
boom period of trade, it could hardly fail to have the effect of
disturbing business confidence; that always occurs when a rising
level of taxation is the outcome of projects in which the governing class does not believe. The danger on this side is the twofold
one of budgetary instability and a party struggle in which the
power of the House of Lords might be invoked by the Conservative Party at a moment deemed suitable. The second reason is
its likelihood of provoking disruption within the Labour Party
itself, both inside and outside the House of Commons. For there
is no doubt that, whatever a Labour Cabinet may propose, an
important section of Labour opinion expects from a Labour government a definite and direct march to socialism. For them social
reform of this kind is an abandonment of the central purpose of
Labour if it stands alone. They have experienced it in the first
two Labour governments. They regard it as exactly that attempt
to patch up the structure of a decaying capitalism for which there
is nothing to be said. It is at least possible that a policy such as I
have outlined would cause a split in the party, might even, possibly, bring down the government. It would be regarded as
"MacDonaldism"; and the contrast between the pledges and the
experiment would cause passionate conflict likely, at the least, to
weaken the hold of the government on public opinion. For if
the policy does not convince a considerable section of the friends
of Labour, it is pretty certain that it will not convince its enemies.

A government under cross-fire from both Left and Right would soon find itself in a critical position.

Now no Labour government can afford the luxury of a third failure. Its implication is the very simple one that the running of a capitalist society is best left to those who believe in it; that it cannot be successfully attempted by men who are seeking to maintain its postulates as the prelude to their replacement. Still less, moreover, can it be successfully attempted by men who ignore the fact that, in a capitalist society, the possession of confidence from those who own and operate the instruments of production is pivotal to successful government. Conservatives and Liberals can secure this confidence because they are willing to abide by the rules upon which it depends. Socialists cannot, without surrendering their claim to be Socialists. It is a perfectly natural instinct which persuades business men to withhold their support from Labour. It is, in fact, proposing a redistribution of income in society incompatible with the postulates of capitalist economics. As a "social reform" government, it is attempting the wholly illogical task of solving the problems of capitalist economy in terms of a moral sensibility in large part irrelevant to them. All its conceptions of policy are derived from assumptions which deny the validity of the capitalist conception of property-rights. It is not merely a question of Mr. Chamberlain's famous doctrine of "ransom." That is an intelligible conception for a radical who accepts the foundations of capitalist theory; the inference of that doctrine, as he preaches it, is only quantitatively different from its results in the hands of a Tory democrat who accepts as valid the same foundations. But it is not intelligible in the hands of a Socialist who makes the right to income a function of personality and not of property, who therefore denies the title of functionless ownership to income, and is insistent that production shall proceed not in terms of profitability but in terms of planned production for social requirements.

I believe, therefore, that an attempt on the part of a Labour government to operate a policy that will win the confidence of its opponents is doomed to failure; the level of that policy would satisfy neither them nor its own friends. And it would still leave wholly unsolved the central question of power. It might work for a brief time in a boom period; it would go right onto the rocks in a slump. That would have the effect, at once, of bringing up again the central question of power; it would then lead either to a split in the Labour Party, like that of 1931 but of greater intensity, or it would mean the re-formation of Labour policy on a decisively socialist basis. The problems, that is, that we face by inference now because the Labour Party proclaims itself as socialist, but with the insistence that this involves no break with capitalist democracy, would be presented to the electorate in a far more acute form when it had become obvious, after this further experience of Labour in office, that nothing could prevent the break. The present attitude of the Labour Party, in fact, can only, as a philosophy of action, postpone, without being able to solve, the problem of the nature of the state, and the political strategy which flows from the view we take of that nature.

For the Labour Party, the capture of an electoral majority is itself the capture of the state-power. It assumes that, having the right through its Cabinet to direct the business of the House of Commons, it is therefore assured the obedience of all the instruments whereby the state exercises its authority over any opposition it may encounter. From its first fatal error of arguing that the state-power is neutral as between contending ideologies, it draws the mistaken conclusion that democracy is secure whatever the economic envelope within which it is enclosed. But all the evidence goes to show that the state-power is not so neutral. The one time in our history in which it has had to choose between contending ideologies which refused to give way, a new equilibrium was reached only after civil war and revolution had decided upon the purposes to which it had to be devoted. Thenceforward, no doubt, it has given the appearance of neutrality, simply because a choice between contending ideologies which refused to give way had never to be made. Now that the unstable compromise of capitalist democracy is breaking down, the question of the neutrality of the state-power depends not upon a postulate assumed but upon an experience tested by the hard facts of life.

My argument, therefore, goes back to those remarkable words of Lord Balfour which I quoted in an earlier chapter. "It is evident," he wrote, "that our whole political machinery presupposes a people so fundamentally at one that they can safely afford to bicker; and so sure of their own moderation that they are not dangerously disturbed by the never-ending din of political conflict." That was, as he pointed out, made a reasonable presupposition because "our alternating cabinets, though belonging to different parties, have never differed about the foundations of society." I have argued here that, if the Labour Party means what its programme says, political parties now do differ about those foundations. Once they so differ, there is no such fundamental unity in the nation as makes possible the continuance of party warfare on the old terms. For with the disappearance of fundamental unity, there goes also the ability to preserve that moderation of temper which is the secret of the ability to compromise; and as that ability is eroded by the absence of the power to bridge differences, all the mutual understandings are suspended by which the parliamentary system has been able to function.

On this view, therefore, the House of Commons in the form in which we know it emerges as the characteristic expression of capitalist democracy in the period in which it is sure of itself. Its political relations, the social habits that it builds, the nature of its procedure all express the fact that its members are aware that its battles are sham battles in which vital wounds are not to be inflicted on either side. Every Cabinet that took office from 1832 was aware, with one exception, that whatever legislation it passed would be obeyed; and that exception, the Home Rule Act of 1914, was for the Opposition a "vital wound," which, it is significant, led straight to the threshold of civil war. What I am urging here is not less true of capitalist democracies elsewhere. It is true of the United States, where the Republican and Democratic Parties have always been agreed upon "the foundations of society," and have therefore been able to work even so cumbrous an instrument as the American constitution; the one breakdown, over the question of slavery and the right of secession, led, it is significant, to civil war. It is true, also, of France; since the foundation of the Third Republic no fundamental has been in question until the Socialists posed the matter of the ultimate constitution of property. When they did, the menace of Fascism was at once apparent; and democracy in France was safeguarded only by an agreement between parties of the Left to postpone the issue of socialism. It is true, also, of the contemporary socialist governments of Scandinavia. These have been able to maintain their position without challenge simply because they have not sought, in their policies, to disturb the foundations of society. They have been advanced social reform administrations which have still to show what effect the transition to socialism will have on parliamentary institutions.

For what is inherent in the habits of the House of Commons is that though parties have been able amply to discuss the goodness or badness of government measures, they have never, until now, had to discuss the central purpose of the state. This they have been able to take for granted. They have had, that is to say, the great ends of life in common, the essential ways by which those ends should be attained. Those who have shaped the central purpose of the state have come, overwhelmingly, from a single class in society—the owners of property. They have understood one another because they lived by the same presumptions. They went to the same schools, and the same universities. People like themselves directed the civil service, the armed forces of the state, the police, the judiciary; they were in charge, also, of all the great public utilities, the banks, the railways, the insurance companies. They were not, indeed, a closed class, in the sense that the older aristocracies were a closed class. But they were a closed class in the important sense that attainment of membership within its ranks depended upon the acceptance of the presumptions upon which, as a class, it was founded. They have set by their needs and habits all the standards of manners, of conduct, of social intercourse in our society; and their needs and habits have, in their turn, arisen out of our system of ownership and the relations of production to which they have given rise. Their life is, so far as its *moves* are concerned, largely without meaning, save in the terms of those relations of production. Now the equilibrium they represent, the foundation upon which our whole political superstructure rests, is threatened because those relations of production are breaking down.

They are breaking down, as I have argued, because they can no longer exploit adequately the forces of production in our civilization; and the governing class is unable, therefore, to satisfy the masses who, having nothing but their labour-power to sell, are dependent upon them. Since the Industrial Revolution these masses have, broadly speaking, passed through three phases of organization. In the first, as the factory-system began to develop its modern amplitude, they built trade unions to protect themselves from undue exploitation in the industrial field. But they found, inevitably, that the conditions of life in the industrial field were determined by the rules laid down by the state-power for its regulation. They therefore, in their second phase, began slowly to assume a political outlook. They fought for the franchise; having won it, they sought to use their votes to persuade parties by legislation to improve the terms upon which they worked. Quite early, they discovered that indirect pressure of this kind was not enough. They were led, therefore, to the formation of their own political party to give to this pressure a tone which indirectness could not confer. Their party, in being formed, coincided with the growing realization that what was wrong with society was not the superstructure of its political institutions but the inner principle on which it was based. Their party, therefore, passed into its third phase—that in which it set itself to transform that inner principle by capturing the political institutions upon which its functioning seemed to depend. It is at this stage that we now find ourselves, and the fascinating question that is set for our generation is whether institutions produced to satisfy one system of class-relations can be so reshaped as to be worked for the ends of a directly antithetic system.

I have not sought here to deny that the parliamentary system, especially in its expression as the House of Commons, was remarkably well adapted to the purposes of capitalist democracy. What I have argued is the very different thesis that at the stage where capitalism, as a system of class-relations, is not able to exploit the forces of production, its logic of profitability is necessarily in conflict with the contrasting logic of the democracy it seeks still to contain. At that point, I have urged, the doubt is raised whether parliamentary institutions are any more appropriate to the expression of capitalism than feudal institutions were appropriate to its expression when society was seeking, as the feudal economy declined, the institutions adequate to the exploitation of the new potentialities which presented themselves. What, in effect, the middle class did, in the sixteenth and seventeenth centuries, was to transfer the seat of sovereignty to Parliament, and especially to the House of Commons, that the supreme coercive power of the state could be in its own hands. The whole apparatus of political institutions has been geared to the central fact that the motive of their operation is the maintenance of middle-class power. The validity of that motive was never seriously questioned until the third of the three phases of working-class history which I have described came into view. That phase implies a change in the residence of sovereignty as vital and as decisive as took place in the transition from feudal to capitalist economy. The point its consideration involves is whether a new class seeking to become possessed of sovereignty can use the institutions of the class it proposes to dispossess to effect that change in residence. Can it do so, I have asked, when the psychological consequence of the effort must seem, to the class that is so dispossessed, like nothing so much as the violation of all the canons of political wisdom and social morality it has slowly built up in the course of centuries, canons, be it emphasized, which tradition has built into the innermost nature of that class? It is upon the answer we make to this question that our view of the efficacy of parliamentary government for the work of transformation will depend.

4

The consequences involved in this conflict for the right to use the power of the state will determine the future of the House of Commons, and all other problems connected with its organization go back, at bottom, to this central issue. It is worth while, therefore, to examine briefly from this angle some of the suggestions that have been made for improving its efficiency. Observers are alarmed at the burden upon the time of the House. They are disturbed at the decreasing place that can be found for the initiative of the private member. They criticize the growth of delegated legislation, the power, that is, conferred upon the departments of state to issue legislation in the form of regulations which have the force of law.

For the first of these difficulties the remedy proposed is usually some form of devolution. Australia has seven, Canada ten legislatures, for a population much smaller than that of Great Britain; the United States has forty-nine legislatures for a population only three times as large. Our Parliament, it is said, is inefficient because we seek to force through the narrow conduit-pipe of Westminster a mass of legislation too big to pass through with adequate examination. If we established separate legislatures for England, Scotland, and Wales, perhaps dividing England into more than one legislative area, we should seriously lighten the load on Parliament. It would then be possible to confine the business at Westminster to the discussion only of questions of major importance.

The solution, at first sight, seems attractive; but the more closely it is scrutinized, the more, I think, it will be realized that in fact it reaches but a little way. The subjects that cannot be developed are all the subjects upon which the main time of Parliament is spent. Foreign affairs, imperial relations, defence, currency, tariffs, the Post Office, the judiciary, the regulation of trade and industry, upon all these uniformity of administration is so important to the modern state that the devolution of them upon local bodies is unthinkable. Indeed, in the federal communities that are offered to us as an example to follow, many of the administrative difficulties which exist are due to the fact that the federal legislature cannot control a subject-matter—labour laws for example—in which uniformity has become urgent. What might be devolved—agricultural control, public health, education, poor relief—would all have to work within a framework of agreed principles the operation of which would necessarily be subject to the financial control of Parliament. These local legislatures, obviously, could not be permitted to tax as they pleased. They could not, either, be permitted to go outside the area of authority conferred upon them. The first would mean that the financial control of the whole scheme would remain at Westminster. The second would mean the acceptance of the principle of judicial review over the acts of local legislatures. Clearly, also, it would have to be provided that all their acts were null and void in so far as they conflicted with the legislation of the Imperial Parliament. This, again, involves the acceptance of the doctrine of judicial review.

Elsewhere, Mr. J. S. Henderson and I have shown that if the proposals of the Speaker's Conference on Devolution were accepted, there would be a saving of parliamentary time of about eight per cent. That investigation is now some thirteen years old. Given the increased prominence of foreign affairs and unemployment since it was made, I estimate that the saving of time, if a parliamentary session like that of 1936–37 is representative, would be about five per cent. If allowance is made for the discussions that would arise on the difficulties emerging from divergent legislative policies in the different assemblies—the problems, for instance, that might arise if there were a Socialist legislature in Cardiff while there was a Conservative Parliament at Westminster, the constant problems which would be involved, and discussed—as a consequence of the complicated financial interrelationships with Westminster, I doubt whether any real saving of time would be effected. On the experience of federal states, moreover, the problem of constitutionality in the legislation of the subordinate legislatures would continually raise issues requiring discussion and settlement by the Imperial Parliament. So, also, in my belief would the treatment of the maintenance of order if, as Mr. Ramsay Muir suggests, its control were devolved upon the new legislatures. A different habit towards miners' strikes in the treatment, for instance, of picketing in one area from that in another would soon lead to a demand for uniform control. It is, moreover, clear that any serious difference in the incidence of taxation by the various governments would tend rapidly to problems of migration which only the central government at Westminster would be able to handle.

The fact surely is that the remedy proposed is largely irrelevant to the issue to which it is applied. The pressure on Parliament arises from the immensely greater area with which modern government has to deal, and this arises, in its turn, from universal suffrage on the one hand, and the growing centralization of economic power on the other. The first means a much greater subject-matter in the demands of the people, demands, further, of a kind which no local authority can handle; the second means that the regulatory power of modern government must be adapted to the character of modern industrial organization. This, it is clear from all federal experience, means uniformity. All over the world, moreover, federalism is breaking down by reason of the fact that any division of power which leaves important subjects in the hands of the subordinate legislatures also leaves the federal government thereby unable to handle its problems efficiently. It is ironical to suggest that a system which attempts to make Great Britain a quasi-federal society would be helpful at a time when the validity of federalism itself is open to such grave doubts.

I believe, indeed, that there is much to be said for a drastic reorganization of the areas of local government in Great Britain and, in the light of that reorganization, the conference upon them of much wider powers of initiative than they now possess. It is absurd that every municipality which wants to start a savings bank, or to purchase a transport system, or to start a municipal laundry, should have to come to Westminster for permission to do so. A Local Authorities Enabling Bill, on the lines of that proposed by the Labour Party annually for many years, is, in the light of the facts, plain common sense. Opposition to it is almost wholly either ratepayers' opposition—the characteristic refusal of the comfortable to pay for the extension of the amenities they themselves enjoy to the poor—or the opposition of vested interests, as in the fight of the laundry industry of London against the municipal experiment in Fulham, or of the joint-stock banks to the extension of the successful Birmingham experiment to other local authorities.

But, even supposing that such a reorganization were successfully attempted, it would still leave the main problem about where it is. Parliament is overburdened, just as the legislatures of all democratic states are overburdened, by the sheer extent of the problems with which it has to grapple. The intensity of debate over those problems springs from the fact that so many of them are vital to what I have called the central problem of power. Parliament, in fact, can always deal rapidly and efficiently with a great emergency when one presents itself; the supreme instance of its remarkable handling of the abdication of Edward VIII is sufficient proof of that. Debate is prolonged, the factor of time becomes urgent, because there are such great divergencies of opinion over the solutions proposed. Normally, a Conservative government cannot drive measures like the Trade Union Law Amendment Act of 1927, or the Incitement to Disaffection Act of 1934, roughshod over the protests of the Opposition, any more than the Liberal government could have so acted with measures like the Parliament Act of 1911 or the Home Rule Act of 1914. It is of the essence of the parliamentary system that the critics of government should have their full say; and the wider their differences from the government, the fuller the say they will demand. The burden on the House of Commons will always be roughly proportionate to the demands it encounters, and the greater the difficulties of our national and international position, the greater will be those demands and, therefore, that burden. The character of our society does not permit that burden to be transferable. Where the residence of the sovereign power is, there, inescapably, will the solution be sought.

The initiative of the private member raises issues of a quite different kind. I have already shown that, in so far as its restoration is sought to mean his freedom from party control in matters of major import, his initiative is, under modern conditions, neither possible nor desirable. But that does not mean that a good deal of the useless and wearying impotence to which the private member is now condemned is either necessary or desirable. The place assigned to him by the procedure of the House is quite largely the outcome of a conception of membership as the unpaid avocation of men whose main concerns are outside the House of Commons. That conception is no longer valid when members of Parliament are paid and when the House usually sits for some eight months in the year. The truth is that our idea of the function of a private member is still built upon the assumption of the "gentleman," in the Victorian sense of the term, as the typical member of the House of Commons, and his relation to its structure has never been seriously revised in the light of the

fact that the idea of the "gentleman" is no longer useful as a
working political hypothesis.

There are at least three important functions which members
of the House of Commons could now perform for which no
provision is made; and the need for one of them, at least, has
been strongly recommended by the Lord Chancellor's Committee
on Ministers' Powers. It is desirable to attach an advisory committee of members to each department of state. It would watch
the process of administration. It would make suggestions on
policy for examination. It could discuss confidentially the principles of bills before the prestige of the minister became associated with each clause and schedule of their content. The value
of the training for members involved in such work needs no detailed proof; it would at least assure us that men who went to
the different departments as ministers had some experience of
what administration implies. I should myself like to see some
members of the Committee related to the Whitley procedure of
the department with which they were associated; the system
stands badly in need of a third-party element of this kind. I am
not, be it noted, suggesting the creation of committees charged
with an executive function; they are, as here conceived, to be
advisory only and at no point to interfere with the authority
of the minister to make his decisions. But there is every reason
to suppose, first, that they would, by their power to ask for information and to discuss policy, be a valuable safeguard against
bureaucracy; and, second, by confidential discussion of measures
before their introduction into the House, they would at once
mitigate a good deal of unnecessary conflict over minutiæ, and
give members material for understanding which ought greatly
to clarify the standard of public debate when the bill is publicly
discussed.

Such committees could also act in an advisory capacity in relation to the issue of orders and regulations under authority delegated by Parliament to the departments. Mostly, no question
would arise over such submission; but the occasional exception

Legislature (Continued from page 1-A.)

would make the Committee invaluable to the minister ____ s officials as a kind of testing-ground for the reception it w___ ke. But if we are to be adequately safeguarded in the ma___ the operation of delegated powers, it is imperative that t ___ould be a standing committee of the House to which a_ ___rs not of an emergency character should go before they ___ ut into operation. The Committee should have its own se___ at to examine them with a view to ascertaining whether the regulations appear normal in the form they have been given. Wherever a doubt arises on this head, the Committee should be entitled to seek explanations from the relevant department; and, wherever it thinks desirable, it should draw the attention of the House to anything exceptional in the procedure proposed by the department. After all, since the House is responsible for the conference of powers on ministers, every reason for the conference of powers is also a reason for a safeguard against their possible abuse. Such a Committee as this could perform an important function in acting as the watch-dog of the House and securing its attention to the forms through which the powers it confers are exercised. Such a committee, once more, would be a privileged check on the danger of any bureaucratic habits in the departments.

The third function I should like to see assigned to private members is an extension of their present opportunities in relation to legislation. At present, as is well known, most of the time spent on private members' bills is largely wasted; only twice in the last generation has any such measure of importance gone to the statute-book. Friday afternoon is usually, in the House, an arid and dreary scene; for when everyone knows that nothing serious is likely to follow from its debate, the temptation is strong either to be absent or to treat it as a festive occasion. I should like to see the system reorganized on a plan which has been attended with remarkable success in the legislatures of the United States, very notably in Massachusetts.

On this principle, private members would ballot, as now, for the time assigned to them. But their bills, instead of being introduced either under the Ten Minutes' Rule or on Fridays, would, if they were backed by an agreed number of the House, be sent to a Select Committee for examination and report. That Select Committee would take public evidence on the matter, whether it be the abolition of the death penalty, the establishment of a minimum wage, or the reform of the marriage laws; and the discussion in the House as a whole would take place on the acceptance or rejection of the Committee's report. The advantages, I think, of this system are great. It enables a considerable number of private members—for the work of the Select Committees could be simultaneous—to engage in social investigation of unquestionable importance. It elicits for their inquiries a continuous public opinion by reason of the circumstances in which the investigation is done. It brings out into the light of day ideas and trends of thought in an institutional atmosphere which assures their adequate consideration. Anyone who has read of the Select Committee on the Combinations Act of 1825, or of that on Indian Constitutional Reform in our own day, will not doubt the value of the work that can be accomplished in this fashion. Where the subject-matter involved was contentious in the party sense of that term, its result would, at the least, be the accumulation of important material upon the subject. Where, as with a subject like the death penalty, there are no party considerations involved, investigation of this character would go far towards creating the kind of public opinion that would compel action. Above all the system would create a legitimate sphere of creative activity for the private member which would relieve him, especially if he sits on the government side of the House, of that sense of continuous frustration which is necessarily incident to the technique of party control.

One of the main features of parliamentary procedure since the war—though its principle is, in origin, much earlier—is the growth of delegated legislation. The pressure on Parliament is now so great that it has become usual to make an act a frame of reference the administrative details of which are filled in by the departments involved. On the average, nowadays, Parliament passes some hundred statutes annually, and the departments issue regulations of from fifteen to twenty times that number.

The system has aroused passionate criticism. We are told that it is the triumph of bureaucracy over Parliament. The latter is given no effective opportunity to scrutinize these regulations; and where objection is taken to them, the placid application of the government majority makes it completely ineffective. Some bills, moreover, contain clauses which actually oust the jurisdiction of the courts upon the question of *vires;* in these cases, the departments are erected into virtually sovereign bodies from whose fiat there is no right of appeal. We are in the toils, a Lord Chief Justice of England has urged, of a "new despotism"; and Mr. Ramsay Muir has argued that Parliament has surrendered its real authority "to the bureaucracy which, behind the veil, wields so much of the reality of power."

Two questions are really involved. The first, and the simpler, is whether in fact there has been any usurpation of power by the departments; the second is whether in principle the system is an objectionable one. The answer to the first is the effective answer that after prolonged investigation by the Lord Chancellor's Committee it was found that the system had proved its indispensability, and that it resulted in no sort of discoverable usurpation. Save where emergency like an outbreak of foot and mouth disease was involved, regulations were made only after the most prolonged consultation with all interests that might be affected by them; and these, from the time-limit usually required by Parliament before regulations became operative, had ample time to protest if they wished to do so. The question of *vires* is more complicated; I shall discuss its significance later, when I come to deal with the position and power of the judiciary in our system. Here, it will be sufficient to say that while the Lord Chancellor's Committee suggested minor safeguards, they found no evidence to reveal a "new despotism" of any kind.

The question of principle raises more interesting considerations. The case against delegated legislation cannot be a case for preventing any executive action which is not strictly controlled by Parliament, for those who make that case do not ask that certain supreme examples of executive authority, the prerogative powers of treaty-making and the right to declare war, for instance, shall be transferred from the Crown to Parliament. It cannot, even, be the claim that whenever a power is conferred upon the departments by Parliament, each exercise of the discretion so conferred shall be reported back to the ultimately responsible body; in things like the administration of pensions, for example, or the Unemployment or Health Insurance Acts, this is a manifest impossibility. The proper way of regarding the problem is to argue that when Parliament confers a discretionary power upon the executive it is entitled to two things. It is entitled, first, to full knowledge, in ample time for objection to be taken, of any general regulations made under the authority of the power; and it is entitled, secondly, to full information, where it is sought, of any individual instance in which the regulations are applied. For this purpose, obviously, the House of Commons needs a procedure which makes this possible. It would be foolish for Parliament to waste its time legislating separately upon applications or extensions of general principles about which it has already legislated. To say, for example, that a poison is a substance declared to be such by the Home Office in consultation with the Pharmaceutical Society is, under proper safeguards, infinitely more sensible than for the Cabinet to ask Parliament for a separate statute on each occasion when it is desirable to restrict the sale of some chemical substance on the ground of its poisonous nature.

This applies, I think, over the whole field of administration in principle, though I should myself argue that it is unwise to confer upon a department any authority to make regulations which had the effect of extending the criminal law; such powers, because of their importance, should be confined to Parliament itself. But, this apart, the only substantial issue raised by the process of delegated legislation is the issue of safeguards against its possible abuse. Here there are no great difficulties. On the side of the individual instance, Parliament has already an adequate technique, in its right so freely exercised, as we have seen, to put questions to ministers. Any survey of the proceedings of the House will show that, in this regard, few aggrieved persons or interests fail to find a member who will ask for information about their case. So far as the control of regulations themselves is concerned, the formal safeguards are not adequate today. But they could easily be made adequate if the two procedural devices I have suggested were adopted. A Committee of the House of Commons could, without difficulty, scrutinize each order or regulation and report upon it to the House; it could satisfy itself that the legislation was normal in form and that the process of consultation before issue had been effective. The Departmental Advisory Committees of members could have the drafts placed before them prior to issue for advice and criticism. The one thing needful in the whole system is the assurance of adequate publicity for its operation, and this is a matter that presents no inherent difficulty of any kind.

5

Subject to the modifications I have suggested, I believe the House of Commons to be an assembly admirably constructed, on the whole, for the work it has been called upon to perform. It is possible, of course, that other modifications are desirable. A strong case, for instance, can be made out for a fuller use of Standing Committees; and it is possible that the operation of these could be rendered more efficient if, as in the similar committees of local authorities, the relevant officials were able to attend them in order to give explanations of detail when required. But, in large outline, I emphasize again my view that the fundamental characteristics of the House, especially its basis in party control through Cabinet control, are essential now, as they were in Bagehot's time, to the success of parliamentary government. Were they destroyed, as I believe they would be destroyed either by the multiplication of parties or by a system of proportional representation, the conduct of government would be far less satisfactory than these characteristics have made it.

But it is important to remember, what this chapter has continually reiterated, that behind party differences, there has always been the safeguard of a common philosophy, and that this has been the prerequisite for their ability to differ without conflict. I have argued here that this common philosophy no longer exists, that it was the expression of a capitalism in its phase of expansion, and that, with its disappearance, the capacity of parties to use the House as an instrument of democracy is at the best a matter of grave doubt. I have sought to show that once men differ about matters of fundamental economic constitution the warfare between parties is no longer mimic in character. This makes effective continuity in the large contours of policy no longer possible. Once this occurs, the condition upon which one government can accept the decisions of its predecessor is suspended. That, as I have sought to show, is the framework within which men form their notions of constitutional action. For those notions are less a precise body of doctrine than a spiritual recognition that the great ends of life are held in common. It is this which, until our own day, has been the flywheel that has driven the whole machinery.

I have argued particularly that this is likely to prove to be the case whether the Labour Party as a government moves directly to socialist legislation or whether, as is at least possible, it strives in the first instance to maintain confidence by large measures of social reform. Either, I have suggested, would after a shorter or longer interval prove incompatible with the inherent requirements of capitalist economics. They would create the conditions that brought financial crisis to ourselves in 1931, as, on a different level, they led to the overthrow of M. Blum in France in 1937. They would reveal, in a word, that the state is an instrument not of the community as a whole—that is, an abstract entity devoid of institutional expression—but of the class which owns the instruments of economic power. I have argued that the Labour Party cannot use the House of Commons, in all likelihood, for socialist purposes save by capturing the state-power; and I have denied that the winning, merely, of an electoral majority is the same thing as winning the state-power. I do not deny that it is an important step on the road to that end—in our present circumstances the most important step conceivable. But it has been the thesis of this chapter that, with all its importance, it reaches but a little way. For the majority-rule of parliamentary government is built upon the prerequisite that the minority will acquiesce in its decisions. I have sought to show how tenuous is this assumption in the conditions we face. Political democracy, I have argued, is seeking always to become social and economic democracy. It cannot so transform itself while it is enfolded in the framework of capitalism, for the economic postulates of this system are in contradiction with the postulates social and economic democracy requires. Since the state-power is, through our system of class-relations, in the hands of capitalists; since, also, their whole way of life, and the immense privileges bound up with that way of life, depend upon their continued possession of the state-power, I have shown reason to suppose that it is at least unlikely that they will co-operate with their opponents in facilitating its surrender. An absence of such co-operation means an inability to maintain the understandings upon which the parliamentary system rests. There, and there only, lies the true problem of its future.

If this be right, therefore, all proposals which seek to improve the House of Commons as a governmental instrument, without finding a way out of this central problem of the state-power, are really irrelevant to the main issue our times have raised. The House of Commons will always be able to do its work adequately so long as capitalism is able to satisfy the demands of the masses. It is, as my argument runs, no longer able to satisfy them. That is what is meant by economic crisis, the prospect of war, the growth of Fascism, and the immense social conflicts to which these have led. It has therefore either to abdicate or to fight; on the evidence, the latter alternative seems the more likely. To seek for a way out of this grim choice by alterations in the mechanics of representation, or in a readjustment of the relation between the Cabinet and the House of Commons, is like using a pill to cure an earthquake. Proportional representation has not saved Germany; and the power of the private member, as in France, to overthrow the government at his discretion has not postponed the magnitude of the same issue there that we ourselves confront. If there is a way out, it is not along such lines that it will be found. There has to be fundamental agreement on all matters of major importance for the life of the House of Commons to continue upon its present lines. Only as we discover how that agreement may be made can we preserve the greatness of its past traditions into a future age.

CHAPTER FIVE

The Cabinet

1

THE Cabinet is essentially a committee of that party or coalition of parties which can command a majority in the House of Commons. Such a description, no doubt, is more functional than formal. It does not emphasize some of those characteristics of the Cabinet to which history and ceremonial alike give prominence. There is a sense, of no great importance nowadays, in which the Cabinet is a committee of certain members of His Majesty's Privy Council to whom the executive control of the state-power is confided. There is a sense, also, in which stress may be laid—though too much stress can easily be laid—on the fact that it is a secret committee. The real function of the Cabinet is to govern the country in the name of the party or parties which provide it with a majority in the House of Commons.

It is, therefore, as Bagehot pointed out in that famous chapter which first revealed the nature of the Cabinet to Englishmen, an instrument for linking the executive branch of government to the legislative. It is the body that directs the latter. It provides Parliament with the policy upon which decisions are to be made. It pushes a stream of tendency through affairs by obtaining for its course the approval of the sovereign organ of the state. But that which enables it to secure that approval is the fact that it is a party committee. Its support comes from the electoral decision that Conservatives, and not Socialists, are to rule. It is by disciplining the House of Commons to its purposes that it carries out its end. But, also, to discipline the House successfully, it must also discipline itself. That restraint is effected by the fact of its party composition. The ideas it will put into effect are, within pretty well-defined limits, the ideas its party supporters expect it to put into effect. It operates always within a framework of established expectations beyond which it can pass only at the peril of forfeiting its majority and so ceasing to be in power.

The success of the Cabinet system has been built upon this fact of party complexion. That is the basis upon which it can count, for at least all the main items of its policy, upon the support of its followers. But, hardly less, that success is built upon the fact that the Cabinet is an integral and living part of Parliament and not separated from it. A House of Commons, so to say, gives the Cabinet life; but normally it can itself live only so long as it is prepared to go on giving life to the Cabinet. It destroys it at the cost of self-destruction. The defeat of a Cabinet by the House involves either a dissolution of Parliament or the resignation of the Cabinet if it takes place upon a major issue; and such a resignation, as we saw in 1931, is almost bound within a brief time to result in a dissolution.

That the Cabinet should be a committee of the legislature is one of the two or three main principles which distinguish our system from that of the United States; it is worth while to reflect for a moment on the consequences of the distinction. The essence of the difference between the two systems is that with us the legislature has no interest separate from the executive; in the United States their separation gives it a separate interest. With us, therefore, the House of Commons must have confidence in, as it were, its board of directors; otherwise there will be either a new board of directors or a new Parliament. But with the Americans, Congress may have a different party complexion from that of the President and his Cabinet colleagues; or he may have a majority in one House of Congress and not in the other. Even with a majority in both, he need not have his way. He cannot control either House directly. He has no power to dissolve it. He can persuade, cajole, threaten, bribe. But the life of the American legislature continues independently of his will. He sends it his proposals; Congress makes up its own mind what it will do with them. It is an authority of equal legal standing with him in the determination of policy. If he cannot secure what he wants from its members, he has no way of appealing to the electorate against its decision. He can advise Congress; he cannot coerce it. And Congress, in its turn, cannot coerce him, unless a two-thirds majority of its members is prepared to override any veto he may impose.

Even when the President's party has a majority in both Houses, he has no certainty that he will have his way. His defeat does not create a crisis in his party; the loss of his prestige may not, necessarily, even injure it. Congress, as it were, is organized for action independently of his power. It broke President Wilson over the Treaty of Versailles; in 1937 it inflicted a heavy defeat over President Roosevelt on his proposals for the reform of the Supreme Court. Managing Congress is an art, in fact, quite different from the art of managing the House of Commons. The one is built on the assumption of distrust in the executive; the other in confidence in him. And this explains, in some degree, the difference in the process of choosing a President in the United States and choosing a party leader in Great Britain. There is no permanence in the first; everyone knows that, at the end of eight years at most, his day is over. The loyalties he can evoke are therefore quite different loyalties from those a party leader is likely to evoke in Great Britain. The President can influence his party profoundly while he is in office; some of his Cabinet may, by their personal qualities, influence it also. But they are not necessarily party leaders, or even men of considerable party experience. The result is that there will always be in Congress itself a little group of men who, in fact even if not in form, are a kind of alternative Cabinet of their own, a Cabinet the special credit of which must not be overlooked in the making of policy. It requires a President of quite exceptional quality to centralize public opinion round himself for this reason. The separation, in a word, makes for the confusion of responsibility. There is not necessarily a clear direction of policy, because there is always more than one interest competing for the right to direct it; and the fact that the President may be compelled to give way means that, even within the ranks of his own party, there will always be cabals to force him to give way. This Senator controls this committee, that Congressman another; the President must, in some degree, compromise with them both. It is not improbable that even so outstanding a President as Franklin D. Roosevelt has never got a bill through Congress in exactly the shape he desired; he has had to sacrifice this clause, soften the burden of that, to meet the will of one or another in Congress with an authority that could rival his own. And since he cannot effectively appeal to the electorate against these candid friends, he is always having to put up with something he may keenly feel to be a second-rate compromise.

This, again, is much more likely to be so in his second term than in his first. The sands of his authority begin to run down. Those who dislike him cannot help remembering that, in four years at most, there will be another occupant of the White House. Something he does arouses fierce criticism; an influential member of Congress may easily think that to head this criticism is to give him a chance of the succession. Another may feel that the time has come to hedge; the President has attacked, it may be, the public utilities, and they are powerful in his state; it will do him no harm in his state to display his independence. The President, to put it briefly, when he deals with Congress is always dealing with a quasi-independent empire his hold over which is never certain. His position is like that of a minority government in the House of Commons without an appeal to the electorate as the contingent sanction of its policy. The time he needs to think out his measures is largely taken up with maintaining a power which ought not to admit of question. And every time he suffers a major defeat, the ability to repeat that defeat is intensified by the loss of prestige he suffers.

From all these doubts and difficulties our system frees the English Cabinet. Broadly, it knows that it can get what it wants. The result is to make responsibility direct and policy coherent. Unless the Cabinet has made a bad blunder, it knows that it can stand by its decisions. No doubt there will be cabals to watch, and intrigues to stifle; Mr. Churchill, for instance, may have his little group of sharpshooters to attack the government's policy over India. But it is rare that the cabal can, or will wish to, pull the Cabinet down. At the best, it may put the other side in office; at the worst, its members may be risking their own seats at the next general election. Parties tend to like reliable men, and even consummate artists in criticism like Mr. Churchill may find that they sacrifice their reputation for reliability in their quest for artistic self-expression. The private member, so long as he is satisfied with the large outlines of policy, is not going to be excessively tender-minded about details. It is only when, as with Sir Robert Peel in 1846, the leap forward goes beyond the frontier within which he expects to dwell, that he assassinates the leaders he has made.

The alternative to this method is not easy to see; certainly it would go to the root of our system as we know it. Probably it would mean the replacement of parties by groups loosely related to one another, and the outcome of this change would rapidly be an assembly more like the Chamber of Deputies than the House of Commons. That would, no doubt, exalt the power of the private member at the expense of the Cabinet, and it would mean, almost certainly, that the right to dissolve would cease to be a prerogative of the Government. The danger of this is, I think, grave. For, in the first place, as in France, it would deprive the electorate of any real power over group-combinations; governments would be built on manœuvres within the House instead of upon electoral decisions outside it. And, secondly, by reason of the exaltation of the private member's power, he would have to be placated by recognition of his influence in wholly undesirable ways. Where the life of a government depends on the will of the private member, as in the American Congress or the French Chamber, there is always the danger of parliamentary corruption. It may be through a method like the American "senatorial courtesy." It may be because, then, the access of the great interests to the private member has a significance which in our system they can hardly possess with any reciprocal comfort. It is not insignificant that the main field of the lobbies in Washington is at the Capitol, and not in the White House; it is not insignificant, either, that they have, in London, to use Westminster as an avenue to Whitehall. Our Cabinet system, whatever its weaknesses, minimizes the danger of sinister influence. And no one who has seen its alternatives at work but will regard this as a gain it is difficult to overestimate.

One other merit, compared with the American, deserves emphasis. The average American politician of eminence is not likely to exchange a seat in the Senate, for instance, for a place in the Cabinet. In the former, in a large degree, he is his own master; he can make the theatre of action to some degree his own. In the latter, he is the servant of any President above the level of the third-rate; and if he cannot agree with the President he must go. An American Cabinet, therefore, is rarely a body of experienced public men who can work together as a team because they have learned to live together in Congress. Some of them are not even names to the public when their appointment is announced, and they cease once more to be names when they leave Washington. Few of them, with a strong President—Mr. Wilson, for instance, or Mr. Roosevelt—have much opportunity to develop a policy of their own. The responsibility is only partly theirs in any case; and, in the public mind, the credit will be the President's because the external responsibility is his. Cabinet office, therefore, is rarely in the United States a supreme prize of ambition for the best minds in the state. Its attainment is as much an accident of private relations as a reward of public service.

With the English Cabinet this is not the case. As a normal rule, membership in the Cabinet will be the reward of service in Parliament; it will have been preceded by a considerable apprenticeship to the service of politics. I do not say that a Cabinet will consist of exceptional men; I do say that the competition for place, the rigour of the selective process, the eminence of the prize, will assure the nation that every Cabinet will contain some exceptional men. And, when formed, it is a team in a sense in which an American Cabinet will rarely be, or grow into, a team. Most of its members will have known one another for years; they will have been accustomed to working together in opposition. More than this: normally, at least, some of them will have had previous experience of Cabinet work, and most of them will have had the experience of deciding policy on problems in opposition upon which they will have also to decide as a Cabinet. To reach the Cabinet at all, they will have had to display, as a general rule, certain qualities of character, common sense, judgment, the ability to make a case, the power to meet an emergency, which are at least the basis upon which the successful administration is built. If it is said that, as compared with the civil servants whom they will control, they are amateurs, there are at least two answers. It is, firstly, highly undesirable for a Cabinet minister to be a specialist in the work of his department; he then runs the danger that is common to all specialists of sacrificing breadth of view to intensity of gaze. And, secondly, his business as a Cabinet minister is not the manipulation of detail but the definition of a general direction. He seeks to co-ordinate the work of his department on the one hand and to assist, in the Cabinet itself, in co-ordinating the work of the departments as a whole into a coherent line of policy. The politician at his best is quite invariably better at this work than any specialist; his training in persuading public opinion makes him so. That is why civil servants, soldiers, and sailors, or business men accustomed to "run their business in their own way," rarely make successful Cabinet ministers.

2

The keystone of the Cabinet arch is the Prime Minister. He is central to its formation, central to its life, and central to its death. No Cabinet can fail to take its complexion from what he is and does in its direction. That is not to say that he is its master in the sense in which the American President is master of his colleagues. The British Prime Minister is more than *primus inter pares* but less than an autocrat. He has, as we shall see, very considerable personal powers; but the condition of their effective exercise is, overwhelmingly, that he should be able to persuade and not to coerce; and the condition of success in that persuasion is pretty effectively dependent upon the success of his government. No doubt he can always compel the resignation of any colleague; but the famous dismissal of Lord Palmerston by Lord John Russell in 1851 is only one instance of many which go to show that the Prime Minister's compulsions are the Prime Minister's perils. It is not merely, as Mr. Lloyd George has said, that there is no generosity at the top; there is always someone willing, and even eager, to take his place. It is even more true that a Prime Minister maintains his leadership of his party by the atmosphere of success which surrounds his policy; and nothing so injures the appearance of success as constant changes by way of resignation in the team that he drives.

In theory, the choice of a Prime Minister rests within the discretion of the monarch; in practice, of course, that discretion is severely limited by the necessities of party politics. Where, for instance, the government has been beaten and the Opposition has its own appointed leader, the King has no practical alternative but to offer him the post. Or, it may be, as on the resignation of Lord Baldwin in 1937, both party and public opinion is so clear as to who is his proper successor that the King must follow the drift of that opinion. For he knows that, in such circumstances, it is wholly unlikely that any other nominee will be able to form a government. Had the King, in 1937, offered the Premiership to Sir John Simon, for instance, it is clear that, even if he had accepted the commission, he would have been unable to persuade his Conservative colleagues to serve under him. Where the wishes of a party are unmistakable, and the political circumstances normal, convention now requires that the King shall act upon the wishes of the party.

However, this apart, it is clear that the King has a small range of discretion in the choice he makes; yet even that small range will, normally, be closely circumscribed by facts that point to a pretty direct conclusion. Though, theoretically, the Prime Minister must be in either House of Parliament, and has been so consistently since the resignation of Lord Salisbury in 1902, it is fairly certain that in the future he will have to be in the House of Commons. George V had the choice between Lord Curzon and Mr. Baldwin (as he then was) in 1923; but the fact that the official Opposition was hardly represented in the House of Lords made all those whom the King consulted advise that it was no longer practicable for the House of Commons to be deprived of the Prime Minister's leadership. The King is not, of course, bound by this precedent in the future; but, unless political circumstances radically change, it is difficult not to feel that the precedent will be conclusive. The House of Commons is now the chamber to which the Cabinet is alone effectively responsible; it is the one in which the maintenance of party organization matters vitally. The Prime Minister, as the head of the party in power, can hardly afford in the future to be out of touch with the chamber where the effective decisions are made.

There are, however, two other situations which need to be considered. A Prime Minister may resign, as Mr. Gladstone did in 1894, leaving no clear evidence as to whom the party wishes as his successor. In that case, the King may, as Queen Victoria did on that occasion, choose the Prime Minister from among a number of possible candidates. His right so to do is unquestionable. But it is, of course, a right the successful exercise of which is dependent upon the ability of the politician so chosen to form a government. In 1880, for example, Lord Hartington was the leader of the Liberal Party in the House of Commons, Lord Granville its leader in the House of Lords; but the party also contained Mr. Gladstone who, though he had resigned the leadership in 1874, was nevertheless universally recognized as the author of the Liberal victory of that year, and expected by public opinion to succeed Disraeli as Prime Minister. The Queen, who disliked and distrusted him, sought to evade the necessity of that choice. She offered the Premiership in succession to Hartington and Granville; each informed her that he could not form a government without Mr. Gladstone, that Mr. Gladstone would not serve under him, and that, in the circumstances, he was the only possible Prime Minister. The Queen then offered the Premiership to Mr. Gladstone, who accepted it and formed his government.

It is clear, indeed, that the King's discretion will, normally, reach but a little way. The number of possible Prime Ministers in a party, at any moment, is limited by party and public opinion, and the King will not be able to go beyond that circle. If he does, his choice will be widely resented as breaking the conventions upon which the governance of parties is based; he will almost certainly find that, normally again, his nominee will not be able to form a government and unlikely to maintain it for long if he does. His failure will be everywhere taken as a criticism upon the exercise of the royal discretion; and it is of the essential nature of the royal functions that they must be so exercised as not to invite public opinion.

The second case in which the King has a discretionary choice is one in which the complexities of the party situation in the House do not directly indicate an obvious government. There have, for instance, been eleven minority governments since 1832, and three periods of coalition government, if we count the

Unionist government which was in office from 1896 to 1906 as in effect a normal Conservative government. In all such circumstances, a leeway for negotiation exists in which the King may well become an influential figure. He must, indeed, proceed under certain fairly well-understood conventions. If the government resigns on defeat, he will be expected to send for the leader of the Opposition and invite him to form a government if he can. The reason for this has been well stated by Dr. Jennings. "The King's task," he writes, "is only to secure a government, not to try to form a government of which he approves. To do so would be to engage in party politics. It is, moreover, essential to the belief in the monarch's impartiality not only that he should in fact act impartially, but that he should appear to act impartially. The only method by which this can be demonstrated clearly is to send at once for the leader of the Opposition."

This has, in fact, been done on every such occasion since 1839; though on the resignation of Lord Salisbury in 1886 Queen Victoria's hatred of Mr. Gladstone induced her to seek departure from precedent, and a long and complex intrigue with those Liberals whom she called "moderate, loyal, and *really patriotic* men who have the safety and well-being of the Empire and the throne at heart, and who wish to save them from destruction," preceded her return to a reasonable frame of mind. It is, further, probable that the King, in sending for the leader of the Opposition, should have no consultations with any other politician. Lord Salisbury, in 1886, gave the Queen quite different advice; but it is in fact clear that any such consultation can only create the impression that the King is seeking to evade the right of the Opposition leader to form a government if he thinks that desirable. Wherever, on the precedents, there has been discussion with some person not the recognized party leader of the Opposition, he has, as in the Lansdowne precedent of 1861, been the Opposition leader in the House of Lords. So, to take recent cases, the King at once saw Mr. Ramsay MacDonald on the defeat of Mr. Baldwin and his consequent resignation in 1924; and on Mr.

Ramsay MacDonald's resignation, together with his Cabinet, in 1931, the King at once saw Mr. Baldwin.

The two coalitions of 1916 and 1931 raise interesting questions, since on both occasions there emerged from the royal discussions a Prime Minister who either had not been or was no longer the recognized leader of a party. In 1916, it is certain that the usual precedents were observed. On Mr. Asquith's resignation, the King sent for Mr. Bonar Law, as the leader of the second largest party in the House, and offered the Premiership to Mr. Lloyd George only when Mr. Bonar Law had refused it and had recommended the course that was followed. The circumstances of 1931 are exceptional and merit more detailed consideration; it must, of course, be added that in the absence of authoritative documentation we are largely thrown back on conjecture. We know that the Labour government, in consequence of financial difficulties about the solution for which it could not agree, authorized the Prime Minister, Mr. Ramsay MacDonald, to resign on August 23. We know, further, that, on the advice of the Prime Minister, the King saw Mr. Baldwin as leader of the Conservative and Sir Herbert Samuel as leader of the Liberal Opposition in order, as the official announcement put it, "to hear from themselves what the position of their respective parties is." No public information authorizes us to suppose that this meeting was concerned either with the resignation of the Labour government or with the formation of its successor. When, on August 24, Mr. MacDonald presented the King with the resignation of his Cabinet, he again advised the King to see Mr. Baldwin and Sir Herbert Samuel. We do not know what occurred at this interview, at which, it appears, Mr. MacDonald was present. "What is said," writes Mr. Sidney Webb, who was Colonial Secretary in Mr. MacDonald's Cabinet, "is that the King, with whom the Prime Minister had been in constant communication, but who never went outside his constitutional position, made a strong appeal to him to stand by the nation in this financial crisis, and to seek the support of leading members of the Conservative and Liberal parties in forming, in conjunction with such members of his own party as would come in, a united National Government. The King is believed to have made a correspondingly strong appeal to the Liberal and Conservative leaders." All that we authoritatively know is that, after resigning as Labour Prime Minister, Mr. Ramsay MacDonald immediately received a new commission to form what became known as the National Government.

But certain other things are known: (1) On August 23, the Labour Cabinet had no knowledge, as a Cabinet, that Mr. MacDonald proposed to desert them. The four ministers who joined the new administration may have been aware of this; the others, until Mr. MacDonald returned to Downing Street on August 24, assumed, and assumed naturally, that, since he was to tender his resignation, Mr. Baldwin would become Prime Minister in the normal way. (2) We must assume that the King was aware that only four ministers would follow Mr. MacDonald, that, certainly, therefore, the bulk of his Cabinet and, presumably, the bulk of his party were in disagreement with him. This, in fact, proved to be the case; only 14 out of 289 Labour members followed Mr. Ramsay MacDonald. (3) We know that the King was never advised to communicate with Mr. Henderson, the leader of those in the Labour Cabinet who dissented from Mr. MacDonald, who was elected the leader of the Labour Party on the former Prime Minister's expulsion from it. (4) We must assume that the suggestion of Mr. MacDonald as the new Prime Minister was made by the King to him, and accepted by Mr. Baldwin and Sir Herbert Samuel in consequence of what Mr. Webb terms "a correspondingly strong appeal" made by the King to them. It has never been suggested that the idea of a MacDonald Premiership in the National Government emanated either from Mr. Baldwin or from Sir Herbert Samuel. Neither is known to have discussed this idea with party colleagues before Mr. MacDonald accepted that commission on August 24.

It is difficult, therefore, in the light of the information we have, not to regard Mr. MacDonald's appointment on this occasion as the personal nomination of the King. He was Prime Minister in no sense as the representative of his party. His majority appears, at least, to have been borrowed for him by the King in that "correspondingly strong appeal" to the other party leaders of which Mr. Webb speaks. He did not recommend to George V any attempt to ascertain the view of the Labour Party which he betrayed; it is, surely, notable that, though he recommended an interview between the King and Sir Herbert Samuel, he did not suggest an interview with Mr. Henderson. His appearance as Prime Minister of a coalition the members of which had been denouncing his government up to the very moment of the new Cabinet has as much the character of a palace revolution as the appearance of Lord Bute as Prime Minister in 1763. Mr. Webb and Dr. Jennings both suggest that the King's action was constitutional. The term is an elastic one. If it is accepted in this implication, it appears to mean that the King can make anyone he wishes Prime Minister so long as his action is subsequently approved in a general election. The leader of one party can be, on this hypothesis, persuaded, unknown to his colleagues, to go over to their opponents, by a royal appeal to "patriotic" obligations; all the normal expectations of the party system may be ignored; and the resulting confusion may be utilized in order to snatch an electoral majority for the new combination. The theory appears to rest upon the assumption that the King does not deal with parties but with men in their individual capacity; and that he is entitled to do so provided that the electorate subsequently approves his action. If this is so, it is necessary, here, only to point out that the King must be regarded as a factor of first-class importance in any political crisis where the direction of events is uncertain. I shall deal later with the implications of this view.

The Prime Minister, when chosen, proceeds to form his government. Here, once again, the fact of party is fundamental to the completion of his task. In all normal circumstances he is

Prime Minister because he is the leader of his party; and if he did not act in terms of that relationship, he would be unable to assure himself of a majority in the House of Commons. Certain colleagues he must choose, because their presence in the government is expected by the party; a few of them, indeed, may be so important that they may be able to insist upon receiving the particular office they desire. It is well known that in 1929 Mr. MacDonald did not wish to have Mr. Arthur Henderson as Foreign Secretary, and only the knowledge that, otherwise, Mr. Henderson would have remained outside the ranks of the government persuaded Mr. MacDonald to offer him the post. He has, of course, a certain amount of elbow-room, which is perhaps roughly proportionate to his influence over his followers. The world was surprised at Mr. Baldwin's decision to make Mr. Churchill Chancellor of the Exchequer in 1924, and perhaps hardly less surprised that this decision entailed a refusal by Sir Robert Horne to enter that Cabinet. Obviously enough, the choice of colleagues must, apart from the small group who nominate themselves, be an invidious task for any Prime Minister; and those who are excluded will rarely be able to see that the grounds upon which others have been preferred are adequate. The Prime Minister has to do the best he can. He is seeking to build a corporate entity, the members of which will be collectively responsible for one another's acts. In general, he will, unless he makes some colossal blunder of omission, have the loyalty of his party behind him in the decisions he makes; and that loyalty will continue unless the Cabinet, as it works, proves a defective arrangement which needs strengthening by reason of the opposition it encounters in the House of Commons.

The Prime Minister must, of course, receive the approval of the sovereign for his decisions. So long as he is a strong man, this he is certain to have if he is persistent in his determination. For if objections to his decision are pressed, he can always resign his commission; and it is at least highly unlikely that the King will push matters to this point. Not, indeed, that the opinions of the monarch are without weight. Lord Derby did not propose Lord Palmerston as Foreign Secretary in 1852 in view of the "well-known personal feelings of the Queen." She was doubtful of the wisdom of appointing Mr. Goschen to the Cabinet in 1866, and persuaded Lord Russell to secure the acquiescence of his colleagues in doing so. In 1868, she tried hard to prevent Lord Clarendon from being appointed Foreign Secretary. She tried, in 1880, to make the appointment of Mr. Chamberlain subject to conditions. In 1886 she told Mr. Gladstone, on the eve of the formation of his Cabinet, that she would not accept the nomination of Sir Charles Dilke; and, in that same Cabinet, she was successful in preventing the appointment of Mr. Labouchere, and in preventing Lord Ripon from going to the India Office. We have no knowledge of later precedents, if there be any. What is clear from the evidence is that the royal right to discuss appointments is fundamental, and that the right to discuss will carry with it, at least in the period for which the precedents are available, a considerable influence in the determination of the distribution of offices.

Just as the monarch has influence, so, also, inevitably do the principal colleagues of the Prime Minister. Theoretically, no doubt, the Prime Minister has an unfettered discretion; "I have never known," said Mr. Gladstone in 1882, "more than a friendly announcement before publicity, and very partial consultations with one or two, especially the leaders in the second House." Even today this is still broadly the rule; though in 1929 a small committee of the Labour Party, composed of Mr. Snowden, Mr. Henderson, Mr. Clynes, and Mr. J. H. Thomas, discussed pretty comprehensively with the Prime Minister the distribution of offices. In fact, though the Prime Minister's discretion is wide, consultation with his personal colleagues is inevitable. He has not only to form a team; he has also to form a team that will satisfy them. He will have to be an autocrat, indeed, to be able to impose his views upon them against their will, since there is always the danger that they may not serve. Mr. Baldwin, for instance, desired to include Sir Austen Chamberlain and Lord Birkenhead as ministers without portfolio in his Cabinet, just before the general election of 1923; but he dropped the proposal when it met with opposition from some of his colleagues. And where a coalition Cabinet is formed, the Prime Minister must necessarily satisfy the leader of the other party. He is limited, too, by the need to provide for representation in the House of Lords, as required by statute. Roughly, it is a fair calculation that about half the Cabinet nominates itself, by the standing of its members in the eyes of the party; and about half of these will be able to bring great pressure to bear in getting the posts they want. It is only with the other half that the Prime Minister really has a free hand.

The Prime Minister is the pivot of the whole system of government. Normally, he is not only the leader of the majority party and the head of what Bagehot termed the "efficient" part of the executive. He settles differences between departments. He can, with the assent of the sovereign, call for the resignation of any of his colleagues. He has a decisive voice in all important Crown appointments. He has to keep a general eye on all departments, in particular that of foreign affairs, and to act as the co-ordinator of policy. He is the leader of the House of Commons, and members there, especially in times of difficulty, will look to him as the reserve power to whom appeal beyond ordinary ministers may be made. He is, further, the effective channel of communication between the Cabinet and the sovereign; and the *Letters of Queen Victoria* bear witness that this function is no sinecure if the monarch is a person who takes his duties seriously.

Obviously, indeed, the office of Prime Minister varies enormously with the character of the man who holds it. Few colleagues ever challenged the authority of Mr. Gladstone; Lord Salisbury, on the testimony of Sir Michael Hicks-Beach, was not good at controlling his colleagues; and Lord Rosebery seems to have been unable to control them at all. His own ability, the range of his interests, his skill as chairman, his capacity for rapid work, his power to distinguish between the significant and the insignificant will all make a great difference. Disraeli is said to have been able to make his own views prevail even when all his colleagues but one were opposed to him. Peel was able—perhaps because the range of administration was so much more narrow in his day—to keep an eye on the work of all the departments; but Mr. Asquith declined even to make this attempt on the ground that it was completely impracticable. It is said, indeed, that during the war he was so little interested in Cabinet discussions that he was accustomed to write letters during their progress, and to assume that, as they died down, agreement had been reached and that the next question could be considered.

It is certain that the modern Prime Minister can, for the most part, hope to do no more than control the large outlines of policy. That does not mean that his authority is less than before. For, in modern democracy, the issues of elections tend to accrete about a person; and there is a real sense in which a general election is nothing so much as a plebiscite between alternative Prime Ministers. The result is to give him a national standing which no colleague can rival so long as he remains Prime Minister. The party is built around his personality, and while he retains the hold of his party no one can really rival his standing. After all, he appoints and dismisses his colleagues. It is to him that ministers go, in the first place, with their difficulties. He has a large share in making foreign policy. He settles differences between departments, and if their dispute becomes a Cabinet question his voice in the settlement will carry special weight. He is the chairman of the Committee of Imperial Defence. He controls the agenda of the Cabinet. He has a special significance in the context of both the Dominions and the League of Nations. His word in the House of Commons is a final word. Revolt against him, in the light of all this, is obviously difficult, unless he has handled his job so badly that there is a widespread feeling of his unfitness for it.

It would be too much to say that the position of a modern Prime Minister has approximated to that of an American President; for the careers of Mr. Asquith, Mr. Lloyd George, and Mr. Ramsay MacDonald all illustrate the fact that his authority is a matter of influence in the context of party structure and not of defined powers legally conferred. But it would, I think, on experience be true to say that the stronger the hold of a Prime Minister upon his Cabinet, the better is the system likely to work. He ought to have his own large conceptions of policy. He ought to make ministers feel that he can decide for them in their difficulties. While detailed interference fritters away his energies, and may even by its repercussions cause grave personal strains, there ought to be no question about the fact of his leadership. There can be no real sort of doubt that the sense that he is driving the team gives it a unity and a coherence it will not otherwise possess. It maintains his prestige with his party, and thereby keeps the party together. And, within limits, to keep the party together is by all odds the best way of enabling it to maintain its hold upon the country.

It is clear that the burden of such an office must be very great. To manage the sovereign, the Cabinet, the House of Commons, and the party, all of them with a view to managing the electorate as the result of managing these, requires qualities that no ordinary man is likely to possess. The answer, I think, is that, with not more than two exceptions, no ordinary man has ever possessed them. A stereotype of Lord Baldwin as a "simple Englishman" was composed for the edification of the electorate, but it is a sufficient commentary on that stereotype to say that no simple man has ever been Prime Minister of England. The apprenticeship he will have to serve even to gain sight of office is a safeguard against the prospect of an ordinary man's arriving there. Discretion, dexterity, the power to rule men—above all, in that power, the knowledge of what men can be trusted— the capacity for effective statement, the intuitive judgment that, while it is ahead of party and public opinion, it is never so far ahead that it cannot be followed with a sense of ease, an ambition that drives, and is yet cautious in the display of its urgency, a relentlessness at the margins where decisions, whether about men or measures, are urgent, these are the qualities no Prime Minister can do without. It is too much, no doubt, to say that a Prime Minister has to hazard his political head every day, but it is not too much to say that every day is a day upon which he may have to hazard his head. To tread a path of fire is inherent in the function. It cannot be performed by a sensitive soul, to whom every decision is a torture—events do not wait; and it cannot be performed by a man who lacks the feeling for the decisive moment. Party loyalties live by success, and Prime Ministers do not last who lack the secret of success. Politicians want office, and no modern Prime Minister has lasted as a party leader who has lost more than two general elections in succession.

The fact that our system has, on the whole, produced a succession of extraordinary men as Prime Ministers is, I suggest, a tribute of a quite special kind to the selective function of the House of Commons. Since 1868, there has been no Prime Minister save Sir Henry Campbell-Bannerman who has not been a person of exceptional intellectual gifts; Sir Henry more than compensated for average mental endowments by a unique combination of sterling common sense and profound moral integrity. The contrast, in this regard, with Presidents of the United States is startling; for, since the Civil War, there have been fourteen Presidents of whom, I think, it is fair to say that only four would have reached the White House had they been subjected to the conditions through which a British Prime Minister arrives in Downing Street. And, in a sense, the tests to which a Prime Minister is subjected are far more severe than those of the American President. The latter cannot be forced to resign. He is the decisive master of his Cabinet. He has never to contend with a leader of the Opposition whom the whole country regards as an alternative to his rule. He has a far easier task in relation to foreign policy. Nor, on a long-term view, has he the same responsibilities as the Prime Minister for the direction and fate of his party; at most, within eight years, the reins of control will pass to another hand.

It is impossible, indeed, to contemplate the office of Prime Minister without the emphasis that its evolution is a signal demonstration of the value of parliamentary government. It confers the responsibility required while it retains upon the exercise of that responsibility a series of controls which have so far worked with remarkable efficiency. The Prime Minister who cannot drive his team goes, as Lord Salisbury went. The Prime Minister who is held, rightly or wrongly, to lack the initiative for his task is driven from office, as Mr. Asquith was driven from office; and it is probably not unfair to say that the main reason for the replacement of Mr. MacDonald by Mr. Baldwin in the summer of 1936 was the wide realization that, under the former's leadership, the future continuance in office of the National Government might well be placed in jeopardy. The system, in brief, provides that office shall test its occupant by the pragmatic test of a successful response to popular demand. The loyalty a Prime Minister can evoke has little about it of constraint or artificiality. No doubt his own press will seek to make him out a superman, but its idealizations will be at least as fully corrected by the press of the other side. He thinks and speaks and acts in an atmosphere in which criticism has every opportunity and reason to reveal his weaknesses, for his opponents prepare the ground for their victory by the ability with which this task is performed. And that is not the case only with his opponents. The Prime Minister is judged, less obviously, perhaps, but not less closely, by his own supporters. The knowledge that they live by his success means a compulsion upon him to bend all his energies to be successful. He knows that despite all personal loyalties there will always be one of his own followers ready, perhaps eager, to take his place. He knows, even, that there is a sense in which his disappearance will make possible the fulfilment of ambitions that are barred so long as he retains power; the campaign of the great press lords against the leadership of Lord Baldwin is only one instance of many of this kind. No Prime Minister can ever say of his office what Clement VII could say of his: "Now that we have got the Papacy let us enjoy it." The first day at Downing Street may give the sense of satisfaction that comes to any man who has fulfilled a lofty ambition; it will also be one of the few last days of mental ease that he will know as Prime Minister. The parliamentary system is conducted on the vital hypothesis that no man is indispensable, and its daily operation is a constant and salutary reminder to the Prime Minister that his fortune depends upon his recognition of this truth.

3

After the Prime Minister, the vital Cabinet positions are, as a rule, those of finance and foreign affairs. It is inevitable that this should be the case. Finance is the key to administrative and legislative possibilities; not a little of the success of the British civil service has been due to the fact that, under the Prime Minister and the Cabinet, the Chancellor of the Exchequer has exercised, through the Treasury, a general supervision of the departments. The special position of the Foreign Secretary is due to different considerations. In part, it is the outcome of an old and dubious tradition of secrecy. In part, again, it is due to the fact that busy heads of departments cannot hope to concern themselves with more than a small part of the area of activity with which the Foreign Secretary must deal. They have no time to read more than the vital dispatches, and they cannot even attempt any detailed supervision of his policy. Action, moreover, has only too often to be immediate; and ministers must be content, in general, to trust to the discretion of their colleague to act within the framework of the policy they have laid down in the Cabinet. They will not always do so; the resignation of Lord Palmerston in 1851 shows what a strong personality may do when he takes the bit between his teeth. They may even approve, and may then be compelled by public opinion outside the Cabinet to repudiate their approval. The resignation of Sir Samuel Hoare, in 1936, is an instance of this kind. But since, as a rule, the Foreign Secretary is working in the closest liaison with the Prime Minister, since, also, the major outlines of policy will be discussed in the Cabinet, his colleagues will know in a general way what the Foreign Secretary is doing; and they have at least the right to exact information even if, as Mr. Lloyd George has suggested, it is sometimes only grudgingly forthcoming.

The Chancellor of the Exchequer and the Foreign Secretary apart, Cabinet ministers stand upon an approximately equal footing; or, rather, the differences in the influence they exert will depend less upon the offices they hold than upon the kind of persons they themselves are. A Cabinet consists of two kinds of posts: there are the departments with heavy administrative functions and there are those like the Privy Seal, and the Presidency of the Council to which no serious burden of administration attaches. In general, every Cabinet functions better if it contains two or three ministers of this sort. It enables the counsel of men to be made available who do not wish to be loaded, for one reason or another, with administrative duties. It sets them apart for assistance in the legislature to a colleague who is pressed with the burdens of a great bill that he is seeing through. They are useful, also, in committees of Cabinet and in general discussion because, like the Prime Minister himself, they can take a more detached point of view than ministers who, in some degree, will always be tempted to attach excessive weight to the departmental interest with which they are charged.

It has always seemed singular to some critics of the Cabinet system that it should be composed of men whose major time is necessarily devoted to their departmental work, and there have been zealous advocates of a return to the War Cabinet system of Mr. Lloyd George. The latter suspended the normal character of the Cabinet and replaced it by a Cabinet of five, among whom only the Chancellor of the Exchequer had departmental duties. The ordinary Cabinet, it was argued, which now contains from twenty to twenty-three members, had become so large that it slowed down the pace at which the war had made it necessary to take decisions. Ministers with departments, moreover, were so buried in the details of their work that the large outlines of policy were, necessarily, a secondary consideration with them; and, in any case, they brought tired minds to that vital task. The fact that the members of the War Cabinet were freed from departmental responsibility had the two great advantages, first, that they were always available for immediate consultation, were, in fact, in almost continuous session, and, second, that they were free from the irritating pressure of minor preoccupations.

There can be little doubt that some such instrument as Mr. Lloyd George devised would be imperative in a period of war. But the evidence also suggests that its practicability is confined to such a period. It works because, in war-time, all considerations are subordinated to the single issue of winning the war, and because the usual processes of opposition are normally suspended in the House of Commons. But as a peace-time expedient it is, at the best, dubious. It is built upon a theory of the possibility of separating policy from administration which is unworkable except under the pressure of such an urgency as war. Departmental ministers cannot be relegated to a secondary place if they are to run their departments efficiently, for the simple reason that their relegation results in the erosion of responsibility. Men of the standing of ministers, moreover, cannot effectively control their policy if the power to make decisions is one in which they do not share. The unity of policy, which the theory postulates, disappears because policy is the expression of an accumulation of minutiæ with which the non-departmental minister does not concern himself; and, further, the policy of one department shades off into the policy of another, so that joint consultation becomes imperative upon a scale fatal to the ideal functioning the system conceives itself to embody. The conflict between the

Prime Minister and the Foreign Secretary during the Lloyd George regime sufficiently indicates the difficulties. There was no real meeting of their minds by the very character of the relation built by the system between them. The result was that, for a considerable period, there were two foreign policies in this country—one in the hands of Mr. Lloyd George as Prime Minister, and one in the hands of Lord Curzon as Foreign Secretary. Neither was fully known to the other; each was worked through a different personnel. The result was an incoherence of attitude for which there was no possible justification.

The return, therefore, to the older system was justified on grounds of both theory and experience. Those men, broadly, must be responsible for the making of policy who will be charged with its administration. That does not mean that a smaller Cabinet is not desirable, or that there are not obvious ways to its attainment. The case, for instance, for a single Ministry of Defence is, under the conditions of modern warfare, an unanswerable one; and it has not been realized less because it has been answered by argument than because it has, so far, been unable to overcome the older tradition of the separate services and the immense vested interests, sufficiently illustrated by the struggle for the control of the fleet air arm, which has accumulated about that tradition. It is probable, too, that Prime Ministers have viewed with some doubt the creation of a single such ministry, for they have been persuaded to see in the immense administrative authority of its head a possible challenge to their overriding authority in the Cabinet. Defence apart, it is possible to contemplate other methods of reducing the size of the Cabinet—the creation, for instance, of a single Ministry of Production in which, as is wholly logical, the functions of the Board of Trade and the Ministries of Agriculture and Labour should be combined; and it is clear that, given such a unification, the need for a separate Ministry of Transport, with, as now, independent Cabinet status, would cease to exist. Changes such as these would reduce the Cabinet to a membership of eighteen; and it would permit a far more logical redistribution of departmental functions than now characterizes our system.

Many of the advantages, in fact, which have been claimed for the smaller Cabinet are in reality achieved by the present system, through the way in which it is organized for its functions. The modern Cabinet, especially in the post-war years, works largely through committees; and it is rare for there to be a Cabinet in which there is not grouped about the Prime Minister a little knot of colleagues who exercise a special influence on its proceedings. The committee-system has very great value. It permits the reference of any special problem to a small number of ministers for special and exhaustive examination. They can go into the problem in detail, examine witnesses, and associate with their deliberations such other persons, including experts, as they may think fit. The result is usually a report which the full Cabinet will find little difficulty in accepting. The committees will usually consist of the Ministers whose problems are directly relevant to the issue involved, with one or two others; and their ability to reach agreement is itself an index to their colleagues that a reasonable compromise has been effected.

The working of the "Inner Cabinet," as it is sometimes called, is less well known to us from the documents; and, in any formal way, it does not exist. But it is broadly true that in any Cabinet there will be five or six ministers upon whom the Prime Minister will place special reliance. They will discuss policy, not officially, but as the Prime Minister's intimates, and in an informal way. They are really preparing the background of debate for the larger body. They assure it a unity and a coherence of outlook which, apart from their relationship, it would prove much more difficult to attain. It is not improbable that the existence of such a group is, indeed, imperative if a Cabinet is to work smoothly. "In most governments," Mr. Lloyd George has written, "there are four or five outstanding figures who, by exceptional talent, experience, and personality, constitute the inner council which gives direction to the policy of a ministry. An administration that is not fortunate enough to possess such a group may pull through without mishap in tranquil season, but in an emergency it is hopelessly lost." It is, in fact, a group such as this which, in most cases, enables opinions to be weighted rather than counted; and it permits the taking of vital decisions suddenly with the reasonable assurance that full Cabinet approval can be obtained later. It is not improbable, for instance, that the Labour government of 1929 was largely held together by the fact that the Prime Minister met his chief colleagues weekly to talk over, apart from the Cabinet, the general direction of affairs.

The working of the Cabinet has been greatly facilitated since 1917 by the institution of the Cabinet Secretariat—an innovation for which the credit belongs to Mr. Lloyd George. Prior to its creation, there were no Cabinet minutes, and no organized method either of being certain of what decisions had been taken or that they would be carried out if resolved upon. The Cabinet Secretariat has ended the tradition of secrecy and informality. It receives all documents which a minister may wish to circulate and sees to it that, subject to the approval of the Prime Minister and notice to the Chancellor of the Exchequer, the appropriate agenda is constructed for each meeting. Its official head is present at all Cabinet meetings to take a note of the decisions reached; these he communicates to the departments affected by them. The advantages of this system are too obvious to need discussion. Broadly, it means that in all normal circumstances Cabinet ministers are fully seised beforehand of the questions they will be asked to decide; in particular, they will know from the Chancellor of the Exchequer any financial aspects these may involve. More, the fact that five days must usually elapse between the circulation of memoranda and the appearance of an item on the agenda gives an opportunity for those informal consultations which usually mitigate the dangers of disagreement. The fact, moreover, that the agenda remains under the control of the Prime Minister means that he will always be able thoroughly to discuss beforehand with any minister a proposal about which he may have doubts, and, if he desires, to associate other colleagues with him in the process of consultation.

Of the enormous value of the Cabinet Secretariat there can be no doubt. It has produced order where, formerly, it did not exist in anything like the degree of today; and the necessity of that order is apparent when it is remembered that Cabinet business is three or four times as heavy as it was fifty years ago. It must, indeed, be emphasized that the value of the secretariat depends very largely upon its being an agent of business and not an instrument of advice. Were it the latter, it would undoubtedly be a danger to the smooth operation of affairs, since it would tend to multiply conflict between departments by becoming an independent source of policy.

Two other reasons reduce in a considerable degree the work the Cabinet has to perform. The Committee of Imperial Defence, over which the Prime Minister presides, relieves it of the necessity of considering all but the largest principles of policy; through the Committee the problems of detail can almost wholly be handled by the relevant ministers and their experts. The Home Affairs Committee of the Cabinet has, once the parliamentary work for the session has been decided upon, relieved it of most of the technical detail on bills by which former Cabinets were oppressed.

The literature of Cabinet government is full of complaint about the pressure the system exercises upon ministers and the heavy burden it involves. It is worth suggesting that the complaint fails to distinguish between burden and responsibility. A Cabinet, nowadays, meets for perhaps two hours on between fifty and sixty occasions in a year. It will have before it an agenda of perhaps fifteen items; and the memoranda connected with that agenda will run, normally, to some fifty pages of folio print, each memorandum being, as a rule, carefully summarized for the convenience of a busy politician who does not feel that he has time to do more than consider the outline of an argument. It is pretty certain either that the substance of each proposal will have been carefully explored beforehand, between the ministers most concerned, or that, if it raises radically new issues upon which there is conflict, it will be referred to a committee for report to the Cabinet. No doubt the responsibility for a decision to accept or reject the Hoare-Laval proposals, for instance, or, as in 1925, to secure the postponement of a miners' strike by granting a subsidy, is a heavy one; and in a period like that of the war the frequency with which great decisions have to be made will induce the strain involved in all great responsibility.

But the actual burden of the Cabinet work can hardly, I think, be called heavy if it is separated from the related pressures of departmental and parliamentary duties. Men of experience in political affairs are trained by the life they lead to make rapid decisions. The direction of the policy within the framework of which they have to decide is largely set by the character of the party expectations they have to satisfy. The material, as it comes to them, has been pretty thoroughly sifted and analysed by the officials in the departments. Where the strain is felt, it is the magnitude of the choice made that constitutes the burden rather than the extent of the materials upon which the choice is built. The very fact that Cabinets so rarely disagree suggests that the large contours of policy are a matter upon which unity is seldom strained to the breaking-point. What causes the pressure is less the strain of making the decisions, or their range, than the knowledge that the nature of our political system will mean that each decision is the starting-point of controversy, and that the fighting of political battles in and out of Parliament is a nerve-racking business. No one need doubt that an experience like that through which the Prime Minister passed on the eve of August 4, 1914, or during the abdication crisis of 1936, is a great drain upon his physical resources. But it is the nature of great decisions to exact their strain; there seems no inherent reason to suppose that there is anything in the Cabinet system itself which adds unduly to it. The paper-work cannot be called excessive, nor is the burden of Cabinet and Cabinet committee meetings larger than will fall upon the executive heads of any large undertaking—the London

County Council, for example. What really constitutes the pressure lies outside the Cabinet, and the strain of the Cabinet itself is psychologically involved in the importance, rather than in the extent, of the material with which it is concerned.

The Cabinet, I have said, is a secret body, collectively responsible for its decisions. The significance of the secrecy may easily be exaggerated. Theoretically, it is safeguarded in three ways: by the Privy Councillor's Oath, the Official Secrets Act, and the fact that, since a Cabinet decision is advice to the King, the monarch's sanction is necessary before publication. But none of these is so important as the fact that men who have to appear before the public as collectively responsible for their decisions could not usefully work together unless they were assured, as normally they are, that the confidences of free discussion will be respected. In fact, indeed, the rule cannot be made an absolute one. Any serious Cabinet division which results in the resignation of one or more ministers always results in a discussion in the House of Commons in which there is revelation, sometimes luxuriant, of Cabinet secrets; that was notably the case after the resignation of Mr. E. S. Montagu in 1921, and after the resignation of the Labour government in 1931, when ministers and ex-ministers vied with one another in hurling Cabinet secrets about the House. Not only is this the case. There are few Cabinet meetings in which the modern press is not a semi-participant, ministers, sometimes the Prime Minister, giving to its organs inspired communications intended to promote opinion towards the direction they desire; and there have been fewer Cabinets still in which some member has not been in fairly confidential relations with one eminent journalist or another. Cabinet ministers, moreover, increasingly publish their memoirs; and though the tradition of secrecy still holds, even for a period as recent as that of the Great War, there are few vital controversies in which we have not been made almost familiar participants.

Collective responsibility is a different matter; the rule was well laid down by Lord Salisbury in 1878. "For all that passes in Cabinet," he said, "each member of it who does not resign is absolutely and irretrievably responsible, and has no right afterwards to say that he agreed in one case to a compromise, while in another he was persuaded by his colleagues." A minister, therefore, must accept a Cabinet decision or resign, and, if he does not resign, it is no less his decision than that of his colleagues even if he protested against it in the Cabinet. He must, that is to say, vote for the decision in Parliament and, if necessary, defend it there or on the public platform. Mr. Gladstone, indeed, took the view that the absence of a minister from a division should be censured, and this appears to apply even to junior ministers not in the Cabinet. The implication goes even further. A minister must not make a speech contrary to Cabinet policy; if he seeks too large a latitude he will, like Mr. Chamberlain in 1903, find it necessary to resign. If he makes a declaration of policy in a speech upon which there is no Cabinet decision, either, like Mr. Lloyd George in the well-known Mansion House speech of 1911, he must have the agreement of vital colleagues who can assure him of Cabinet sanction afterwards, or, like Sir William Joynson-Hicks, when in 1927 he pledged the Cabinet to women's suffrage at twenty-one with no such consultation, he must take the risk that a refusal of *post hoc* consent will put him in a position where he has no alternative but to resign. The Cabinet is by nature a unity; collective responsibility is the method by which this unity is secured.

The rule is not only salutary; it is also a necessary one. There is no other condition upon which that team-work which is of the essence of the Cabinet system becomes possible. Not only this. Collective responsibility begets mutual confidence, and it makes possible that give-and-take in the shaping of policy without which any effective mutual confidence is rarely attained. It is clear that ministers could not easily live together if any Cabinet minister could at any time divest himself of responsibility for an unpopular decision or for one pivotal to the Cabinet's outlook, and it is clear, further, that no minister can speak on those topics, especially foreign affairs, on which his colleagues are acting, without seriously implicating them in his pronouncements. How inescapable the rule is was shown by the notorious "agreement to differ" of 1932. For the logic of that situation would have involved the destruction of any party basis for Cabinet government. The "exceptional circumstances" by which Lord Hailsham justified the departure from what he described as a "very sound constitutional principle" would, if they ever became regarded as a precedent, mean that no method would exist for satisfying the supporters of the government in a coherent way. That would mean either a series of short and weak governments, which would discredit parliamentary institutions, or a system of coalitions of persons devoid of any principle of unity. Along that road, as Dr. Jennings has insisted, men march to a Fascist state. It is to ask for trust in men regardless of the principles they profess. That trust is what the party system exists to deny. That is why the suppression of political parties is one of the first measures taken by a dictator who suppresses parliamentary government.

This leads us to the conclusion that the secret of collective responsibility is, in all normal circumstances, the fact that the Cabinet is rooted in the party system. It is its party complexion that gives it its unity of purpose. It is its party complexion, also, that provides the sanctions by which that unity of purpose is maintained. The party assures the presence in the Cabinet of like-minded men with similar objects who will contemplate from a similar angle the problems they will have to deal with. It is the party, also, which makes it possible for the Cabinet to follow a policy which, predetermined in its large outlines, is likely to command a continuous majority in the House of Commons. That is why Disraeli could rightly say that England does not love coalitions. For a coalition is essentially a suspension of the normal principles of our political life for objectives disturbing to the habits by which men seek to live. It involves a suspension of those habits; by its very nature, it involves a suspension of principle also. Either it breaks down rapidly, in which case the normal process of politics is resumed; or it continues. And if it continues over any considerable period, as with the National Government of 1931, it becomes quickly apparent that it must result in either a realinement of parties (in which case it ceases to be a coalition) or the destruction of parties. But to destroy parties is necessarily to destroy representative government, since they are the active principle of its life. From this angle, therefore, the collective responsibility of the Cabinet is central to the whole structure of our parliamentary system. To jeopardize it is to risk all that the system secures for effective discussion of the governmental process in this country.

4

I shall discuss in a later chapter the position of the sovereign in our system. But it will be useful here to analyse briefly the relation between the Cabinet and the Crown. Theoretically, just as the Cabinet is a unit before, and collectively responsible to, the House of Commons and the country, so also collective responsibility determines its relations with the Crown. But the working of that relation involves delicacies and complexities about which there are few established rules.

It is, of course, clear that since the King must act upon the advice of his ministers, the Cabinet can always have its way by making resignation the alternative to the acceptance of its policy. Since resignation unconnected with a defeat in the House of Commons, or some similar external crisis, would mean that the King was involved in the struggle of parties, once he has put his view and the Cabinet remains firm, the King must necessarily give way.

But there is, obviously, a wide intermediate ground. The King is in constant touch with the Prime Minister on all the vital aspects of policy; he sees other ministers with some frequency;

and he has as a matter of course the Cabinet minutes and the main official documents relevant thereto. He will be aware of all proposals before decisions are taken in the Cabinet upon them. He has the right to comment upon them and, where he so insists, to see that the Cabinet is fully informed of his opinions before it decides. It is clear, therefore, that a King who so wishes can play a considerable part in the process of government. No doubt his influence will depend to a large extent upon the quality of his mind and character. A comparatively idle king like Edward VII will have much less influence than a hard-working monarch like Queen Victoria. But it is clear from the documents that even a bad king, like George IV, or a stupid king like his successor, is far from being a negligible factor in the process of Cabinet government.

Mr. Gladstone took the view that the Prime Minister ought not to disclose to the monarch any division of opinion in the Cabinet; he is bound, he thought, "not to counterwork the Cabinet; not to divide it; not to undermine the position of his colleagues in the royal favour. If he departs in any degree from strict adherence to these rules, and uses his great opportunities to increase his own influence, or to pursue aims not shared by his colleagues, then, unless he is prepared to advise their dismissal, he not only departs from rule, but commits an act of treachery and baseness." It is difficult not to feel that Mr. Gladstone was right; but the evidence runs directly counter to his principle. Lord Melbourne, Lord Russell, Disraeli, and Salisbury all gave the Queen details of Cabinet discussions; so did Mr. Asquith on the Naval Estimates of 1909. In other ministries, particular Cabinet ministers have given the Crown information of this kind which it has not otherwise obtained; Lord Granville and Lord Rosebery both acted in this way, and, on at least one important occasion, even Lord Morley. There have been cases in which the Crown has by means of these private relations brought pressure to bear on one side of the Cabinet against another. On at least one occasion in the Labour government of 1929, George V was able to appeal

to the Foreign Secretary against a proposal the latter was about
to put to the Cabinet by urging that the Prime Minister agreed
with the royal view.

It is obvious that any departure from Mr. Gladstone's view
will tempt a monarch with strong views to intrigue within the
Cabinet, and I shall show in a later chapter that this possibility
of intrigue is deepened by the fact that every monarch has his
secret and unofficial advisers with their own political connexions.
Any such departure, moreover, leads the monarch into differentiation between ministers in terms of their accessibility to his
influence. It is certain that any knowledge that the royal views
tend in a particular direction makes it difficult for a Cabinet,
and especially a Cabinet whose unity is threatened, to maintain
its position. It is irrelevant, in this regard, that the King's view
may happen to be right. The point is that as soon as he tries to
get what is virtually a group to favour his view, he is abandoning
that neutrality in action which is of the essence of his position.
From intrigue within a Cabinet to intrigue with the Opposition
is a gravely short step. I shall show later that it was a step that
Queen Victoria, at least, did not hesitate to take.

The King has not merely the right to comment upon Cabinet
proposals; he can also raise questions for discussion before it. So,
too, he has the right to be consulted before any bill or public inquiry is announced. Queen Victoria went even further and argued
(after consultation with the leader of the Opposition, Lord Salisbury) that a Cabinet minister cannot speak upon a grave public
question not before the Cabinet without preliminary discussion
with the Palace. King Edward VII complained of Mr. Lloyd
George's attacks on the House of Lords and of his support for
women's suffrage. The Crown has also the right to see important
dispatches in all departments and to have its comments thereon
considered. "His Majesty," wrote Edward VII, "directs me to
point out that it is his constitutional right to have any dispatches
of any importance, especially those initiating or relating to a
change of policy, laid before him prior to its being finally de-

cided upon." We have a picture from Lord Morley of the efforts
required to persuade Edward VII, in 1909, to agree to the innovation of appointing Indian members of the Secretary of State
for India's Council in London.

From all this it is clear that the power of the Crown in relation to the Cabinet is a real one. Its exercise, no doubt, depends
upon the characters both of the monarch and of the Cabinet. It is
one thing with Disraeli, who was able to transform the Crown
into a kind of pocket borough for his own purposes; his correspondence with Queen Victoria, when he was out of power, shows
the kind of problem his impact upon its influence could raise for
his successor. The point is that under no circumstances can the
monarch's influence ever be negligible. It may be dangerous
with a weak Prime Minister; it may be important when the position of the Cabinet is uncertain; and it may be far-reaching when
parties are fairly evenly balanced in the House. It reaches strata
of opinion which are not always free from a dangerous bias against
the government in power, and there is no evidence that it may
not become infected with that bias. On any showing, the position
of a constitutional monarch is, *vis-à-vis* the Cabinet, an extraordinarily difficult and delicate *métier*. The evidence, as I shall
show later, tends to suggest that it is through ministers, rather
than the monarchs themselves, that he has functioned reasonably
well.

5

"The Cabinet," writes Mr. Ramsay Muir, "has arrogated to
itself, half-blindly, a series of colossal responsibilities which it
cannot meet, which it will not allow Parliament to tackle, and
which are not met at all except in so far as they are assumed by the
bureaucracy behind the cloak of Cabinet omnipotence." These
responsibilities, he suggests, are: (1) "surveying and controlling
the whole vast mechanism of administration"; (2) "co-ordinating
the work of the various departments, and overcoming the vice of

departmentalism"; the transfer of these responsibilities from Parliament to Cabinet, Mr. Muir urges, is fatal to the adequate working of the parliamentary system.

Cabinet control of the administrative process is effected through the fact that most ministers in charge of departments are members of the Cabinet and have its authority behind them in the decisions they make about departmental matters. They are always free to bring up in Cabinet any issue which, in their judgment, is large enough to require its sanction; and they are expected to bring up any matter which represents a considerable innovation in policy, the more especially if it represents a departure from some principle previously agreed upon. Where finance, moreover, is concerned, each item of activity will be discussed between the department and the Treasury, and, if unsettled by that discussion, will normally, with the Prime Minister's consent, become a matter which the Cabinet will decide. It is difficult to see what better mechanism of control could be devised; particularly, it is difficult to see how this aspect of administration could suitably be settled by the process of debate in Parliament. For the latter body is too large and miscellaneous in character to debate the infinity of detail out of which administrative decisions emerge; its business is to discuss the general principles which underlie them. In so far as it goes beyond this function, the evidence, particularly in the United States and France, suggests that the result is definitely inferior to what is achieved by the method of Cabinet control.

Mr. Muir's point, however, has a wider bearing. We live in an age of vast problems of population, of technological change, of economic relationships. Busy ministers have rarely the time, and seldom the energy, to think out the applications of new knowledge in these fields to the day-to-day issues they have to decide. The pressure of immediate issues weighs so heavily upon them that they lack the leisure as a Cabinet to tackle the issues which go to the foundations of our society. Unless a government is constantly thinking of these things, there is grave danger of an omission to apply the findings of science to our problems.

There is, no doubt, a real truth in this view; though it is diffi-cult to imagine that a revival of independent authority in the private member of the House of Commons would lead to the kind of change Mr. Muir desires. Indeed, as he frames the issue, it is misconceived as an attack upon the functioning of the Cabinet. The latter, by its nature, can deal with problems only when they have emerged at that level where they become politically signifi-cant. A body of politicians is not an organization of specialists fol-lowing the drift of research; it must use the results of research as these become apparent in the problems with which it has to deal. Its ability, moreover, to use those results is necessarily con-ditioned by the values it attaches to them. In a complex com-munity like ours, there is little universal agreement upon these values. One group in the community may feel strongly, with much medical evidence behind them, that the reform of the abor-tion laws is an urgent matter; another may insist that the aboli-tion of the Means Test for the unemployed brooks no delay; a third may insist that the problems of electric power are not soluble save as the industry is nationalized. But each of these views en-counters objections from interests which no government can neg-lect, interests, indeed, with the outlook of which it is so closely articulated as to make impossible the retention of its supporters if it accepts the insistence of the particular group concerned. From the nature of parliamentary democracy the point, normally, at which a government must deal with a problem is the point where a significant element of the electorate expects it to be dealt with. At that point only does it begin to possess political significance.

Criticisms of this kind forget that a Cabinet is not, like a com-mittee of the Royal Society, engaged in the pursuit of knowledge whatever may be the results of its discovery. It has to deal with knowledge the fruits of which are deemed to be of instant po-litical significance. It is fair, for example, to ask a Cabinet which, like that of Mr. Chamberlain in 1937, has embarked upon a great programme of rearmament to consider now what it will do with the large numbers likely to be unemployed when that programme is complete; it is not fair to ask it to consider what steps it will take to deal with the heavy metal industries if, as seems possible in the next generation, the light metals largely replace the heavy metals for industrial purposes. A Cabinet can be forehanded so long as actuality surrounds its forehandedness; it cannot be expected to be forehanded in a vacuum where most of the factors in the equations involved are either unknown or only half known.

A variant upon this theme of Mr. Muir is provided by those who are unhappy at the relation of research generally to Cabinet planning. In recent years, two methods have been tried for bringing the results of new knowledge to the attention of ministers. The first was the Committee on Civil Research instituted by Mr. Baldwin in 1925. The model of that body was the Committee of Imperial Defence. Its chairman was the Prime Minister, and its members such ministers or others as he might choose to associate with him in consultation. It was, therefore, a flexible body to which reference could be made on any subject the Prime Minister might think desirable. There were obvious advantages in the method, as there were obvious weaknesses. There was no assurance, of course, that the Prime Minister would see that the right questions were discussed or that the right persons would be asked to discuss them. The flexibility had the decisive weakness that it made both the volume and character of the research dependent upon the will and energy of the Prime Minister. Obviously, it was likely that he would refer to it questions of short-term significance rather than of long-term importance; and there was no assurance, save his personal feeling about them, that the findings of the Committee would become the basis of Cabinet action when they were made.

The Committee on Civil Research was replaced in 1929 by the Economic Advisory Committee—a device of Mr. Ramsay MacDonald. This body, of which the Prime Minister was nominally chairman, was given a definite body of members chosen by the Prime Minister and provided with a small but permanent secretariat. The members consisted of eminent business men and trade unionists, like Sir Josiah Stamp, Sir Walter Citrine, and Mr. Bevin, economists like Professor Pigou and Mr. G. D. H. Cole. It worked in two ways. Some problems were referred to it as a whole; others were referred to sub-committees which drew upon advisory panels of experts who were not necessarily members of the full Committee itself. The Committee made a number of reports; and some of the work of its sub-committees is said to have been of high value. But, after 1931, it fell into semi-obsolescence; in recent years there does not appear to have been any effective revival of its activities.

It is, I think, clear that the Economic Advisory Council was ill-conceived for the purposes Mr. MacDonald had in view. It was futile to expect a large mixed body to arrive at agreed conclusions upon large general issues about the very premisses of which they were not agreed. It was a mistake, further, to superimpose a general advisory body of this kind, charged with no administrative responsibility for its findings, upon a civil service which was, in a number of departments, already duplicating its work. No proper organic relation was ever established between the Council and its committees; and none was established, either, between the Council and the departments. It was, in fact, no more than a permanent Royal Commission, of highly miscellaneous membership, unlikely, therefore, to agree upon any fundamental matters referred to it. Moreover, when it did report, it could do no more than offer a body of advice which required to be dissected, from an administrative point of view, in the departments before it was ready for submission to the Cabinet. It was an ideal body, for example, to investigate the problem of a protective tariff which became significant in 1931. The fact that the Cabinet never referred this to the Council is evidence enough that it never acquired an effective status in our administrative system.

More recently, Sir William Beveridge has sought to meet this problem by the device, originally put forward by Mr. H. D. Henderson, of an Economic General Staff. Exactly, it is urged, as the Imperial General Staff plans in peace-time for all the problems that may arise in the emergency of war, so we need a body of economists who will work out for the government the large general problems with which neither the Cabinet nor departmental officials have time to deal. The Economic General Staff is, it appears, to be a body of permanent officials without departmental duties; it is to be free, so to speak, for long-time planning and research. It is to be an advisory body; but it is to have sufficient authority to be able to compel attention to its findings. In this way, we are to presume, the Cabinet will be made aware of those large secular changes—all the problems, for instance, raised by the fall in the birth-rate—to which, at present, neither itself nor its advisers are able to give adequate attention.

Superficially, the conception is an attractive one; but it can hardly be said that its protagonists have seriously thought out the administrative problems involved. Is the Economic General Staff to decide what questions it shall investigate? Or is it to decide the questions referred to it by the Cabinet? In either case, it is clear, the value of its findings depends upon the view taken by the Cabinet of their practicability; and this, in its turn, is partly a matter of their immediate urgency, and partly of the political complexion of the government of the day. These findings, moreover, become relevant to action as they are examined by the different departments in the light of the consequences they will have for each. A fall in the birth-rate, for instance, may mean, from one angle, fewer schools and fewer teachers; from another, it may be a maintenance of the present number of teachers with a smaller number of pupils in each class. The decision upon the findings of the Economic General Staff must be based, that is, upon financial and social considerations to which the views of the Economic General Staff are largely irrelevant. And findings of this general kind are, in fact, being made every day by economists, both within and without the civil service, without the device of a quasi-department of state for their discovery. The problem we confront is not the problem of discovering new knowledge; it is the problem of clothing that new knowledge in appropriate form for government action.

It is difficult to see that Sir William Beveridge has attempted seriously to discuss this question. Nothing in his scheme explains the relation the Economic General Staff is to bear to the appropriate government departments. Every recommendation it can make involves their views; it is hard to see why its recommendations are more suggestive, in the form in which they are bound to be made, than the recommendations of the Royal Commission. Nor can I see how the Economic General Staff is to be clothed with the authority to "compel" attention to its findings. If it is to be a normal government department, it must be advisory to the minister who is charged with its direction. It can no more "compel" him to take action upon its views than can any other body of officials compel a minister to do so; it is indeed incompatible with the idea of civil service neutrality that its members should be in a position to do so. If it is to be a body resembling the Statutory Unemployment Insurance Committee, with a quasi-independent status and the right to publicity for its findings, it is clear that its power to "compel" attention to itself will be dependent partly upon the public support it elicits for those findings, and partly upon their coincidence with the general views of the party in power. An Economic General Staff, for example, might well work out proposals for the reorganization of the coal industry akin to those of the Samuel Commission of 1925–26. But, however able the report it makes, that is no guarantee, and should be no guarantee, that its findings will be accepted by the government of the day. Not even an oligarchy of economic experts, supposing them to be agreed, is entitled in effect to have the sovereignty of the state transferred to its hands.

The truth is that the conception of an Economic General Staff is false in its analogy with the Imperial General Staff, on the one hand, and based upon a complete misconception of the relation of thought to administration on the other. The Imperial

General Staff, or, for that matter, the Committee of Imperial Defence, is set a series of definite and concrete problems. Granted, they are told in effect that such and such are the objectives of our foreign policy, and are asked what defence forces we require for their maintenance in the light of any possible combination of powers against their attainment, and how the proportions of those defence forces can best be distributed among the different branches of the services and organized both within themselves and in their interrelationships. The vital fact about the problem of war is that the objectives of foreign policy set the boundaries, at any given time, of the equations to be solved. The naval experts reach their conclusions on the size of the navy needed to maintain imperial communications, and the volume of armament that navy requires. Within the postulated size, they make their recommendations upon the number of ships of each type which, in their judgment, will produce the required result. So, similarly, with the army and the air force. It is, indeed, not impossible that the experts of the General Staff are inexpert in their measurement of the economic repercussions of their recommendations; that is an issue which raises interesting questions about the type of training they receive. What is important in this context is that, granted their recommendations are unanimous—and this is rare—the civilian Cabinet has still the problem of evaluating their cost, on the one hand, and their social and economic consequences upon the other. The vital fact is that they remain recommendations until the Cabinet has made up its mind about them. If they did not, the defence forces would be masters of the state in the sense in which they are its masters in Japan and Germany.

Obviously, there is little analogy between work of this kind and that which Sir William Beveridge proposes should be undertaken by the Economic General Staff. The work it would undertake would be no more than very generalized preliminaries to the more detailed examination of principles which, as they claimed application, would have to be undertaken by the departments themselves. In so far as the proposed General Staff attempted that detailed application it would either require a large investigating personnel of its own, or would have to depend on the intelligence sections of the different departments; and either of these would result both in friction and in unnecessary duplication of work. The kind of research Sir William Beveridge has in mind is, no doubt, of high importance. But it is certainly not the type which is now undertaken by the Imperial General Staff or by the Committee of Imperial Defence. It is not concrete; it is not definite; it is introductory to the making of policy. It assumes that thought in a vacuum divorced from responsibility for action directly clarifies the work of men who have to take decisions. It mistakes, in short, academic arguing for government investigation. The importance of the former needs no emphasis; the work done, for example, by the University of Liverpool in its report on Merseyside, by the London School of Economics and Political Science in its survey of London life and labour, or by the University of Manchester in its inquiry into juvenile labour, is all of it of the highest importance; and the more of it that can be undertaken, the wider will be the basis of knowledge upon which policy is built. But the whole point of such inquiries is that they form the groundwork for policy; they are not policy itself. A government which receives such reports has material upon which to build action; it has still to relate that material to a hundred different considerations which academic investigators do not, because they need not, take into account. But it is exactly those considerations which are vital to the formulation of a government decision.

A simple illustration will clarify this point. The Imperial General Staff may be alarmed at the decline in recruiting for the army. It expresses its alarm, through the appropriate channels, to the Cabinet, and indicates possible ways of enlarging the supply of men. It may urge the desirability of conscription; it may suggest improved conditions of service for recruits; it may suggest compulsory enrolment in the territorial forces; and so on. The point of importance is that, when all the possibilities have been put forward, there still remains for the Cabinet the vital task of considering their implications, social, economic, political, psychological, and evaluating them. The Cabinet does not simply have to take an expert report and say yes or no to its conclusions. It has first to make up its mind about the premisses upon which the conclusions are based; they have to set the result in the proper relation to their political policy; and they have to judge, as best they can, the probable impact of that policy, as so shaped by the conclusions put forward, upon public opinion. Moreover, they may not be dealing with experts who favour one point of view and one only. During the war, says Mr. J. A. Spender, "from beginning to end civilian ministers found themselves compelled to choose between rival and competing military plans, each of which had highly expert authority behind it, and to adjust whatever plan was chosen to the policy and strategy of the Allies. . . . In whatever way the ministerial pack was shuffled, it was not to be supposed that active and conscientious men who accepted responsibility for the results would remain mere spectators of the conflict, or refrain from expressing opinions which they held with conviction."

Sir William Beveridge, in short, has forgotten the significance of Burke's famous remark that "the ideal lines of politics are not like the ideal lines of mathematics: they are broad and deep, as well as long." This has led him wholly to mistake the relation of thought to administration. In the world of politics there does not exist a body of facts which point irresistibly to inescapable conclusions; about them, always, are "ifs" and "buts" which have to be supplied from without in order that they may be properly evaluated. An Economic General Staff would, therefore, be valuable precisely in so far as it discussed and evaluated those "ifs" and "buts." But to do so usefully, it would have to be composed of the men responsible for that discussion and evaluation. It would have, that is to say, to be composed of the ministers and their departmental chiefs who have to take the decisions upon the facts they receive; for, in the process of government, it is no more possible to divorce thought from responsibility for action than it is, in the realm of war, to divorce the principles of strategy from the tactics by which they are given effectiveness.

At the back, indeed, of the idea of an Economic General Staff there are, I believe, two "inarticulate major premisses," to use Mr. Justice Holmes's term, neither of which Sir William Beveridge has ever consciously examined. The first is the assumption that there exists a body of expert knowledge which ought to be made available for political use; the second assumption is that the politician cannot see the significance of this expert knowledge unless its meaning is assessed for him by a special type of investigator able to prevent the politician from evading its conclusions. For Sir William Beveridge that investigator attains objective truths the validity of which compels to action in the Platonic sense of the compulsion of knowledge. None of these assumptions is more than a dubious half-truth. Knowledge in the realm of social affairs is in a wholly different category from knowledge in the realm of nature; the considerations which apply, for example, to the determination of a population policy are not *in pari materia* with those which apply to the strains and stresses of a steel girder in a bridge. And the expert formulation of social knowledge never takes us very far; its meaning is learned far more from a quality of mind and heart that I can only call wisdom than from the possession of *expertise*. That is why Lord Haldane was a great Secretary of War, and Lord Kitchener was not; the first had the indefinable quality I have called wisdom, and the second lacked it. Nor do the "objective truths" of social science take us any distance in the formulation of policy. All of them depend upon postulates within the framework of which they are developed, and their validity is as great, but no greater, than that of the postulates upon which they depend. The student of population problems, to take my former example, is able to show that, given the continuance of present conditions in Great Britain, ours will be a half-empty island a century from now. But the calculation is dependent upon the postulate that present conditions will continue, and it is obvious that there is no reason to suppose that this will be the case.

I do not mean here to suggest that it is unimportant for the results of social investigation to be brought home to a Cabinet; quite obviously it is. The more a Chancellor of the Exchequer is made aware of the unorthodoxies of Mr. Keynes, or a Minister of Health of the discoveries of Dr. Kuczynski, the more he will be able to see that policy is shaped only after their implications are taken into account. But it is one thing to argue this position; it is a quite different position to argue that this end is best achieved by the kind of institution Sir William Beveridge has in mind. It will be inadequate because its deliberations are not directly related to responsibility. If it independently decides the problems with which it proposes to deal, it will of necessity tend to side-track itself unless they are urgent, or, where they are so, to be no more than a supplementary arm of research to already existing bodies, to which it will have secondary importance just because it is not responsible. If, on the other hand, it investigates problems assigned to it by the Cabinet for study, it will have to work through and with the departments to be effective; and it will then be found that, in order to carry its proper weight, it will require to embody the personnel of the departments. And it is worth while noting that such a body offers no guarantee, once it is a staff of officials, that it will not develop a line of its own unreceptive to what it may well consider heterodoxies from outside. Just as, in the post-war years, the British Treasury has been hostile to great schemes of public works, such as those advocated by Mr. Lloyd George, so an Economic General Staff would, if it were organized like a government department, tend to develop "isms" of its own, and to be hostile to other "isms" which contradicted its own outlook. From this angle, the more distinguished its personnel, the greater the difficulty it might well create for new ideas of which the Cabinet ought to be seised; for its temptation would be great to use its authority to stifle innovating doctrine. If, on the other hand, its members did not constitute a hierarchy, and were independently free to put their ideas before the Cabinet, the position would be simply that which now exists in the Defence Ministries, where the Cabinet has to choose between the rival views of experts. That would not, of course, be a novelty; but it is difficult to see that the result it proposes is precisely that which the advocates of an Economic General Staff have in mind.

The real truth surely is that the relation of ideas to policy is both different from and more complicated than anything Sir William Beveridge appears to have realized. New theories in the field of social politics do not make their way as they do in the natural sciences. A discovery like Einstein's has the kind of immediate relevance in its own nature which assures it of consideration from his fellow-physicists. A book like that of Adam Smith, or a theory of banking like that of Mr. Keynes, has to meet a wholly different universe of discourse before it emerges at the level where it acquires political significance. Like the theory of Einstein, it is an endeavour to predict the behaviour of phenomena; but unlike Einstein's theory, its adoption demands an alteration in the way in which governments will respond to the interests they encounter. The considerations involved in the acceptance of such ideas are obviously different from those which apply in the world of natural science. A government is not, in the parliamentary system, a dictator that can announce truths to be applied independently of the public opinion which receives them. It has to make sure of the support it requires to carry its proposals. It has to recognize that, if it is to receive this support, it must work within the framework of the expectations its party will look to it to satisfy. For it to announce, especially in a matter of first-class importance, that, whatever those expectations, they must be completely disappointed, is always a difficult adventure. They must, normally, either wait for a sufficient conversion among those upon whom they depend, or, alternatively, leave the problem involved as one which the nature of their support does not enable them to tackle. If it is urgent enough, its discussion will produce among their opponents the claim that the failure to deal with it is a proof that the government is unfit for its task. Out of that claim will emerge public discussion of the kind that makes the issue of that level of importance where the idea becomes a policy. So it has been, at least, with all considerable changes in social constitution, whether in the tariff, or currency, in the problems of industrial regulation, or those connected with an issue like birth-control. The climate of opinion their appearance produces must be such as to impose upon a government the need for decision before they have the "pungent sense," as William James termed it, of effective reality about them.

Above all, it is important to remember that there is no field of social policy in which, as I believe Sir William Beveridge unconsciously assumes, the specialists have an esoteric body of truth in their possession the importance of which politicians fail to recognize or which, from the exigencies of party conflict, they suppress even when they recognize their importance. Most specialists feel that they have remedies for our social ills which are insufficiently recognized by the government of the day. Most of them are tempted to feel that if only they could bring them to the attention of the Cabinet—even better, if they could, as Cabinet ministers, apply the remedies themselves—the world would be a better place. In fact, there is no such body of esoteric truth; and the specialist who is insistent that government needs the aid of "thought" usually means that the politicians do not place upon the remedies the same importance as he attaches to them. But at the point where he makes his judgment, he in fact ceases to be a specialist; for he is then establishing a scheme of priority in value for ideas—a matter in which wisdom, and not specialism, is the test of validity. It is the essence of our parliamentary system to make the responsibility for such priority in value one that the Cabinet must take. Any alternative would destroy that system because it would ultimately place the responsibility for action outside the area where it can be controlled by Parliament and the electorate. That road, ultimately, leads to dictatorship, however benevolent in purpose. For it rests upon the assumption that, whatever the popular will, it must accept the specialist's conclusion of what is good for it. It is a view, no doubt, capable of powerful defence; but, so far, it is contrary to the traditions upon which the government system of this country has been built.

I believe myself that what is valid in criticisms of this kind about the operation of the Cabinet system is more likely to be corrected by a device like the Committee on Civil Research than by either of the alternatives we have explored. The value of such an experiment, no doubt, depends upon the will and energy of the Prime Minister under whose auspices it operates; but so, also, will either of the others. His chairmanship of the Committee gives the one effective assurance available that, when he is impressed by its inquiries, their result will be properly considered by the Cabinet. Its composition under his presidency, moreover, is the best guarantee we can have of two important things: first, that the subjects it considers will be sufficiently actual in character as to be directly relevant to foreseeable policy; and, second, that, apart from outside experts, the men who will be called into consultation will be those who, under their respective ministers, will be responsible for applying the results of its deliberations. Lord Baldwin's proposal of 1929, in fact, was administratively better conceived than any other that has been so far suggested. It would prevent the danger, inherent in and fatal to Mr. MacDonald's Economic Advisory Council, of a large and fixed body of miscellaneous composition, incapable directly of research, and so composed as to be unlikely to reach agreement about its evaluation. It would avoid further the weakness of the proposal for an Economic General Staff by refusing to separate research and administration. The channels through which its results would reach the Cabinet are those which can alone attach proper weight to their substance.

One further remark it is perhaps worth while to make. It is at least unlikely that such an institution will be able to do its work adequately until the government is, both within and without the departments, far less niggardly in its attitude to research than it has been in modern history. It is clear that much important work, especially of a statistical character, remains to be done which cannot be even attempted with the funds at present available for social inquiry. It has been known, for instance, for years that the government cost-of-living index was hopelessly out of date; yet it took a generation before its reconstruction was determined upon. We probably need a body in this field like the Council of Medical Research which can allot in detail an annual grant to research bodies that are now inhibited by lack of funds from embarking upon large schemes of inquiry, especially those which, like the *London Survey*, transcend the possibilities of individual investigation. If such a Committee were given a grant of, say, half a million pounds a year, and planned investigations, in conjunction with the Committee on Civil Research, on the basis of a five- or even ten-year programme, there is little doubt that it could achieve results of extraordinary importance which would rapidly require legislative attention. The economics of housing, the implications of the population problems, the measurement, along the lines so notably begun by Gray and Moshinsky, of educational opportunity, the results of our system of workmen's compensation, the economics of agricultural resettlement, these are merely illustrations of the kind of problem about which we know little, and about which, also, we need to know a great deal. Our inattention to them is largely the outcome of the fact that while, over an increasing area, state-intervention is forced upon us, we still largely have to research the attitude of mind characteristic of the *laissez-faire* period. We think of it, that is, as a gentlemanly pursuit, undertaken by amateurs in quest of knowledge out of a spirit of detached and disinterested curiosity, instead of conceiving it as an integral part of the function which the state must make it possible to perform if its intervention is to be wise. Partly, also, no doubt, our investigators are anarchic and haphazard because we have not seen, in a civilization of which the predominant spirit of those who govern is still individualist, that knowledge, to be effective, must be harnessed to social purposes. The best example of this attitude is the fact that nowhere within the framework of our legal institutions is there any body whose business it is seriously to concern itself with the results of the operation of the law, and of its reform in terms of those results. That a country like Great Britain should lack both a serious criminology and a serious penology is a sufficient index to the cultural lag between the needs we face and the provision we make. Not until we bring ourselves adequately to confront the costs implied in the positive state will the Cabinet be in a position effectively to deal with the problems it has to decide.

6

The second part of Mr. Muir's indictment of the Cabinet was its inadequacy for its task of departmental co-ordination and, in particular, of overcoming what he calls the "vice of departmentalism." In one way or another it is a common accusation. Cabinet ministers, we are told, come to their departments with but little knowledge of them; they are ruled by their civil servants, whose puppets they really are. Within the large outlines of party policy, what ministers really do is what the officials tell them to do. The minister, at best, is in his department for a few brief years. For most of his time there he is an amateur in the hands of professionals. Above all, he is anxious not to make mistakes; and he must largely depend upon his officials if he is to be saved from mistakes. The result is that, in most cases, the policy he will adopt is their policy. All Chancellors of the Exchequer become imbued with the Treasury outlook; all First Lords of the Admiralty get the naval point of view. "In a majority of cases," writes Mr. Muir, "he [the minister] has no special knowledge of the immense and complex work of the department over which he is to preside. . . . He has to deal with a body of officials who may be, and often are, men of far greater ability than himself, and who have been giving their whole time in quietness to the study of the problems of the office, during the years when he has been making his position in the world, or talking hot air on platforms. They bring before him hundreds of knotty problems for his decision; about most of them he knows nothing at all. They put before him their suggestions, supported by what may seem the most convincing arguments and facts. Is it not obvious that, unless he is either a self-important ass, or a man of quite exceptional grasp, power, and courage (and both of these types are uncommon among successful politicians), he will, in ninety-nine cases out of a hundred, simply accept their view, and sign his name on the dotted line? . . . On the whole, the policy of the 'Office' will nearly always prevail; its powers of quiet persistence and of quiet obstruction, and its command of all the facts, are irresistible except to a man of commanding power."

This view is superficially plausible. But, before I examine it from the angle with which this chapter is concerned, there is one preliminary observation it is worth while to make. Mr. Muir's own remedy for the danger of that bureaucratic power he here paints in such lurid colours is the restoration to Parliament of its control over the Cabinet. But it is surely obvious that if the rigorous selective process of the House of Commons does not throw up enough men with the grasp, capacity, courage and knowledge (even when they have as Cabinet ministers the formal power) to control their officials, the remainder of the House, who have not been selected for leadership because they have, *a priori*, not convinced their party that they possess those qualities in the same degree, are unlikely to display them. What Mr. Muir's case, if it were true, would really prove is that we have either passed beyond the stage where anyone can control the civil service or that, on his own showing, it is better to have it controlled by men who are unlikely to possess the qualities necessary to control, and will therefore be unlikely to control wisely, than to have no control at all.

We need not, indeed, face this dilemma at all, for the simple reason that in the form in which Mr. Muir poses it, it is quite remote from the facts. There are certain truths in his indictment. Most departments do have a policy of their own which evolves naturally out of their experience in the course of years; just as writers grow a style, actors a favourite gesture, doctors a favourite remedy, and so on. Able men—and, as Mr. Muir rightly says, most high officials are able men—cannot spend years dealing with a subject without developing views about the best method of its disposition. It is also true that every Cabinet contains ministers who are either not particularly able men or devoid of any particular direction in which they desire to move in the realm of policy. The temptation, to either class, to live by official suggestion is clearly great. Where such ministers are in charge of a department the hand that guides the helm will be only nominally theirs.

The real question involved must, clearly, be differently formed. It is, at bottom, a twofold question. Can a Cabinet which takes office with a policy which it desires to carry out, and for which it has the requisite support in the House of Commons and the country, carry that policy to the statute-book? Secondly, can a minister who goes to a department impose his personality upon his officials when he has made up his mind what he wants to do? I shall discuss the second question first because the issues it raises admit of a fairly simple and direct answer. In the history of British administration it is, I think, quite clear that any minister who has known with any precision what he wants to do has been able, if he had the will to do so, to become the master of his officials. In our own day, to take obvious examples, that has been true of Lord Haldane and Mr. Lloyd George, of Mr. Churchill and Mr. Wheatley, of Sir Kingsley Wood and Mr. Herbert Morrison. Ministers, broadly speaking, may be divided into three classes. There are those who come to office with a fairly detailed picture in their minds of the policy for which they propose to be responsible. There are those who come to it with no particular direction, but with a desire to make a name as ministers. There are those, thirdly, who may, without offence, be described as somewhat startled to find themselevs in office at all, and mainly intent on living their lives there with the minimum of adventure.

Of the first type, I have given six examples; Mr. Arthur Henderson's tenure of the Foreign Office is another notable illustration of the type. In each case, there has never been any question of the minister's power to dominate his officials. He knew what he wanted and he knew how to get what he wanted. In at least three of the cases I have named the minister concerned met all the "persistence" and "obstruction" of which Mr. Muir speaks and had no difficulty in triumphing over them. The case of Lord Haldane is especially famous. In the years in which he held the War Office (1906–11) he converted a difficult department, largely staffed by men steeped in a deep-rooted professional tradition— the type which is of all the most difficult to change—into one which it is fair to call enthusiastic for the new habits to which he reshaped it. The Foreign Office has rarely had a chief more alien to its classic traditions than Mr. Arthur Henderson; and a good deal of what he sought to achieve ran counter to the policy in which his department had confidence. Yet it is well known that Mr. Henderson emerged from his post with the reputation, among the officials, of having been the best Foreign Secretary in recent years, some would even say the best Foreign Secretary in modern history. I have heard Sir Robert Morant say that the mere presence of Mr. Churchill in a department transformed the spirit of the officials there. There was a new sense of energy, the eager feeling that comes with the recognition that something important is to be attempted. It is said of Mr. Wheatley that in his brief career at Whitehall he contributed a similar drive to the department; and anyone who compares the record of Sir Kingsley Wood at the Post Office with that of his predecessors for something like a generation will see that neither persistence nor obstruction can deter an energetic minister who has made up his mind.

It is, of course, true that this type of minister is the rarest type encountered in politics; that is surely not surprising, since really outstanding men are rare in any political system. The more usual type is the second of the three I have enumerated. He wants to do something; he is not wholly clear what precisely he wants to do. So long as he really desires achievement, and is persistent in his desire, it is not in the least surprising that the contours of his policy should be largely shaped by the departmental tradition. Any department worth its salt has measures in view which it is eager to promote. It takes the view—it rightly takes the view—that its administrative work cannot be done efficiently without those measures. It is perfectly natural for officials to urge their desirability on a new minister, and it is equally natural that a new minister in search of a reputation should accept the departmental policy as his own and seek leave from the Cabinet to push it to the statute-book. It is said, for example, that the Home Office has, in the post-war years, urged the amendment of the Factory Acts upon each successive Secretary of State. It is wholly right that it should do so; and that Secretary of State who cannot see the significance of this reform in terms of the happiness it brings to individual lives must be a poor person indeed. To elicit ministerial support for the policy of the department is an official obligation. For it is above all the business of the civil servant to draw the attention of his political chief to the absence of powers he believes to be necessary for the successful conduct of the administrative process. If this is bureaucracy, there is no state that can afford to do without it.

The type of minister who is largely or wholly in the hands of his officials exists, of course, in every Cabinet. Partly he is there because the Prime Minister has chosen him. He may be a "representative" man, as when a Labour Premier selects an ageing trade-union official who, it is felt, should receive official recognition and whose personal status makes the offer of a minor post inacceptable. Or he may be a member of some eminent family whose influence in the Conservative Party is won for the government by his elevation to Cabinet rank. Every Prime Minister, it is important to emphasize, is trying to make a team which will work as a unity. It is doubtful whether one composed wholly of "strong" personalities, in Mr. Muir's sense of the term, makes the most efficient Cabinet; a ministry of prima donnas, so to say, is usually difficult to keep together. That was the trouble with Lord Rosebery's Cabinet of 1894; once the strong hand of Mr. Gladstone was withdrawn, the Prime Minister's authority was not adequate to his task. His real problem, accordingly, is not merely to find men who are set on an ample programme in every department of state; the digestion of the public, and the time-table of the House of Commons, may easily be overtaxed by a too luxurious fare. What he requires is a number of colleagues who can think out and carry into effect big measures, sufficient to maintain his support, and others who, satisfied with a relatively secondary position, can nevertheless be expected to keep their departments going at a normal level of efficiency. Their essential contribution to the Cabinet is their common sense, their ability to put before their colleagues that judgment about decisions which public opinion, and especially party opinion, will make after they have been published. A Cabinet that does not contain half a dozen such men is likely both to lack balance and to fall rapidly out of touch with the opinion with which it needs to keep in contact. For a Cabinet of extraordinary men is always liable to the danger that just because its members are extraordinary they fail to think as the man in the street thinks. They lose, as it were, the common touch. They fail to realize what is being thought and said about them because they are too set on their own ideas. In quiet times, especially, the parliamentary system requires these "secondary" men in order that Cabinet judgment may not outrun the pace it must keep if it is to satisfy the constituency upon which it depends.

There are many instances of this type in British Cabinets. Lord Althorp, Mr. Walter Long, Lord Bridgeman were all good examples of it. None of them was a really able man. None of them had any of the dynamic qualities which we associate with

Gladstone or Disraeli, Mr. Lloyd George or Mr. Churchill. What each supremely was I can perhaps best put by saying that he was, in his generation, the average House of Commons at its best. He had common sense, a very real shrewdness, an important representative capacity. What he said and did was never distinguished in itself. But what he said and did about his more dynamic colleagues' measures was what the lobbies of the House were likely to say when public opinion began to shape itself about those measures. They were, so to speak, Voltaire's *M. Tout-le-Monde* in the Cabinets in which they sat—a type for which, in its proper proportion, no Prime Minister can be too grateful.

For it is worth noting that the most successful Cabinets in our history have always been those in which a number of dynamic personalities have been balanced by secondary men of this kind. Mr. Gladstone had Lord Hartington; Disraeli had Cross; Mr. Asquith and Mr. Lloyd George were, before the war, as useful a combination as were the latter and Mr. Bonar Law after 1917. This, it may be noted, is one of the reasons why, again, above all in normal times, the most successful Prime Minister is unlikely to be a genius but rather, as Bagehot said of Peel, and, as has been true in our own day of Lord Baldwin, an uncommon man of common opinions. The policy of a government department is not, under the parliamentary system, a thing of which the basic outlines ought to be made afresh with each new ministerial chief. Its basic assumption is continuity of general principles; and what is therefore required in any department where great innovations are not in contemplation is exactly these secondary men about whom critics like Mr. Muir are so contemptuous.

That is the inner meaning of a great remark of Sir William Harcourt to which too little attention has been paid. "Political heads of departments are necessary," he said, "to tell the civil service what the public won't stand." That, in general, is a function which men like Althorp and Long and Bridgeman perform to admiration. They are not themselves overburdened with ideas. But they have been accustomed by education, by position, and by experience both to expressing judgments on other people's ideas and to giving orders about them. The exercise of authority is not for them a luxury they enjoy for its own sake; *ne pas trop gouverner* is a central maxim of their behaviour. They have a certain large placidity, an innate shrewdness, to which it is rare for the vices of bureaucracy to be able to accommodate themselves. They have been used to dealing with men in long years of country business, affairs in the city, the instructive relations of the House of Commons. They know how men jostle one another in life; and I do not think they are easily taken in. Official "smoothness" is more likely to seem to them an absence of frankness, and official persistence the kind of obstinacy that must be "put down." I do not think anyone who ever watched Lord Bridgeman dealing with officials would have regarded him as in the mental class of the best civil servants; but I do not think, either, that anyone could have doubted that, when he had decided to have his way, he knew how to get himself obeyed.

The critics of the system make, it seems to me, certain erroneous assumptions about the whole ethos of Cabinet government and its implications which vitiate all the conclusions they form about it. They assume, first, that a Cabinet minister ought to be as expert about the material of his department, if he is to run it effectively, as the officials who have spent all their lives in it. That is not, of course, the case. The best type of Cabinet minister is a really intelligent man of the world who can think rapidly and in an orderly way upon the multifarious questions he has to decide. His first quality is common sense; his second, the art of judging men. He must know how to give orders and to see that they are obeyed. The very nature of the competition for political place assures us that most Cabinet ministers will have these qualities; and, when they do, they are rapidly able to adjust themselves to the business of running a great department. I do not mean that every Cabinet will not contain men lacking in these qualities; the system produces, by way of exception, inherently stupid men, like the late Lord Brentford, who are incapable of the qualities this kind of work requires. But, given the selective process, they tend to be the exception. Even when, as with the Labour Party, a new class comes to high political office, its members will have had a valuable training in these qualities in their trade unions, their local councils, and—in Great Britain a matter of real importance—in the government of their churches.

The second assumption made by the critics is that civil servants in this country are a race of exceptionally able men, highly expert in their special fields, and singularly lustful of power. They are dealing, we are asked to believe, with a simple race called politicians who are amateurs in those fields, driven by their ignorance to accept blindfold the proposals that the civil servants put before them. No picture could be further than this from the truth. There are, no doubt, extraordinarily ambitious civil servants with a will to power so strong that they will stop at little to get their way; just as, equally no doubt, there are both lazy and incompetent politicians who will accept whatever the officials tell them as a gospel. In fact, both types are rare. The heads of departments with whom the politicians deal are not experts in the sense that a great physicist, a great surgeon, or a great artist is an expert; they do not live in a realm into which the ordinary man cannot enter. They have spent their lives working out the ordered details of processes which, in their large outline, any politician of importance handles every day in the House of Commons; their quality is his quality applied to details with which, in so far as he needs them, he can familiarize himself rapidly as the occasion requires. The best analogy is with a first-rate barrister. Anyone who, in our generation, has seen counsel of the quality of Sir John Simon or Sir Stafford Cripps handle the complicated details, say, of a case in contract which turns on the intricate technique of modern manufacturing industry will not feel that he is likely to be at a loss when he comes to cope with the memorandum of a civil servant. Rapid judgment, the eye for the weak and the strong points, the ability to "feel" the impact the whole will make on that outside world which is his judge and jury, these are the qualities the minister requires in his relation with his department. To display them to advantage is, no doubt, a great art. But it is not a mystery into which common men cannot enter if they have had the experience which trains them for admission to it.

And the politician who becomes a Cabinet minister, let us remember, is himself unlikely to be a simple amateur. He will have spent a number of years in the House of Commons occupied with the large outlines of political problems about which, as to principle at least, he will have to make up his mind in much the same kind of way as when he becomes a minister. Not improbably, he will have been a member of the front Opposition bench; and, as such, he will have helped to work out, with his colleagues, the policy which they will set alongside the decisions of the Cabinet. He will have been in pretty constant contact with the interests outside Parliament that seek to obtain expression there for their views, especially if these are critical of the government of the day. He will have been, in fact, immersed in a stream of fact and opinion about which he has to make up his mind for public purposes in much the same kind of way as a minister has to make up his mind. My point is not, of course, that any experience compensates for the actual knowledge a man gains as head of a great political department. It is rather that the politician who becomes a minister is, as such, an experienced man of affairs; and that the affairs in which he is experienced set for him a technique of judgment comparable in character to that which he will require as a member of a Cabinet.

Upon one point here it is worth while to make a remark. The critics of the Cabinet system seem to assume that there is little relation between the qualities required to become significant in the House of Commons and those which enable a man effectively to run a department of state. "A newly appointed minister," writes Mr. Ramsay Muir, ". . . has obtained this position because of his achievements in the general field of politics—because he is a good platform performer, or a good parliamentary debater, or commands a great deal of social influence, or is a prominent trade-union organizer." We need not argue that any of these qualities is a guarantee of administrative power. But it is at least equally important to insist not merely that they are not incompatible with its possession but that they are not unlikely to offer assurance that administrative capacity might at least reasonably be expected in their possessor. A man does not become a significant debater in the House of Commons, he does not even long remain a good platform orator, unless he has something to say. Not merely this; the effective parliamentary debater is subject to a continuous test of his judgment and critical power which are a preparation of high importance for his later work as minister. The same is true of an important trade-union organizer. Most of their work before they come to political office is a training in the art of persuasion, in the ability so to say what they have to say as to make a successful impact upon public opinion. They live by their ability to achieve this success. What, I suspect, the critics forget is that this art is central to the working of a democratic system. The view that it is almost a disqualification, that we should begin by suspecting the minister's ability because he has survived the tests a politician must face, is a cynicism which ultimately leads to the rejection of democracy itself. For it implies the belief that the qualities which enable men to become political leaders are a disqualification for successful government. I know no evidence to support this thesis.

And it is worth noting that we base our confidence in the administrative class of the civil service upon qualities which are not notably dissimilar to those by which we judge politicians. We send men into the Treasury because they have good general minds, not because they are trained economists; so also in the Ministry of Agriculture or the Board of Education. They are valuable as administrators less because they have expert knowledge of a technical subject-matter but because we believe, on the evidence rightly, that their training will endow them with qualities of judgment and initiative without which no government can be successfully run. But these are exactly the qualities a politician must have if he is to be successful, normally, in the struggle for place. No doubt he has to exercise them at a different, though not necessarily a higher, level. He has to relate the recommendations of his officials to the direction in which he (and his party) think that the country ought to travel. That is the meaning in Sir William Harcourt's phrase that I quoted earlier. The judgment and initiative of the official are checked and controlled by the judgment and initiative of his political chief. The latter may succeed or fail, but the system compels him to attempt the exercise of both. It trains him for that exercise by asking him to offer proof that he possesses them as a condition of attaining office. It penalizes him for his mistakes; and a bad mistake may even cost him (like Mr. E. S. Montagu) his career. No doubt politicians are rarely great men. But the apprenticeship they serve is at least an equal assurance with that we have in the official's case that they will emerge from it competent to the task to which they are called.

I do not mean by this to deny the important influence that civil servants exercise; I am anxious only that it should be seen in its proper perspective. Where it is large, it usually is so for a number of solid reasons: (1) The policy recommended to the minister is one for which the material itself calls, or is judged by him so to call. (2) The policy recommended, whether negative or positive in character, is one about which neither the minister nor his Cabinet colleagues have any particular view. If they are satisfied with its *bona fides*, they see no reason to alter the decision that is proposed. (3) The policy recommended is accepted, not because the minister wholeheartedly approves it, but because, for one reason or another, he is not prepared for an alternative. That alternative may be too expensive; it may entail risks of opposition he is not prepared to take; it may involve a call upon the time-table of Parliament which his colleagues are unwilling to attempt. What, clearly, is involved in the whole relationship is the need for the minister to know his own mind. Once he does, he is in a position to control his officials. Once he is uncertain, he is bound either to rely upon them or so to inform himself as to enable him to discover grounds upon which a different certainty from that of his officials may be attained.

But this is to say two things. It means, in the first place, that a Cabinet must take office knowing what it wants to do and that its Prime Minister must so distribute the posts at his disposal as to constitute the team most likely to effect its purpose. The weakness of a Cabinet in this regard usually arises from the fact either that the Cabinet has not made up its mind or that what it wants to do encounters a body of criticism at the point where the decision to act is being taken which causes it, as it is faced with the responsibility of action, to change its mind. This, at bottom, goes back to the relation of the Cabinet to the party basis of parliamentary democracy. If a party has not taken office knowing both the major general tasks to which it wishes to set its hands and the methods by which it proposes to deal with them, it is, to say the least, not surprising that its ministers should tend to accept the best advice they can get from their officials. Or if, like so many ministers in the Labour Cabinet of 1929, they find, when taking office, that they shrink from the risks of implementing the policy to which they are committed, it is natural that its place should be taken by that which the officials recommend to them. If a Home Secretary, for instance, has never thought about penological methods, it is inevitable that the absence of any important public demand for their revision should lead him to assume that the old tradition of our prisons may reasonably be continued.

Effectively, this is to say, a party must know where it wants to go, if it expects the civil service to co-operate with its leaders in going there. And this gives rise to the second consideration it is necessary to bear in mind. The minister, with party decisions or some personal policy in mind, may indicate changes he desires to make. It is the business of his officials to see to it that he is aware, as he embarks upon his task, of all that is involved in the action for which he proposes to be responsible. The case for this view has been stated once for all in the Report of the Dardanelles Commission. "It is the duty of the official," it said, "not to resign, but to state fully to the head of his department, and, should any proper occasion arise, to other members of the ministry, what is the nature of his views. Then if, after due consideration, those views are overruled, he should do his best to carry out the policy of the government, even although he may not be in personal agreement with it. . . . Undue loyalty would tend to cripple independence of thought, and would leave the parliamentary heads of the various departments without that healthy assistance which they have the right to expect, and which is at times much more likely to be rendered by reasonable and deferential opposition than by mere agreement resting wholly on the ties of discipline."

If there is to be a creative intellectual co-operation between the minister and his officials, that argument is, I think, unanswerable; and the best results of our system have resulted from the fact that this has always been the relation between the able minister and the best officials. Sir Robert Morant and Sir Eyre Crowe, to name only the eminent dead, never hesitated to put their views before their political chiefs with the full vigour of which they were capable. But this leads to the second point I have to make in which, as I think, the critics of the present system have a good deal on their side. There are two situations in which a minister, when dealing with his department, is undoubtedly in a difficult situation. The first is when he wants to innovate rapidly on a big scale. The second is when he wants to pursue a policy that is contrary to the tradition of the department over which he presides. And the position may be even more complicated by the fact that the two situations may well, in a given instance, be combined into one.

Let us take them separately. It is clear that innovation on a big scale requires something more than broad heads of proposals if it is to be effective rapidly. The proposal has to be financially and administratively sound. It has to be looked at from every angle, not least the psychological. The department cannot but be aware that if there are loose ends in the policy as it emerges into a bill, it is bound to suffer a serious loss of prestige. Its temptation, therefore, is to play for delay in order that the bill that emerges may be in all respects as water-tight as possible. It wants to investigate the material; it seeks to sound the interests likely to be affected; there is the grim business of drafting; and so on. From the angle of a Cabinet, these delays may be highly dangerous. It loses the advantage of its "honeymoon" period—always a factor of importance in the life of any government, not least of a government of the Left. It gives the Opposition, and quasi-political interests hostile to the measure, time to organize attack against it while it is being prepared. The mere fact of delay, moreover, jeopardizes the place of the measure in the parliamentary programme. It is well known, for instance, that the postponement on these grounds of its Education Bill by the Labour government of 1929 was the main reason of its failure. Its agreement to postpone its introduction meant the loss of the initiative in this field; and when, in the second year of its existence, it was at length brought forward, the vultures, so to say, were already prepared for a creature known to be destined for an early demise.

There is, I think, no remedy for this situation save through the ability of the party organization to be ready, when its leaders take office, with proposals in such a form that there can be no question of delays of this character. A simple illustration will serve. A Labour government which proposed to embark upon a great housing programme which it intended rapidly to push to fruition would need to have ready when it took office not merely a body of general principles but all the details of its policy in such a shape as to be able at once to go forward to drafting. It would have had to make up its mind about the financial limits within which it was prepared to act. It would have had to determine how far, if at all, it would depend upon the co-operation of local authorities. It would have had to have settled in its own mind its methods of compulsory purchase of land, its relations with the building-trade unions, its price-policy for building materials, and so on. To come into office without concrete views on each of these matters—to take illustrations only from this particular field—is, in effect, to trust to the ingenuity of the civil service to improvise a policy after office has been taken. That position is not, perhaps, so desperate as Mr. Tom Shaw's despairing protest, in 1924, at being asked "to produce rabbits out of a hat." But it is spiritually akin to that protest. It means the replacement of policy-making by that most time-consuming of all administrative processes—departmental discussion to discover methods which will clothe ministerial policy in concrete terms.

It is here, obviously, that the mechanism of party organization is, under the conditions of the parliamentary system, vitally related to the proper direction of the departments by the Cabinet. There cannot be that direction unless, behind the King's speech, there is not merely a declaration of intentions, a pious hope of fulfilments sought for, but the solid investigation already made which has resulted in a Cabinet effectively prepared to begin its voyage. Of course, this predicates for the modern political party something like a civil service of its own. It must have at its disposal not merely men who can write well-sounding propaganda leaflets. If it wants, for instance, to reform the prisons, it must have at its disposal not merely the knowledge embodied in the famous Hobhouse-Brockway Report but also the actual proposals it desires its Home Secretary to operate. He must, this is to say, not merely have the plan in his head; he must have lived with it, argued about it, considered it, in such a way that his sense of its implications is deep-rooted enough to withstand the official scepticism he may encounter. He must be prepared, that is, for action and not for investigation. He must have a plan to be criticized, not a direction to be explored.

And this perspective of the first situation relates closely to the problems of the second. Every department worth its salt has a policy of its own; a body of able men cannot long have direction of an administrative process without seeking to define the latitude and longitude of that direction. It is perfectly proper, also, as the

Report of the Dardanelles Commission emphasizes, that they should feel entirely free to urge upon the minister the importance of their views, the dangers and difficulties attendant upon his taking any views but theirs. But it is at least as proper, and certainly as important, that he should be aware that, underlying this sense of direction, there is a body of premises, not always conscious, which, when brought to the light of day, may be incompatible with the views it is his business as minister to impose. In the British tradition, there is no doubt at all that certain departments, while fully living up to the spirit of the Dardanelles Report, have shown remarkable pertinacity in shaping ministers to suit their own conceptions of political wisdom. That has been particularly true of the Foreign Office, the Treasury, and the Defence Ministries, in part because of the special delicacy of the problems they handle, and, in part, also, by reason of the special complexity of the material with which they deal. The power, particularly, in the last hundred years of the British Treasury to impose its own orthodoxies upon successive Chancellors of the Exchequer is one of the most remarkable feats in the history of modern administration; and it has not been due to the weakness of personality in the Chancellors so much as to the energy and pertinacity of the officials with whom they have dealt.

It is easy to see how the tradition can be imposed. The new minister does not inherit a clean sheet; he has to begin making decisions upon policies already in operation from the day he takes office. Many of them relate, necessarily, to matters about which he is either not informed at all or about which he can only have very general views formed without relation to vital documents. He has to make those decisions quickly; and he has, as I have said, to make them after discussion with able men who feel pretty confident about the direction in which they want to go out of long familiarity with the problems concerned. If his mind marches along with theirs, his problem, *a priori*, is a pretty easy one; if his decision is challenged, he will be able to defend it in Parliament with all the power and ingenuity they can place at his disposal.

But his position, clearly, is far more difficult if they believe that the decisions he proposes to make are fraught with danger, even, in an extreme case, with disaster to the country. Obviously, in such a case he needs to be very certain of himself, to have at his disposal an assurance that is not merely the emotion of conviction that he is entitled to his certainties. In the field of politics the roads to disaster are manifold; and no minister is entitled to innovate upon a large scale without full certainty of his ground.

A single illustration will suffice. Let us suppose a Foreign Secretary takes office who is confronted, as Sir John Simon was confronted in 1931, with an incident like the rape of Manchuria by Japan. He has a general faith in the League of Nations Covenant, a genuine desire to implement the obligations his country has assumed under the Covenant. He has never specialized in the details of Far Eastern affairs. He is informed that, under Article XVI of the Covenant, support for China may well lead to war with Japan. The degree to which such a war may jeopardize the immense interests of Great Britain in the Far East is emphasized to him. The complexity of the naval and military problems it will raise is put with all obvious force by men able to enlarge with expert knowledge upon their implications. The war, he quickly sees, may blaze into a world war; in its aftermath may easily come revolution and all its consequences. He may, if he so please, give a full-hearted lead at Geneva. He cannot be certain that the League will stand the strain of his lead. He may incur, he is told, the ill-will of the most powerful Far Eastern state with no commensurable return to Great Britain. There is, of course, much to be said for the League view. But this is a hard and grim world, in which Foreign Secretaries have to be realists. The risks of a League policy, he is told, are incalculable. A sober realism now may not only save a possible war. It will gather goodwill from Japan in relation to British interests it is dangerous to jeopardize. It is far from certain that the British people would favour action in behalf of China that may involve the loss of British lives and British property. Much of the difficulty is less the fault of Japan than of the organized anarchy of China; it is even conceivable that a strong hand in Manchuria will be good for British trade. Some day, no doubt, the policy of sanctions must be tested. But it is not wise to select for that test such a case as will unite behind the British Cabinet the whole force of an opinion as solid as that ranged behind the Asquith government over Belgium in 1914? The Foreign Secretary will, of course, remember how the instinct for neutrality, so strong in the last days of July, shrank into nothing as the issue of Belgian neutrality came into discussion. Is not this, he is told, the true pattern he ought to see? Can a general faith in the League transcend the obligation to confront the possible outcome of these grim contingencies? In the quite special circumstances of this instance, is it not the part of wisdom to avoid the risks involved in a warm-hearted but wrong-headed League policy?

I have taken, of course, an imaginary argument. But it is, I think, easy to see how a Foreign Secretary confronted with this persuasiveness can be induced to submit his general faith to the proposition that this is not the time to bring it to the test. He may have an uneasy suspicion that he is wrong, that he is sacrificing the long view to the short view. He may, above all, feel that he would like to hear the case against the departmental recommendation put with the same cogency and persuasiveness. This is, I suggest, the case for the adaptation to British practice of the custom traditional in French politics of the minister bringing in with him, when he succeeds to office, a small and intimate group of men of his own party, or, at least, his own way of thought, in whose knowledge of his departmental problems he has confidence, and with whom he will feel able freely to discuss them in an atmosphere wholly apart from that of the official hierarchy. That relation has sometimes developed in this country between the minister and his private secretary—between Mr. Asquith and Sir Vaughan Nash, for example, or, it is said, between Viscount Grey and Lord Tyrrell. But the best example of the kind of adaptation I have in mind is provided by Mr. Arthur Henderson's tenure of the Foreign Office. He went there, in 1929, with a fairly definite body of objectives in view, and he was clear in his own mind about the way in which he proposed to attain them. He knew, further, that there was a substantial difference between his own principles and those of the department over which he was to preside. He recognized, also, that if he stood alone in the department he might not find it easy to maintain his own line. He therefore quite deliberately took with him into the department three men who had not only specialized in foreign affairs but who, as he was aware from long intimacy, shared his own views. They were invaluable to him in the fulfilment of his task. Not only did they give him a sense of assurance about his general direction. They were able to examine official memoranda with a capacity not less than that of the officials themselves. They made possible the maintenance of the general line amid the mass of detail in which a Foreign Secretary can so easily be overwhelmed. It is well known that Mr. Henderson's period at the Foreign Office was an outstanding success; and though, unquestionably, much of that success was due to his own sterling integrity and shrewd common sense, he himself did not doubt that this special secretariat was essential to his achievement.

I believe that such a technique has everything to commend it as a method of helping the minister to find his way through the labyrinth he will encounter. A rare minister, Haldane, for example, may not need such assistance; an average minister will almost always be assisted by it. Obviously, there are difficulties. It is not in the tradition; the officials will regard it with scepticism, perhaps, at first, with suspicion. The answer, of course, is that every innovation is so regarded at the outset. Old-fashioned soldiers disliked the Committee of Imperial Defence. Old-fashioned civil servants were critical of the Cabinet secretariat. The scheme implies no lack of confidence in either the capacity or the *bona fides* of the existing civil servants. It does imply the need to surround the minister with men who are able to look at official recommendations, to scrutinize official arguments, from the angle he has adopted and not from the departmental angle. The success of the system in France gives us every right to suppose that it will be successful here also. The very fact, indeed, of the ability of the departmental heads is one of the strongest arguments for its adoption. It gives the minister eyes and ears that are, as near as may be, his own. It offers him the kind of organization in supplement to the official world into which he has to plunge that the experience of men like President Roosevelt has shown to be urgent under modern conditions. It makes possible, particularly, ministerial and party interrelationships not easy to maintain through the medium of the official hierarchy. It is a safeguard that the minister's line of action will be determined with a full sense of all that it implies. If Sir John Simon, to revert to my imaginary illustration, had adopted his Japanese policy only after its basis had run the gauntlet of a full and frank examination by Lord Cecil—as it would have done under Mr. Henderson's regime—one would have had a confidence not otherwise easily available that it had been adopted only after rigorous analysis from an independent angle. To subject the departmental tradition to this kind of analysis cannot, I submit, but be both helpful to the minister and healthy for the officials. Certainly it is at present one of the outstanding defects of our system that no such technique is available.

Along lines such as these, I believe that the major criticisms of the Cabinet system can be fairly met. I do not, of course, mean that office will not continue to be, for all but the extraordinary man, an intense strain. The evidence of almost everyone who has held high place, from Peel to Lord Baldwin, is too emphatic to make any other conclusion possible. The final answer is the simple one that the governance of interests so massive as those upon which ministers have to pass cannot be otherwise. When peace and war hang upon their decisions, when a bill may make such changes in our social contours as were effected, for example, by the Unemployment Insurance Act, when a Cabinet has to find wisdom enough to grapple with an issue of the magnitude of the general strike of 1926, Oxenstierna's famous "better be a shepherd and tend one's sheep than meddle with the government of men" comes at once to the mind. There are no institutional devices which will permit a minister the leisure to think out in office in the luxury of silence the policy he ought to have determined upon out of office. There is none, either, that will make administrative co-ordination achieve more than half of what we hope for it. The range and intensity of our problems do not permit us to paint the conditions of government as less grim than the facts inevitably make them. To rule men responsibly has always been a wearing business; and the more sensitive the minister's imagination, the more intimately he will be aware of the gap that separates his hopes from his achievement.

The drawbacks to the Cabinet system upon which the critics have fastened are less, I have argued, drawbacks removable by institutional devices than difficulties inherent in the complex art of ruling men. The direction of affairs is not, under that system, divided, as so many of its critics seem to suggest it is divided, between what Graham Wallas called "an uninstructed and unstable body of politicians, and a selfish and pedantic bureaucracy." Most politicians, with all their defects, not only aim at the general good as they see it, but work hard and persistently for the achievement of that good. The official tradition is one that, in general, will be more fully admired the more fully it has been experienced. The time the Cabinet lacks for the hard business of thought is not traceable to weakness in men, any more than the "vices of departmentalism" are due to that weakness. Both are limitations set by the material with which we have to grapple. The best we can do is to make all the provision we can to assure ourselves that when a Cabinet does take office it is aware, so far as may be, of what it wants to do on the widest intellectual basis upon which its generalizations may be framed. But not less important is the courage to go on with the policy to which it has set its hand. Parliamentary democracy can outlive a good deal; it cannot survive over any long period a lack of courage in its rulers. For, thereby, the institutions through which it lives are permeated by an energy and purposiveness which elevates the moral stature of the whole people. Good government, in the long run, is always courageous government. But courage in the ruler is not merely a matter of willing what is right; it is also, as Plato said, knowing what it is right to will.

The Cabinet system, as we have inherited it, provides at least the basis upon which that knowledge may be made available. By being set in the context of party, it moves from the plane of concept to the plane of action. No other context, granted the framework of the system, could adequately take its place. Granted all the weaknesses inherent in the party structure of representative government, we have seen that it alone makes possible such an organization of the people as permits the articulation of preferences. It relates, that is, not merely concept to action; it relates those concepts to action which have behind them the driving power of number. The Cabinet is the trustee of that driving power. It is essentially on the faith of its trusteeship that it becomes a Cabinet; and its power to govern is, at bottom, determined by the continuance of that faith. Here, no doubt, as in each element of the parliamentary process, the secret of the faith depends upon the degree to which the mutual confidence of parties is maintained. They must, as I have pointed out, speak the same language. More: they must, in their form as Cabinet, speak a language also which their civil servants speak; upon this network of reciprocal understanding depends the power of the system to maintain the goodwill among its parts without which it cannot work.

So far, in large part, this goodwill has been maintained. But it is confronted by dangers today which it would be folly to deny are a grave threat to its continuance. They do not, I have argued, lie within the actual machinery itself. There is nothing to support the view either that, in a basic way, the relation of the Cabinet to the House of Commons is wrong, or that the relation of the Cabinet to the departments is wrong. Innovations are possible, even, as I have sought to show, desirable; but they are not innovations which at any point touch the spinal cord, as it were, of the system's anatomy. In particular, I have argued that there is nothing to be said for abrogation of Cabinet control of Parliament, and little to be said for the view that the minister is a helpless *fainéant* in the hands of his officials. Both arguments are based upon an unconscious desire to return to a wholly different environment from ours, governed by the ability to apply thereto rules that would rapidly wreck the system as it confronts its present necessities.

The central danger of the modern Cabinet system lies in the threat to the goodwill upon which its operation depends inherent in the present wide abyss between party purposes. That is not, I add again, an abyss that can be bridged by electoral devices like proportional representation. It is a factor of disunity produced by the disproportion between the forces of production and the relations of production in our society; it cannot be transcended, within the postulates of parliamentary democracy, save as that disproportion is transcended. It is not met, as Bagehot saw, merely by the constitution of Cabinets of "moderate" men. The danger of that conception is in its invitation to ministers to avoid the action to which their principles call them in the hope that their abandonment may, in some mystic fashion, discover a formula of social peace. Such a conception can lead to success only in periods of economic expansion when capitalist confidence permits the extension of concessions to the masses. Where it does not obtain, the result of the attempt to concede is, as is shown by the experience of England and America and France, the inevitable suspension of capitalist confidence. A socialist party, in a word, cannot operate capitalist democracy successfully except upon the postulates of its opponent; and its Cabinet is, therefore, unable to attain the conditions under which it can both know what it wants to do and do that courageously. It, therefore, either becomes a weak government, or, alternatively, by the fact of its courage to act upon its faith, it suspends the confidence of capitalists in its purposes which is necessary to the maintenance of that continuity which the functioning of the Cabinet in a parliamentary democracy requires. I see no escape from this dilemma; certainly no escape that is available in terms of institutional machinery. For at this point we are back, as the earlier chapters of this book have sought to show, at the foundations of our society. We cannot agree about its institutional superstructure until we have agreed once more about the nature of those foundations.

CHAPTER SIX

The Civil Service

1

THE influence of the civil service in Great Britain is a comparatively modern phenomenon. When Bagehot made his analysis seventy years ago, he did not think it necessary even to discuss the influence of the officials; and even the interesting treatise of Sir Sidney Low, now just over a generation old, hardly gives them more than a passing notice. Mr. Lowell's *Government of England*, which made its first appearance in 1908, is, I believe, the first considerable treatise on our political system which recognizes the immense part played by the civil service in its functioning. In the thirty years that have passed since its appearance, it is not untrue to say that no other part of the system has received or deserved so much attention from commentators.

That prominence is due to a number of reasons. The first, undoubtedly, is the fact of the greatly increased importance of the service itself. The change from the negative state to the positive state has brought with it so vast an extension of public business that the minister is compelled to leave to his officials all but the largest decisions on major policy. The days when Sir Robert Peel could, as Prime Minister, seek seriously to acquaint himself with the inner working of all departments, or when Lord Salisbury as Foreign Secretary could write all important foreign dispatches himself, have gone for ever. The second is the immense improvement in the quality of the service. After the abolition of patronage, in 1870, by Mr. Gladstone's famous Order in Council, the service was able to attract to its ranks a body of men as capable as there is to be found in any walk of life in this country. Their standards of conduct rapidly became a model for the whole world. They were incorruptible. They served the government of the day, whatever its complexion, with equal zeal. They made possible the organization of knowledge for the business of administration at a level completely different from anything that had gone before. It is not, I think, true to say that they consciously sought for power. Rather the *Zeitgeist* created the opportunities for power of which, because they were able men, they naturally took full advantage. And the fact that they demonstrated their efficiency reflected, in its turn, upon the situation they had to handle. From 1870 onwards, there are few failures in the handling of the big problems of civil administration in Great Britain; the officials proved equal to dealing with each issue as it arose. Out of the sense of that ability, there grew up, even in men who were dubious about the wisdom of attending state functions, the sense that the official knew how to perform his task. As the new electorates, in 1867, 1884, 1918, asked that the state relieve the pressure upon their lives by an extension of social amenities, it became natural to look to these men to handle the extensions so demanded. And as each extension proved itself by its results, so, quite inevitably, it created the presumption that where defect was found, state-action had the means of remedy at its disposal.

No doubt some, at least, of this change from the negative state to the positive is due to the efforts of civil servants themselves. What Veblen has called the "instinct of workmanship" is an inherent part of the equipment of any civil servant worth his salt. You cannot ask an able man to concern himself with questions like education, public health, factory legislation, safety in mines, without two consequences following. To ask him to discover facts is to ask him to indicate conclusions; and the very fact that he reports conclusions necessarily indicates a theory of action. It is significant that no small part of the socialist indictment of English industrial conditions in the nineteenth century was based upon the findings of government documents. Ministers could not escape the meaning of the knowledge for the publication of which they were themselves responsible. And as soon as they began to recognize that there was no escape from it, they were bound to listen to the advice of the men who had dug that knowledge from the raw material, framed it into generalizations, lived with their implications, developed about these that sense of compulsion which, as Plato insisted, is always inherent in knowledge that has become a living part of personality.

There is not, I think, as some of the critics of the civil service have suggested, a conscious lust for power on the part of those who direct it. If housing is bad, if standards of public health have to be set, if there are trades in which wages are unendurably low, if the public conscience demands certain minima of sanitation and safety in factories, then there must be the assembling of knowledge to permit action. There must be principles of action decided upon; and the civil servant whose life is passed in dealing with that knowledge will naturally advise upon those principles. Because, moreover, he has ability, he will also have views; he is not, and cannot be, a die to impose without discussion the imprint of ministerial direction. It is his business to tell the minister what, in his judgment, are the probable consequences of any policy for which the minister proposes to be responsible. He must warn against this line and urge the wisdom of that. The minister must make up his mind; but he cannot make up his mind, he cannot, certainly, make up his mind wisely, save as he considers the burden of the experience upon his proposed line as that experience is interpreted for him by his officials. There is nothing in this of conspiracy; it is plain common sense. A policy which was separated from official experience would almost certainly be ignorant and, not seldom, disastrous.

The civil service, in a word, has the influence it exercises because that influence corresponds to the needs implied by our political democracy. Once there is universal suffrage, political parties naturally seek to win the largest vote they can. They construct their programmes with a view to its attraction. When, after they gain power, they have to implement their programmes, successful administration means the shaping of policy in terms of a knowledge and experience for which they are largely, though by no means wholly, dependent upon the departments. For wholesale improvisation is impossible in any society rooted in traditions and accustomed to certain ways of life unless in terms of revolutionary change. A system intended, like ours, to offer uniformity of treatment and satisfaction of established expectations, can afford to innovate only within a framework the outlines of which are known and accepted; and vital alterations in the framework can be made successfully only when the public mind is habituated to the idea of their necessity. What the civil service really does is to maintain the government as a going concern. It corrects the risks of popular election by subduing its results to a medium where ascertainable knowledge is the protective envelope of action. It oils the machinery of politics by relating the popular will, as the party in power reflects the impact of the popular will, to what a detached and disinterested experience believes to be practicable. Its authority is that of influence, not of power. It indicates consequences; it does not impose commands. The decision which results is the minister's decision; its business is the provision of the material within which, in its judgment, the best decision can be made.

This, at least, is, I am confident, the spirit in which all the really eminent civil servants of the last seventy years have approached their task. The change in the perspective of their function is, in part, the outcome of changed electoral expectations, and, in part also, of the important fact that the civil service has become, especially since the war, not an inchoate series of departments, but a unified administrative mechanism. The first is the direct consequence of the enlarged electorate. Those who have to be satisfied have different wants today from those to whom Russell and Peel, or even Gladstone and Disraeli, sought to respond. The second is due to the fact the necessities of efficient administration have compelled the departments to think of themselves, in Sir Warren Fisher's phrase, as "units of a complete and correlated whole." We have witnessed, above all in the last generation, what he has well termed "the evolution of a service conception in contrast to a departmental one." It is, indeed, far from complete; the struggles between the three Defence Departments is evidence of that. But the stage is beginning to be reached where the lines of general administrative policy are the outcome of a continuous co-operation, conscious, if informal, between the heads of departments. The machinery of administration moves much more deliberately on a single plane of purpose than at any previous time.

2

The civil service, in its modern form, is now some seventy years old; for the essential character that it now possesses was determined when, in 1870, Mr. Gladstone gave effect to the recommendations of the Trevelyan-Northcote Report by establishing open competitive examination as the central highway of entrance to its ranks. Since then, naturally enough, there have been greater or lesser reorganizations of its structure. But every investigation since 1870 has merely confirmed the wisdom of Mr. Gladstone's decision. To it we owe not merely the abolition of the major evils of patronage. With that abolition has come what is virtually an incorruptible service, and one which has been able, for relatively small reward, to attract some of the ablest men in the country to its membership.

I cannot attempt here even to describe the organization and functioning of so complicated a mechanism. It must be sufficient to draw attention to the chief characteristics only of the service. Of these, two are, I think, outstanding in their significance. The first is the fact that the different classes in the service are roughly co-ordinated with the different stages of the educational system of the country. The second is the fact that the method of examination for entry is a test not of special qualifications for a particular

department, but of a general intelligence which, after appointment, is trained and disciplined by practical acquaintance with the
problems it is called upon to handle.

It is easy to see how natural was the impulse to that first principle. But its results were far more profound than its makers could
have conceived. What, in effect, it did was to divide the service
into four great classes which reproduced, in their relations, the
social structure of the general population. There was a large class
at the base whose life would be spent in routine work which,
while demanding both application and accuracy, would at no
point really call either initiative or responsibility into play. There
was the great army of clerical officials, for the most part doing
routine work, but from whom, save at the apex of the pyramid,
little was expected save the application of well-worn precedent
to new material. Above them, again, was the executive class, responsible, indeed, but, for the most part, rather preparing the
materials for policy than initiating policy itself. Above them,
finally, was the administrative class, almost exclusively university-
trained, who were the advisers of ministers and the makers of
policy. Of some half-million persons who are in one way or another civil servants, 330,000 are absorbed by industrial establishments, such as the Arsenal and the Dockyards, and the Post Office.
Of the remainder there are some 70,000 clerical, some 16,000
executive, officials; and the administrative class comprises some
1300 members. To these must be added, of significant officials,
some 2500 inspectors in different departments, and nearly 7000
professional, technical, and scientific workers, who range from
architects, barristers, physicists, and doctors to experts in old
furniture at the Office of Works.

From this pattern, especially in the post-war period, certain
things immediately emerge. The effective power in the civil service is in the administrative class. That is the brain of the whole; it
is there that the decisions which count are made. Effectively, also,
that class is composed of men with a university training; most of
its members come from Oxford and Cambridge. An analysis of

the social composition of the administrative class will show, further, that its members come mostly from parents whose range of income permits them to send their sons to the great public schools. This is especially true of the Foreign Office. While, moreover, there is some degree of movement between the clerical class and the executive, there is very little between the executive class and the administrative; perhaps an average of fifty cases in a year. There are, this is to say, gaps between the different grades of the hierarchy which are rarely bridged. For all but an infinitesimal minority of the service, the grade of entrance determines a man's official career. But since his entrance grade is, in its turn, almost wholly determined by his educational opportunities, which are, in their turn, largely determined by his parental circumstances, the official career is mainly settled by the class into which a man is born.

All this, it may be urged, very largely explains the character of the British civil service. Those who govern it belong, effectively, to the same class that rules the House of Commons. Largely, they go to the same schools and universities; after admission to the service, they belong to the same clubs. Their ideas, that is, or, rather, the assumptions upon which their ideas rest, are the same as those of the men who own the instruments of production in our society. Their success, as a civil service, has been mainly built upon that fact. Their ideas of the margins of possible action are much the same as those of the ministers who have been responsible for their decisions. The kind of society they have naturally envisaged to themselves as attainable is the kind of society similarly envisaged, in more or less degree, by the ministers with whom they have collaborated. There is little or nothing in the experience they bring to the interpretation of their environment which would lead them to question the assumptions upon which our system rests.

This explains, I think, both why the civil service has been able, in these sixty-odd years, to maintain its neutrality and why the measures they have recommended have proved equally accept-

able to Cabinets of either party. They have been neutral because
their ultimate principles of action have been those upon which
the policy of both political parties in this country were based before the war; and since, after 1918, neither of the Labour governments has sought to depart from those principles in action, their
neutrality has not been questioned. So, similarly, in relation to
policy. No government, in the period of the modern civil service,
has embarked upon measures which have called into question the
foundations of the state. Succeeding governments have differed
in degree; they have not yet differed in kind. The neutrality of
the civil service has not yet been tested by the need to support a
policy which, like that of a socialist party, might well challenge
the traditional ideas for which it has stood.

I do not for a moment suggest that the civil service would not
meet such a test with adequacy; I note only that, so far, the need
to meet it has not arisen. But I do suggest that no small part of
its remarkable success as a service has been the outcome of the
virtual agreement between parties upon the foundations of policy.
That has made possible a rapid and harmonious co-operation between ministers and officials which has been built upon the fact
that they were united to apply broad principles of policy held in
common by them. The real problems will only begin to emerge
when this is not the case. Would Sir Maurice Hankey, for example, who has testified before a Royal Commission that he believes the nationalization of the armaments industry would be a
"disaster," be able easily to collaborate with a Labour government determined upon that policy? Would a Treasury which has
been so continuously hostile to a big policy of public works be
able easily to collaborate with a Cabinet which had no sympathy
with its hostility? Would a Foreign Office so largely responsible
for the Hoare-Laval proposals be able to put all its mind and
heart behind a minister who built his whole policy upon the
socialist interpretation of the principles of collective security?

It would be excessively naïve to return a simple affirmative
to these questions. That the *esprit de corps* of the service has built

a strong tradition favourable to collaboration in the letter and in the spirit is undeniable. But there is an important difference to be noted. It is one thing to put through a policy the assumptions of which you accept. It is a very different thing to put through efficiently a policy the very foundations of which you believe to be disastrous. The subconscious tendency, then, is to maximize all the difficulties it will encounter. That attitude acts as a paralysis of the will in a degree it is very important not to underestimate. And that paralysis inevitably communicates itself to the minister concerned. He begins to see the doubts and dangers which attend his policy in quite special proportions. He has to be a very exceptional man not to play for time, to consider the wisdom of possible concessions which go to the root of his schemes. His officials, in all this, are perfectly sincere; constitutionally, also, they are playing a perfectly proper part. They are simply assuring themselves that the minister does not act until he has looked all round his proposed innovation. Quite rightly, they do not want him to make a mistake; it is their business to secure for him the easiest possible path. What it is vital here to realize is that the problem involved is not the kind of quantitative adjustment that the normal working of our system requires. The difference is a qualitative one due to a conflict of major premises; and we cannot judge just what the neutrality of the civil service really means until it has been tested on the plane of qualitative difference.

So far as we have knowledge, it does not exist in Whitehall properly so called. Our evidence relates to the army in the Ulster crisis; and, no doubt, both the traditions and the psychology of the army are very different from those of civilian officials. But it is certainly of major importance in this context that Sir Henry Wilson, then the Director of Military Operations at the War Office, did not think it incompatible with his official position to intrigue against the government he served both with officers to whom that government was issuing orders and with the leaders of the Opposition who were seeking, by similar intrigues, to wreck the government's plans. Nor is it less important that Sir John

French, while Commander-in-Chief in France, intrigued with the press in order to force his views upon the government which had appointed him to the post. I have taken two instances only; the reader of Sir Henry Wilson's *Diaries* and of Mr. Lloyd George's *War Memoirs* will know that they are not unique. The problem they raise is the grave problem of an army whose officers —so to say, its administrative class—have strong convictions directly opposed to those of the government they serve. Assuming —as parliamentary government assumes—the necessary supremacy of the civil power, can a government in critical circumstances rely upon the undivided loyalty of its officers? Can it do so, remembering the relatively narrow class-horizon they represent, the habits that class-horizon has meant in Russia, in Germany, in Italy, and in Spain? These are delicate, even dangerous, questions. They lie, no doubt, at margins which no one will desire to reach in political controversies. But because, in a crisis, they are reached, no one who speculates upon the issues of political power can fail to keep them in his mind.

It is, of course, true that the civilian official is schooled both to a detachment of view and an interest in ideas which are far more rare in the soldier. That is because predominantly our army is still, as it was in Wellington's time, a class-army in which, as Mr. Lloyd George has said, "the ablest brains did not climb to the top of the stairs . . . seniority and society were the dominant factors in army promotion. Deportment counted for a good deal. Brains came a bad fourth. Men of great intellectual powers are not tempted to join a profession which offers so little scope for the exercise of their powers, and where the awards have no particular reference to special capacity." That is not merely the judgment of a radical Prime Minister; it was put, also, if with more urbanity, yet with equal emphasis, by so experienced an observer as Lord Esher, who made, in this regard, a significant comparison between the qualities brought out by service in the army and navy respectively. In the latter case, as he noted, the material which was the medium of the profession brought out the highest qualities of character and intelligence; in the former this was not the case. It is at least possible that these criticisms apply, if in a less degree, to the diplomatic service. It is, of course, no longer true to say, as Bright could fairly say, that the Foreign Office is "the outdoor relief department of the British aristocracy"; change in the method of recruitment has, since 1919, brought a slow change in the sources from which its personnel is drawn. But it may still be legitimately doubted whether the implications of the divorce between aristocracy and government which is today characteristic of most states is reflected in the habits of either the Foreign Office or the diplomatic service. It is certainly rare for a British embassy abroad to have any wide or continuous contact with sources of opinion outside what Bagehot called the "highest social circles"; and any survey of the Foreign Office personnel will show that its selection is still largely based upon the assumption that about sixty-five per cent of the natural diplomatic talent in Great Britain is to be found in one or another of eleven leading public schools. "Despite the reforms," writes Mr. Nightingale, "environmental advantages still weight the balance heavily in favour of the propertied and the professional classes."

The point of this is the simple one that all the leading figures in the public services, whether the civil service or the defence forces, come, in fact, from an extraordinarily narrow class within the community. With individual exceptions, they bring to their work an attitude which accepts the fundamental assumptions of the present social order as outside the realm of controversy. Their range of thought, the limits of the decisions they think wise are therefore largely set by the fact that they arise within the framework given to them by those assumptions. Within them, I do not doubt that they are capable of great imaginative insight. Granted the assumptions, the men who have built the Health Insurance system, the Unemployment Insurance service, and the Factory Inspection system, have little need to apologize for themselves. But the real test comes not when work has to be done within the assumptions but at the margin where those assumptions are changed. Here we dwell in a twilight world of guesswork simply because the strain involved in the acceptance of new assumptions is one to which no branch of the service has been subjected. They may survive it brilliantly. But it is vital to realize that, so far, the success of our system is mainly due to the fact that it has not yet been necessary to meet it.

I shall deal in a later part of this chapter with some of the criticisms that may, as I think, be legitimately passed upon the habits of the official world. Here it is worth while emphasizing one other point to which I referred earlier. One of the great qualities of the civil service is its flexibility; and this, I have suggested, is due to the method by which the members of the administrative class are chosen. No greater contribution has been made to administrative technique during the nineteenth century than that insight of Macaulay's which insisted that general intelligence, rather than special training, should be the basis of choice. It may well be that the present weighting of examination subjects is, at least in part, educationally obsolete; it may well be, also, as Dr. Finer has incisively shown, that too much importance is attached to the interview in the selection of successful candidates; and I think that a strong case could be made for recruiting a number of candidates at the post-graduate stage upon the basis of an original contribution to the social sciences such as a really able doctoral dissertation; granted all the possible improvements of the present system, its main principle is right beyond question. What is needed in the control of the administrative process is the general mind, and not the specialized mind. So large a part of the civil servant's work depends upon judgment, common sense, wisdom—qualities which have little connexion with *expertise*—that the confinement of the highest posts in the departments to men whose training is, in the best sense, humanistic has, I think, been the salvation of the service. I do not mean, of course, that the specialist is incapable of these qualities. I do mean that specialism is open to the danger that its possessor loses in width of horizon what he gains in intensity of gaze. It is not accident that soldiers and sailors have rarely made good ministers; it is not accident, either, that engineers, doctors, teachers have rarely made successful statesmen. And, at the top of the departments, the great official is nothing so much as a statesman if he is to be successful. He has to judge not merely where the material leads, but also how it is to be wisely related to that public opinion which will be affected by the result of its translation into statutes. His business as administrator is the art of relevant selection and significant emphasis. I doubt whether any but the exceptional specialist possesses this art. It is, I think, produced by the best kind of humanistic training. I do not mean that such a training is a guarantee of its possession. I do mean that, as between two able men, the specialist is less likely to become a successful administrator in the modern state than, say, one who has been trained in the honours school of *litteræ humaniores* at Oxford.

On the evidence, this is to say, I believe that, at its best, a humanistic training produces greater flexibility and greater open-mindedness than is the case with a specialist's training. The danger of the specialist is that he takes the truth relevant to his special field of knowledge as wider in its implications than the facts will warrant. He takes his postulates for granted; and he is too likely to be unaware that, at its highest, the main art of administration consists in the examination of postulates. A good deal of what I am trying to convey is contained in the subtle change which, in the last generation, has transformed political economy into economic science. In the one, as the reader of Mill or Marshall will be acutely conscious on every page of their work, the writer is fully aware both of the fragility of the hypothesis from which he starts and the degree to which "friction" renders imperfect the conclusions at which he arrives. In the other, the writer tends to construct a logical pattern, an essay in deduction, in which, quite unconsciously, he takes for granted human nature, the legal relations of the modern property-system, the finality of the sovereign state, and other such matters. When, therefore, he comes to transfer the conclusions of his logical pattern to the real world of stark fact, the irrelevance of his conclusions is almost startling. Too often, indeed, they read like nothing so much as the reflections of a saddened believer in the Ptolemaic astronomy who refuses to be aware of the Copernican hypothesis.

I believe that the civil service has been safeguarded against this danger by the acceptance of Macaulay's principle as its basis of selection. But that safeguard is not, in itself, enough. There remain two other dangers to which, in the evolution of the past seventy years, I do not think sufficient attention has been paid. The first is implicit in the narrow class from which the highest civil servants are drawn. It is the danger that they are not able imaginatively to penetrate the experience they have to encounter. The ways of life they know, the habits of thought in which they have been brought up, the departmental traditions in which they are immersed, all represent a mental climate so different from the one whose results they have to handle, that it is far less certain today than it was a generation ago that they can handle it successfully. There was a grave failure of imagination, for example, in the new scales of the Unemployment Assistance Board in 1934. There has been a similar failure in the whole realm of penal reform. There has been a similar failure, as the evidence in the Gresford Colliery tragedy makes evident, in the service of mines inspection. There has been, if not failure, at least a lack of requisite persistence, in the development of technical and secondary education. I choose examples only of a whole range of grave problems which have come to the forefront in the post-war years in which the official mind has not, on the evidence, adjusted itself to the scale of the problems involved. Perhaps the most striking problem of all is that of the distressed areas where it can hardly be said that the civil service has begun to grasp either the proportions or the urgency of the issues.

Why? Let us make allowance for the fact that civil servants must adjust their proposals to the political possibilities they confront. Let us make allowance, also, for the fact that, up to some point, the maxim *quieta non movere* is an index to an important part of the art of public administration. Even when these discounts have been made, it is yet evident that a good deal of official thinking is circumscribed by the fact that the experience it encounters does not bring home with adequate pungency the scale of our problems in such a way as to make it think out afresh the implications of that scale. The kind of awareness of which I am thinking does not come from an occasional contact with the unemployed areas, a meeting with a trade-union deputation, the occasional friendship that, happily, grows up between high officials and Labour members of the House of Commons, even from the fact that, as a young man, the civil servant has spent six months in residence at Toynbee Hall. What is lacking, despite every device (the advisory committee, for instance) we have so far invented, is continuity of interpenetration of one class-experience by that of another. "A wise system of official training," wrote Graham Wallas, "would consist in 'seconding' young officials for experience in the kind of work which they are to organize." In an effective and coherent way, we have made no such provision on any serious scale in the working of our system.

But the issue lies deeper than the "seconding" of young officials, important though this is. It lies deeper even than the interesting proposal (which, originally, we owe also to Graham Wallas) of leave of absence for officials on full pay to acquire, outside the department, knowledge that may be useful to its work. The issue is the acquisition of those habits of mind which, in a period of rapid change, are capable of going back without fear to the foundations of tradition, and being able, in the light of their examination, to see the full significance of the need for innovation. With all its virtues, I venture to doubt whether our civil service possesses this type of mind, or is, indeed, favourable to its emergence. And I am suggesting that the reason why it does not possess it is in the interrelation between the tradition of each department, on the one hand, and the narrow class-range from which officials are drawn, on the other.

The tradition of the department makes, in almost every case, for continuity of policy; it tends, therefore, in a period of rapid change, to be a brake on innovation. It looks rather to the past than to either the present or the future. It tends to look at new ideas from the angle of how best they can be fitted into the existing scheme of things when the real need may be to depart from it. There lurks in this the historic danger of bureaucracy—the danger, namely, of unconsciously suspecting all innovation it has not itself originated. That suspicion has been well exemplified in the history of army reform in England; there, at least, the documents are on record. But it is not less true, either, of penal reform; it is, I think, true to say that, minor changes apart, every serious impulse to prison improvement in this country has originated outside and not inside the Home Office. It is seen, also, in the fact that after thirty years the rules governing workmen's compensation should have remained unchanged, and that it should have taken almost a decade of agitation to persuade the Ministry of Labour to embark upon the revision of the cost-of-living index. I believe myself—though this is far more controversial ground—that it is seen also in the Treasury's relentless opposition to a great public works programme. The need for far-reaching improvements in electrification, water supply, housing, roads, especially in rural areas, is largely a matter of common agreement. But every attempt at development along these lines has broken down in the face of opposition from the Treasury. It is at least legitimate to doubt, in the face of available foreign experience, whether the postulates of the Treasury position are as satisfactory as successive Chancellors of the Exchequer have been persuaded to regard them.

But I believe that the narrow range from which the administrative class is drawn is still more important in this context. High officials are hard-worked men, immersed in the grim daily burden of their task. Living the same kind of life, meeting, for the most part, people who lead lives similar to their own, seeing problems not in the pit and mine, in the slum house and the condemned school, but in the massive dossiers which come to them in endless procession, it is at least not clear that they are driven by their work to that examination of fundamentals which, as I have argued, is so urgent a task for our generation. They can see the problem of juvenile unemployment as an administrative and statistical problem; it does not impinge upon them, as parents, as it impinges upon the parents of the working-class boy who, twelve months after he has left school, sees nothing ahead but a choice among different blind-alley occupations. They see that the terms of enlistment must be made more satisfactory if the army is to be maintained at full strength; but they do not see, they do not even think of seeing, that so long as the army is not a career really open to the talents, in this generation a few pence on the day's pay is not going to make the really able and ambitious working-class youth think of the army as a career in the sense that he thinks of engineering or schoolmastering as a vocation that will give his energies their full scope. He does not himself pass through the kind of experience which burns on every page of Mr. Walter Greenwood's *Love on the Dole*. He is rarely visited by the kind of passion which led John Cornford and Ralph Fox to die in Spain as volunteers in the International Brigade.

Men think differently who live differently; and unless we can somehow fuse alien experiences into a common understanding, not the completest body of factual materials is approached from that angle of insight which gives them their proper perspective. The danger of what Graham Wallas called "narrowness and rigidity" in official life is, in this context, painfully real. At the top of the hierarchy, the civil servant hardly knows—no doubt there are exceptions—at first hand what unemployment does, what the Means Test implies, the effect on an able boy of a decision to economize on the number of free places in the secondary schools. He will, indeed, even tend to persuade himself that an insistence that the system he operates should be made to confront its failures not less than its successes is the mark of an extremist or a crank—both words of horrific import in the dictionary of official practice. He confronts the danger that he will accept the immense pressure of the whole system towards conformity in the essentials of thought with the knowledge that if he is reasonably efficient and reasonably intelligent the chances are that he will get his promotion and that the system will last his time.

A civil service, I am arguing, needs not only the able routineer; it needs also the ardent inventor who can disturb the routine; and my own doubt is whether the system either breeds that type or is able adequately to assimilate it when it rarely discovers one. There is no lack at all in the civil service of energy and devotion, of self-lessness and public spirit. The degree and quality of the team-work discoverable, not merely when some big adventure is on hand but in the normal round of daily duty, are alike remarkable. But there is, from the nature of its construction, an absence of that ultimate imaginative scepticism, that passion for constructive in-novation, which would enable us, in Wallas's noble phrase, "to teach those distant impersonal masters of ours who are ourselves how to prevent the opportunity of effective thought from being confined to a tiny rich minority living, like the Cyclops, in irre-sponsible freedom." The best way for the civil servant to "teach those distant masters" is for him first to teach himself; and it means, above all, a kind and a direction of intellectual effort and experience which, at present, the service itself tends to minimize.

3

The civil service, as a career, offers certain solid advantages to its members. Granted good behaviour and efficient service, the official has security, a salary with increments which compares not unfavourably with what the best outside employment of a similar kind can offer, modest holidays with pay, sick leave, and, on re-tirement, a non-contributory pension which is roughly equal, in normal circumstances, to about two-thirds of his salary in the last years of his career. In all the lower grades of the service, more-over, he has a share, through the system of Whitley Councils, in discussing and in some degree determining the conditions of his employment. He can belong to one of the staff associations which function as his trade union, though, since 1927, these bodies are not permitted outside affiliations of any kind. If he is not an industrial worker, he is debarred from political activities; his acceptance of a parliamentary candidature, for instance, has operated, since 1928, as automatic resignation from the service. In some departments, however, he may be permitted, under suitable circumstances, to serve on bodies such as local councils. He may not, however, without express permission of his superiors, express publicly, by speech or article or book, his views on controversial public questions.

Taken as a whole, no one can say that the civil service is an expensive service. Three-quarters of its members receive less than four pounds per week; and, throughout the service, there are only some five hundred posts of which the salaries are £1000 per annum and upwards; even heads of departments receive only £3000 per annum. There can be no doubt that, at the base of the pyramid, the essential attraction of the service is the security and the pension it offers; at the apex, the dignity and influence it confers upon those who reach the highest posts. Except on grounds of age, it is very rare for men to leave the service; in 1929, for example, 2205 did so. But of these nearly 1400 left through ill-health or death, and 271 only through inefficiency or misconduct. Of others who left for no given cause, there were 523, and one must assume that, among them, were those who found, as they believed, the opportunity of a better career outside the service.

Obviously, from this angle, the civil service is regarded by the youth of the community as a career which compares favourably with outside vocations. The permanence, the increments on pay to the maximum of the grade, the prospect (even though small) of interclass promotion, the holidays with pay, and the pension on retirement all constitute solid advantages which are rivalled only by the best of private establishments. The highest class of civil servant, however, apart, there are, I think, two conclusions to be drawn from this. The first is that the service tends to attract to its ranks, at least for the most part, the unadventurous, plodding type who is content, knowing his probable destination from the start, to accept a well-defined routine. The second is that so small a number of departures from the service must mean, compared with outside employment, a general satisfaction with its conditions.

But, again looking only at the service below the administrative class, there is one weakness in its organization which is impressive. In these classes, there are some hundred thousand officials of different kinds; the proportion of interclass promotions is very small. Does this mean that the methods of promotion in the service are so satisfactory that the channels through which men may move from the base to the apex of the pyramid are sufficiently wide to give us assurance that there is no wastage of ability? Are there, to put it in another way, such adequate methods of assessing ability as to make us sure that the lower ranks of the service do not contain men who, given the opportunity, would prove their fitness for work of the highest kind?

Obviously, this is a question of proportion. I can only record my own conviction that is based upon a twofold experience. I have been for ten years a member of the Civil Service Tribunal in which I have come into contact with every grade of the service in a large number of cases; and I have, as a university teacher, had nearly twenty years' experience of teaching civil servants, both as undergraduates and as research workers in their spare time. My own view is definite that there is, in each of the lower grades of the service, a small, but nevertheless significant, number of officials whose ability would fit them for the best class of work, but who remain either undiscovered or unused in the working of the system. Largely, I think, this occurs because (1) the grades of the service are too rigid, (2) because promotion methods below the administrative class are too mechanical, and (3) because not enough encouragement is offered by the system to those who, with such encouragement, would quickly demonstrate their capacity. Each of these conclusions needs a separate word.

The grades of the service are too rigid. The intake is, of course, determined by considerations of public business; and an official's fate must mainly be determined by the educational opportunities of which he can take advantage. But too much reliance is placed upon the opportunity for serving officials to compete, at a somewhat higher age, for better posts; the competition is unreal partly because they lack the opportunities for the training received by those with whom they compete, and after some such age as twenty-five examinable capacity begins very definitely to decline. It is, therefore, a pity that experiment has not been attempted with alternative qualifications for entrance to that of the competitive examination. I see no reason, for example, why, up to some such age as thirty, a young official who has taken a good university degree, or qualified himself with distinction for the Bar, or done, as some have done, an interesting piece of social investigation, should not be given a temporary "acting" appointment in a higher grade to see whether he cannot justify exceptional promotion. The burden upon the taxpayer would be small; and the experiment would at least have the important merit of offering to the really able man in the lower grades the knowledge that he has an effective chance of recovering from the handicap of inadequate educational opportunity. At present, as anyone acquainted with the service will be aware, there are in its ranks men who would be eager to make the effort involved in this attempt, did they not believe that the steepness of the hierarchical slope makes the relation between labour and reward too small to justify the sacrifice of leisure involved.

The methods of promotion are too mechanical. It is, I think, a fair estimate that, below the administrative class, an overwhelming proportion of promotions go by seniority; the Promotion Board is less a real search for merit than a safeguard against the fear of favouritism. Obviously, there is a case for this view where a considerable part of the work to be done is routine work, even if routine work that sometimes calls for a real degree of personal initiative. My point is that, by and large, until one reaches the executive grade, the nature of the material upon which most civil servants are working will not lead to the evocation of the kind of capacity required in the highest grades; with the result that it is only exceptionally, as where a man has made his mark on a Whitley Council or Committee, that the Promotion Board, with its not very illuminating report before it, will really know the full range of the young official's abilities. The present system is satisfactory for the bulk of routine promotions. It does not touch the problem of the exceptional man with whom I am here concerned.

The system, thirdly, does not sufficiently stress the need to discover exceptional talent. This is due to a number of complicated causes. In part, it is the outcome of the historical fact that, before the war, it was rare for the heads of departments even to think it likely that men of exceptional talent were to be found outside the products of Oxford and Cambridge. That tradition has been discouraged since the war; but it is not, I think, unfair to say that it has been found by no means easy to break it down. In part, also, it is the outcome of the obvious truth that it is not easy, in the classes devoted to routine work, for really exceptional talent to make itself known; and, even when it does, there is always the danger that staff jealousy will view with disfavour any exceptional promotion. In part, therefore, the third difficulty arises that when the exceptional man does, as he moves up the hierarchy, display his ability, unless his movement has been unusually rapid, it is far from easy to fit him into the fairly rigid categories of the service. I have known young men of quite first-rate ability in the clerical class who have gone into the service eager to climb up its ladder. After two or three years at a routine job they have become discouraged, simply because its daily performance offers them no real prospect of proving what they can do. Such men tend to find in leisure the chance of self-expression they ought to find in the service; or, as in one or two notable cases, they leave it either for private employment or to organize the trade unions which have become so notable a feature of the post-war civil service.

It is, of course, clear that, with all the goodwill in the world, no great organization can expect not to make mistakes of this kind.

The service is a hierarchy; the work is apportioned out with meticulous care in terms of a carefully watched grading; and the staff is quick to note departures from fairly well-settled routines. An establishment officer, no doubt, is eager, above all, to avoid the accusation of favouritism in promotion; nothing so easily disorganizes the morale of an office. It is, no doubt, for this reason that the elaborate system of reports has been devised that, in the choice of men, there may be safeguards against its intrusion. Granted all this, I can only record my own conviction that the service has been inadequately experimental in this regard. Certainly there are methods of choice it might have explored of which it has not taken full advantage. A considerable number of civil servants have devoted their spare time to taking university degrees; that is, at least, a proof of energy of mind with which it would be worth while to experiment. Others have shown considerable administrative ability in negotiation with the officials above them. Some of these I have known; and the cases they have prepared for the Civil Service Tribunal were able and effective pieces of advocacy. Again, little advantage has been taken to notice the presence in a routine class of ability not being used to the full extent of its powers. And a small number of civil servants in the lower grades have made contributions of distinct importance to the literature of public administration without arousing in their superior officers the sense that such contributions at least warrant the inference that the talent so revealed demands the recognition of a title to experiment.

I emphasize this because it is certain that an infusion of lower-grade ability into the upper hierarchy would do a great deal of good. It would break down that enclosure within traditional postulates which is still too characteristic of heads of departments. It would enable new views to be considered, new points of criticism to be borne in mind. It is very difficult for any upper-class Englishman to know what is being thought in the classes below him; and, unless he is a very exceptional person, he is rarely imaginative enough to see the urgency of finding out. And since the administrative class is largely shut off—and the higher in its ranks the more shut off—from contact with those below it, especially in a social way, its knowledge of the psychology which underlies the wants it encounters is all too likely to be external and second-hand. What this affects, above all, is the civil servant's conception of the limits of possible action. The attacks made on his primary conceptions appear to him inacceptable because he has never had direct and continuous contact with the experience that has led to those attacks. Yet there exists within the service itself a good deal of that experience which, if only it could receive expression at the point where policy is formulated, would inject into the traditions of the departments something, at least, of the scepticism about fundamentals it is urgent for the civil servant to possess. At present, I do not think he tends to possess it; and the narrow stratum from which he predominantly comes does not encourage its possession.

It is, of course, clear that there can be no rapid internal change in these matters; alteration must wait upon fundamental changes in the character of the educational system. What we have gives us, at least in most of those mainly concerned, a remarkable capacity for detachment, a disinterested zeal for the success of any measures it is ordered to take, which are both of high importance. But, even taken together, they are not enough to secure the positive success of any wholesale experimentation with the postulates of a new social order. That cannot be made to work either by detachment or by disinterested zeal. It needs rather a positive conviction not only that the postulates are in themselves worth while but also that it is imperative that they should work. Just as something, at least, of the breakdown in the administration of the Palestine Mandate was due to the fact that some of the chief civil servants concerned did not believe in its principles or purposes, so a civil service such as the British might easily fail because it did not believe in the experiment it was asked to attempt. And were that to be the case, I believe the source of the failure would largely be due to the fact that most of those responsible for the administrative measures necessary to implement it would be at best sceptical and at worst intellectually hostile to the purposes of those measures. And this, in its turn, would be due to the fact that the main personnel in the service is too narrowly class-conditioned in the social experience it represents.

This would not, I must add, be a failure of will on the part of the civil service. There can be little doubt in the minds of any who have had contact with the chief permanent officials of the reality of their faith in the central principle of neutrality. But that principle is set in the perspective of an environment far more narrow than they are likely to realize, even less to admit. Their notions of what I have called the limits of the practicable are set by their experience of the present system as a going concern. Their minds have rarely bent themselves to the speculative task of considering its transformation. Interventionism, regulation, even the planning of some specific area of the national life, these they fully understand. A fundamental change in social motivation is a different matter. How hard it is for that change to be appreciated came out with clarity in Sir Maurice Hankey's evidence before the Royal Commission on Armaments. It came out, again, in the evidence of the Board of Trade before the Royal Commission on the Localization of Industry, where the effect of the department's evidence was the insistence that any control of the right of business enterprise to determine its own geographical habits was economically unthinkable. It is implicit, once more, in the difficulty of persuading the Home Office seriously to confront the problems of penal reform; after the remarkable achievements of the Soviet Union in this realm there is little excuse for the indefensible complacency of recent years. It is evident, again, in the "superior" attitude, far, as yet, from being broken down, of the diplomatic to the consular service. Once again, it is not less true of officials than of politicians that men who live differently think differently. The environment from which the main bulk of the leading officials is drawn in itself creates half-conscious intellectual presumptions against change. Until the road up its hierarchy is in reality an open one, it will be very difficult to overcome the immanent psychological consequences of the present situation.

4

The ethos of the civil service is detachment and neutrality; for that reason a long tradition, extended in recent years to the Defence Forces, prohibits a civil servant from a parliamentary candidature; and certain departments, the Ministries of Health and Labour, for example, which have special relations with the public prohibit their officials from candidatures for local government bodies. Hardly less strict is the rule which prohibits a public servant from comment upon public affairs by way, for instance, of a book or article. A recent case, in which an official of the Ministry of Health was dismissed from the service for a pseudonymous article criticizing the policy of sanctions in the Italo-Abyssinian War shows how rigorously the rule is applied.

There is a large body of evidence to suggest that the strictures of these regulations is deprecated, and even resented, by the lower ranks of the service. They appear to admit that they are necessary where the higher ranks are concerned. But they believe that there is no case for their application to the lower grades, and that the virtual deprivation of civic rights for several hundred thousand officials, which the rule entails, is indefensible. In their judgment, there would be no abuse if the matter were left to be determined not by rule, but by the discretion of the individual officer. He would act, it is argued, with all proper regard for the traditions of the service; and, in any case, the numbers affected are so small that they do not constitute a problem big enough to warrant the severity of the present procedure.

A distinction, clearly, must be drawn between political activity in the full sense of the term and written comment, by way of a book or article, on contemporary problems. So far as the first is concerned, the matter seems to rest upon the paramount principles, first, that the confidence of the public in the neutrality of the service must be maintained, and, second, that the administrative discipline of the departments is not interfered with by the freedom in politics that is permitted. It is, I think, clear to everyone that no civil servant engaged in the making of policy could possibly be permitted the luxury of a parliamentary candidature. The relations between, say, a Labour government and Sir Maurice Hankey would, to say the least, rapidly become strained if he were at one and the same time the Secretary to the Cabinet and a Conservative candidate for the House of Commons. No public could be induced to believe in the *bona fides* of any service whose leading officials were engaged in the promotion for themselves of a political career.

It is, therefore, clear that down to some point in the hierarchy of the service, there must be prohibition. How far should that extend? The Treasury itself agrees that it does not extend to industrial workers in, for example, one of the dockyards or in Woolwich Arsenal; though postmen, whose work is more or less comparable in character, are excluded from the non-prohibited area. I do not myself believe that the presence among the fifteen or sixteen hundred candidates at a general election of a score or so of civil servants would jeopardize public confidence in its general neutrality, so long as they were not members of the higher classes of the service. But I think the situation would become very different if the great bulk of the great army of officials were allowed, without actually becoming candidates themselves, to participate in the general activities of party warfare. Even a clerical officer in the Unemployment Assistance Board would become a centre of wholly undesirable discussion if, on a Labour platform, he were to denounce the regulations of the Board; and the Labour Party would, I am confident, rapidly begin to ask angry questions if, at the annual conference of the Conservative Party, an official of the Mines Department were to denounce with bell, book, and candle the policy of nationalizing the mines.

I see no way in which, in the field of party politics, it is possible to draw lines between one grade and another in any logical manner. That impossibility seems to me to imply that to leave the matter to individual discretion would mean the danger that any grave lapse on the part of an official would tend pretty easily to be regarded, if it were punished, as a case of political victimization. The present rules, therefore, stringent as they are, seem to me to represent the necessities of the position. Anyone who is aware of the pressure brought to bear upon members of Parliament, even local councillors, to take up individual cases will, I think, realize that the greater the degree in which the official is separated from this pressure, the more likely is the public to feel confidence in the justice of the system. Granted all the historic *esprit de corps* of the service, it would not be difficult to lose that quality if its members took, on any wide scale, a full part in the party battle.

The administrative problem, moreover, raises real complications. If civil servants were permitted to embark upon a political career, grave difficulties would arise if, at any time, they were defeated in their election. Are they to have the right, in that event, to return to the service? Is the right to be absolute, and without regard to the time an official has been in the House of Commons? It seems to me obvious that the relations of a department are too delicate to make this kind of reabsorption a possible adventure. A Foreign Office clerk, who had spent some years in the House ardently attacking his department, would not easily go back to the discipline it imposes; and the situation would be still more difficult if he continued to hope, as he well might, for a return to active politics.

The problem of the written word is much more complicated. It is, I think, clear that a civil servant could not easily be permitted publicly to criticize the policy of the department of which he was a member. A strong attack on Mr. Eden's foreign policy by a junior official of the Foreign Office would strain relations to the breaking-point. Even an anonymous attack would be incompatible with the loyalty and detachment that are the hall-mark of a competent official. From the angle of the kind of confidence a minister must be able to feel in his permanent officials, it is not, I think, debatable that a vow of external silence imposes itself by the nature of his task.

There is, however, a middle ground in which I believe that the right to self-expression is a wholly desirable thing. No one, for example, would object to the works in which an eminent Treasury official, Mr. R. G. Hawtrey, has revealed himself as one of the best English economists of the present time. So long as a civil servant is contributing generally to the structure of knowledge there is, so far as I can see, no reason why any official ox should tread upon his tongue. Provided that he is reasonably discreet, the contribution his experience can make may be of exceptional value; and it would be a pity if prohibitions compelled him to silence. Just as I think there is everything to be said for allowing naval and military officers to develop in print their view of strategy and service organization, so I think that as full a liberty as may be for the civilian officer to develop his theories of social and administrative organization is desirable. No doubt there ought to be an imprimatur from his superiors. But a treatise, for example, on Treasury control by one who has practised it, or on the relation of government to industrial arbitration by an officer with experience of the conciliation department of the Ministry of Labour, has everything to recommend it. We underestimate, I think, the importance of encouraging civil servants to think organically and fundamentally, as it were, about the problems with which they have to deal; and excessive discretion in this realm is a hindrance, and not a help, to the discovery of truth. To allow a civil servant to write a book, for instance, on the prison system without allowing him to discuss the major criticisms that have been made of its functioning is almost worse than to allow him to write no book at all. We run the very real danger, unless there is a measure of genuine freedom in this regard, that civil service work is written about and criticized by men who do not know the facts, and tend therefore somewhat easily to misjudge the habits upon which they have to pronounce. After a certain point, the quasi-anonymity with which the service surrounds itself is harmful, rather than beneficial, to its proper relations with the public.

Something of this has been realized in recent years, though the method adopted to meet it has not, in my own judgment, been a wise one. The method is that of appointing a "public relations officer" for the department whose business is to explain, or to explain away, its procedures to the public. The title is a formidable one. It covers a reality which may extend from the wholly proper communication of news to handling the press so that the criticism of the department therein may be minimal in character. My own feeling is strong that this is the wrong kind of development. It had led to efforts to hinder criticism, to the retailing of inspired gossip, to the conversion of what is in fact propaganda into what appears to be genuine news, for which there is nothing to be said. Where a department seeks to explain what it is doing, or to defend itself from attack, the proper person to explain or defend its policies is the minister responsible for them; and nothing justifies the modern method of allowing hints to appear in the press which are intended indirectly to create what the public relations officer regards as the "right" attitude on the part of the public. No department, in the long run, loses anything by the maximum possible openness in its relations. The modern publicity expert, whatever he may specialize in, is hardly a specialist in straightforward dealing. Like an advertising agent, he has a commodity—the policy or the personality of his department—to sell, and he takes the quickest means he can to that end. Above all, I suggest, he takes the utmost pains to convey the impression that the chief characteristic of the department he represents is infallibility.

Civil servants, like other human beings, do in fact make mistakes, even grave ones; and the best method of convincing the public of their *bona fides* is the fullest openness about their habits. A failure in this is bound, in the crucial instance, to have serious repercussions. The suspicions of the police which followed on the Savidge case have not yet died down. The public is far from feeling that it has heard the real facts about the Dartmoor prison mutiny. Sir Samuel Hoare's attitude to the dockyard dismissals of 1937, where men of blameless record were sacked upon unknown charges formulated by unnamed accusers whose description seemed uncomfortably close to that of Oliver the Spy, may have convinced the Colonel Blimps of this world; they have certainly failed to convince the trade-union movement. And when, in 1937, Mr. Frank Griffin formulated a series of specific charges against the army, one cannot help feeling that the proper way to deal with those charges was not to dismiss the man who made them from the Reserve—a clear endeavour to create the public impression of his undesirability—but to have the charges investigated by a small committee in whose impartiality the public would have had full confidence. Sir Warren Fisher's notable inquiries into the Gregory case and the Bullock case are classic examples of the kind of forthright dealing with the public out of which the right kind of confidence develops. It is, I think, a pity that this method of full communication is not followed in the rare, but usually significant, instances in which the public is left dissatisfied by the course taken by the department concerned.

And this leads me to the insistence that just as the maximum publicity is desirable for what may be termed official thought, so is the maximum relation between civil service and public desirable wherever the exercise of a discretionary power, especially one that is secret in its nature, is entrusted to a department. The whole difference between public and private administration consists in the fact that in the first sphere the citizen is entitled to know the reasons for any decision by which he is affected. That is why the Lord Chancellor's Committee on Ministers' Powers recommended the publication of the inspectors' reports to the Ministry of Health in such matters as slum clearance. That is why I should like to see the conference upon aliens of a right to appeal, say to a judge in chambers, against any decision of the Home Secretary to refuse a certificate of naturalization. The present system, in which the grounds for the refusal are always denied, is unsatisfactory simply because there are many instances in which the friends of an alien may get the decision reversed by appealing from one Home Secretary to his successor. The argument that Parliament has conferred an absolute discretion in this realm does not really take us very far. For the purpose of Parliament is that the discretion should be rationally used; and there are certainly many instances in which the curious habits of a particular official, wholly screened from the public view, are allowed a weight which a judicial-minded scrutiny would destroy in a few minutes' close examination.

I have already, in an earlier chapter, urged the desirability of advisory committees of members of Parliament in connexion with each of the departments of state. I believe that not the least service they could render lies in the continuity of contact they would afford between the responsible legislator and the administrative specialist—a contact which, for reasons given earlier, I believe to be of great importance. But every reason for committees of this character seems to me a reason also for building about the departments advisory committees of citizens whose interests are relevant to the work the departments have to do. We already have committees of this character; and some of them, most notably the Consultative Committee of the Board of Education, have done very valuable work. Not its least valuable aspect is the kind of bridge it builds between lay opinion and the administrative process. The real danger that confronts the official is his constant liability to be separated from this lay opinion. He lives seeing his problems so largely through the miasma of files that he may easily lack a sense of proper proportion unless they are translated into the eager, palpitating lives of the men and women whose needs they embody. It would be a good thing for Home Office officials to see representatives of the Shop Assistants' Union not on an occasional deputation when two or three speeches are followed by the polite promise of further consideration but in an organized monthly meeting in which both sides learn in personal contact the range of their common problems. It would be a good thing, too, if there were an advisory committee on slum clearance at the Ministry of Health where in continuous exchange of criticism and idea the officials had a constant sense of the urgency of the issue. I should like, indeed, to see the changes in army regulations, as they affect the common soldier, promulgated, not from on high as the army council has of itself seen fit to make them, but after they have passed through the sieve of criticism and suggestion of a really good committee of ex-soldiers who learned where the shoe pinched during their years of service; this applies, of course, to the navy and air force as well. I do not think, to take an obvious example, that Invergordon would ever have occurred if the Board of Admiralty had been made to feel the repercussion of its decisions as they would be felt by the men to whom they applied. So, also, I believe, it is a pity that the Ministry of Labour has made no effort to associate the unemployed with its local Labour Exchanges, and the trade unions with their central administration. There is an immense fund of social experience, deeply relevant to the process of administration, which, under the present system, is never brought into organic relationship with the men who direct that process. It is important to bring it into that relation. Were that to be done, it would, I venture to believe, do more than a score of public relations officers to make the work of the civil service fully understood by the public.

For despite all the eulogies that are passed on the service from time to time, it is important to emphasize that little of its real work is yet understood by the citizen. That is partly due to our defective education; we still do not realize the importance of what Aristotle called a "training in the spirit of the constitution." Most of the population grows to maturity with little conception of even the purposes, let alone the methods, of modern administration. They believe (quite wrongly) that all officials are well paid, that they have security and short hours of work, and that they are enmeshed in a red tape which makes them slow and cumbersome about getting things done. Even a committee like the Anderson Committee on Pay showed itself, as its comments on inspection work made clear, quite unaware of the nature of the civil servants' work; and it is a habit with some critics of the civil service to move deliberately from ignorance to misrepresentation. There is far greater interest displayed in an occasional instance of administrative pathology, like the Bullock case, than in the steady performance of tasks upon which a very large part of the public welfare depends.

The urgency of effective civic education speaks for itself. Ignorant democrats will not be able to defend democracy, simply because they will not know what they have lost until it is too late. But I think it is important to remember that the more people we can actively associate with knowledge of the administrative process on its positive side, the more fully the value of the work will be grasped. That was, it is worth remarking, one of Lenin's major insights. He realized that the larger the public actually associated with the process of administration, the profounder would be the quality of its performance simply because it would meet so much wider an area of responsible criticism. Here, as I think, has been one of the great failures of imagination in British democracy. It has failed to see how wide a public there is to be interested in its processes if only it will invent the institutional devices necessary to elicit that interest. We have been able to do that successfully in other walks of our national life. The co-operative movement, the trade unions, the Labour Party, to a lesser extent the friendly societies, have literally lived upon their ability to exact voluntary service from their members. I believe that the advisory committee, both centrally and locally, is, properly organized and fully used, essentially the device that could elicit the same kind of service for the process of public administration. It would be necessary, of course, to convince the committees that consultation with them mattered; to allow them to degenerate into formalism would be worse than not using them at all. But it is so important to prevent the modern citizen from degenerating into what the French call *l'administré* that all the effort and burden it would involve is amply worth while. The citizen knows that he pays taxes; he ought to be made far more continuously aware of what he pays them for. Until he has that realization as an intimate and living part of his personality, he is not, in a full sense seised of his citizenship. For few people, outside the really active members of the political parties, will feel that they are really citizens if their part in the process of politics is confined to marking a ballot paper once in three or four years.

I am not, let me emphasize, seeking in any way to depreciate or to diminish the central principle of ministerial control by anything this argument implies. Decision must still remain the minister's task. But it is surely obvious that the wider the range of experience that can be collected for him as the basis of his decision, the more likely it is that what he decides will be wisely decided. In a sense, what I am suggesting is only a logical extension of the part played in our political life by the Royal Commission; and the aid that device has given to clarity in both policy and administration is literally beyond estimation. My thesis is, after all, the essentially simple one that democracy is government in terms of the consumers' choice, and that the best way to get at the consumer is to organize him for the purpose of consultation. No amount of paper knowledge, hardly any amount, even, of skilled administration, will compensate for the absence of effective interest in the results of policy. The civil servant too easily assumes that the absence of criticism is the presence of satisfaction. That is far from being the case. The real way to know what the public wants is to organize it to say what it wants; no amount of *expertise* will ever compensate for the absence of that pronouncement. And the real way, too, to get to know what it wants is to associate it with criticism of what it is receiving. The more fully that, again, is organized, the more effective will be our safeguards against the major ills of bureaucracy.

5

The daily experience of the average citizen testifies to the growth of executive power in this country. Some of it has been achieved at the expense of Parliament; the increase in delegated legislation is one of the most notable procedural changes of the past thirty years. Some of it, also, has been achieved at the expense of the courts of law; ministers have been increasingly entrusted with quasi-judicial, and even fully judicial powers, which have partly, or even fully, excluded the operation of the rule of law. We have been offered grave warnings against the consequences of this evolution. It is the "new despotism"; it is "bureaucracy triumphant." So eminent a protagonist as the Lord Chief Justice of England has descended into the arena to insist upon the importance to public liberty of a return to the ancient ways.

The protest against the growth of delegated legislation collapses as soon as it is submitted to serious scrutiny. There is everything to be said for seeing to it that Parliament confers no rule-making powers which, an emergency like foot and mouth disease apart, it has not the opportunity to scrutinize before they go into operation. That is not, as the Lord Chancellor's Committee on Ministers' Powers pointed out, a difficult matter to arrange. It would be easy to set up a Standing Committee of the House of Commons to which all orders and regulations were submitted before they went into effect; it would be easy, also, for that Committee to draw the attention of the House to anything exceptional in their character of which the House should be aware before it confirmed them. Granted such scrutiny, granted, also, the assurance—which has not so far been lacking—that no department makes regulations without full consultation with the interests likely to be affected by their operation, there is everything to be said for, and little effective to be said against, the process of delegated legislation. Anyone who examines the kind of subject-matter with which it deals, will find that it saves a good deal of valuable parliamentary time which can be better used for other matters. An extension of the list of poisons, a change in the schedule of fares for taxi-cabs in London, these, to take typical illustrations of the use of regulatory power, are not really a threat to our freedom if they are made, under suitable safeguards, by a body of ministers rather than by the House itself. The vital thing is that Parliament should be in a position to take objection to any use of the power when it deems fit, and that it should be so able to examine what is done in its name as to make it certain that nothing to which objection can be taken escapes from its purview. That achieved, the system of delegated legislation which is, in fact, far older than its critics like to make out, is an elementary procedural convenience essential to the positive state.

The conference of quasi-judicial and judicial powers upon the departments raises far more difficult questions. Englishmen schooled in the famous doctrine of Professor Dicey have been taught to believe that no issue of law is properly settled until it has been disposed of by a court of law independent of the executive of the day; and they tend to look with suspicion and, in the case of the Lord Chief Justice, even angry dislike upon the growth of a ministerial jurisdiction which ousts the authority of the courts. Lawyers, particularly, obviously resent the notion that any issue can be properly determined outside a court of law into which justiciable matter enters. They complain, therefore, that the growth of this jurisdiction is proof of an intent in the civil service to make ministerial policy supreme over legal power. This, they argue, is the new despotism in all its arrogant panoply. The rule of law has been, at least since the time of the Stuarts, the essential safeguard of Englishmen against arbitrary authority. To relax its vigour is to risk the intrusion of discretion into a realm where it ought never to enter.

This, obviously enough, is a realm where every student of the new tendencies must tread delicately. There are certain types of power the conference of which upon the executive would, quite certainly, place public liberty in danger. It would be a dangerous surrender of principle to allow the executive to designate certain behaviour as an offence and to decide whether a given individual's conduct fell within the category so established. It is essential, further, that when any type of quasi-judicial power is conferred upon the executive, its methods of decision shall be such as to establish reasonable confidence in their *bona fides*. It is important, again, that the grounds for any executive decision in this realm shall be public and that a full assurance shall be available of proper scrutiny by the officials concerned of all the material relevant to the making of a fair decision.

Where these criteria are satisfied, the fact that power of a judicial kind is conferred upon the executive ought not to create the alarms and excursions upon which so much attention has been concentrated in the post-war years. There is no reason, in experience, to suppose that a court of law is better or more fairly able to decide a dispute between School Managers and the Local Education Authority than is the Board of Education; [1] on the contrary, granted that the latter body is fully seised of the facts, the presumption is all the other way. There is no reason, either, to suppose that a court of law is better able than the Minister of Health to pass upon the validity and wisdom of a closing order made against the owner of an insanitary house by a local authority; [2] on the contrary, once more, granted the character of the issues involved, the presumption is again the other way. What is really involved in the jurisdiction of these ministerial tribunals is the evolution of adequate administrative standards; and the root of such standards is, by its nature, far more a matter for the executive than for the courts. In the conference of such a jurisdiction, the requirements of the rule of law are amply met when Parliament, in conferring the jurisdiction, sees to it that the standards of investigation observed in such tribunals are such as to assure fair play. This has been well put by Kelly C.B. in the classic case of

[1] *Board of Education v. Rice* (1911), A.C. 179.
[2] *Local Government Board v. Arlidge* (1915), A.C. 120.

Wood v. Wood.[3] "They are bound," he says of such tribunals, "in the exercise of their functions by the rule expressed in the maxim *Audi alteram partem* that no man should be condemned to consequences resulting from alleged misconduct unheard, and without having the opportunity of making his defence. This rule is not confined to the conduct of strictly legal tribunals, but is applicable to every tribunal or body of persons invested with authority to adjudicate upon matters involving civil consequences to individuals."

Nothing in the history of administrative tribunals suggests that this principle is flouted in application. So far as our knowledge extends, though their methods may be different from those of a court of law, they are not less scrupulous in the protection of private rights. Very largely, they are concerned with technical matters the decision of which requires a special knowledge rarely available either to magistrates or to judges. Their work is swift and cheap. Anyone who compares its results with the unhappy consequences of allowing the ordinary courts to have jurisdiction over workmen's compensation or the powers of the district auditor will, I suggest, be inclined strongly to the view that, in the positive state, the ordinary courts of law are rarely suitable for work of this kind. Their canons of statutory interpretation are wholly defective for the purposes of the modern state;[4] and they lack the knowledge necessary for the construction of proper administrative standards. It must be remembered that most of this jurisdiction is concerned with questions of "reasonableness" in policy; and it is difficult to see why a judge's view of "reasonableness" is more likely to be right than that of a minister who may have to answer for his view in the House of Commons. If, moreover, every case involving such questions could be transferred to a court of law the process of administration would become impossible, and the courts would be overwhelmed with base-

---

[3] (1874) L.R. 9 Ex. 190.
[4] See my memorandum of dissent in the Report of the Lord Chancellor's Committee on Ministers' Powers (193).

ness. One instance of this must suffice. Under the Widows', Orphans', and Old Age Pensions Act of 1926 there were in the first eleven months of 1926 some 4000 appeals under the procedure provided by the statute. It is surely obvious that reference of these to an ordinary court would be a fantastic procedure.

The truth is that Professor Dicey's conception of the rule of law and his profound hostility to *droit administratif* were both based on the postulates of an historic period which have now passed away. His rule of law was the expression of an atomic individualism in which state and citizen were regarded as antithesis, an objective and impartial court holding the balance between them in terms of the eternal principles of the Common Law. But, in fact, those "eternal principles" were no more than devices adopted to protect the owner of property from arbitrary interference by the state-power; and their character, so far from being permanent, shifted, as the evolution, most notably, of the law of torts makes evident, in terms of the social pressure to which they were subjected. His account, moreover, of *droit administratif* was a caricature even when he wrote it; certainly since the Third Republic, the administrative courts of France have given to its citizens a protection against abuse of power by the executive far more ample than anything they receive in England. But, until quite recently, Dicey's strictures on the French system have been accepted by English lawyers and, above all, by English judges as a conclusive argument for the view that the conference of judicial power on officials is bound to bring freedom into jeopardy.

Under suitable safeguards, there is no reason to suppose that this is the case. It is important to see that officials who exercise this type of jurisdiction are free from the pressure of their political superiors to decide in one way rather than another; and it is important, also, to ensure that their methods of investigation are fair as between the parties to the issue. Obviously, also, the question of *vires* is fundamental; a department ought not, as a general rule, to have an absolute and final right to determine the limits of its own authority. Granted that the growth of administrative law is implicit in the nature of the modern state, the problems it raises turn upon the institutional answers we make to these questions.

The second of them is comparatively simple, and the evidence already suggests that it has been satisfactorily solved. Granted a full opportunity to state a case, granted, also, that the decision made reveals the grounds upon which it has been built, on this side the citizen is at least as likely to obtain full consideration before an administrative tribunal as before a court of law; and he is likely to receive it more swiftly and at far less cost. The real heart of the problem is in the first and third of the questions I have noted. A jurisdiction entrusted to a minister is, of course, one that he cannot exercise in person; he merely confirms a finding that will be made by his officials. They are pretty certain to be unknown to the general public; and it is a good rule that a judicial function should be entrusted only to known persons. Since, further, there enters into the exercise of this function an element of law, it is important, also, that their administrative knowledge should be linked to a legal training. It is, I think, important also that the public should be assured that they have some security of tenure in their performance of a function which, on any view, has judicial attributes in its exercise.

From this angle, it seems clear that we are driven to the conception that those who advise the minister in the exercise of his judicial powers shall be set apart for this work by special nomination. Their experience of it should be continuous, and they should have the normal legal qualifications as a precondition of their appointment. The interested public should be as aware that X or Y advises the Minister of Health about closing orders as it is that a particular judge is the vacation judge. The more difficult issue is the problem of *vires*. It is, said Scrutton L.J., "of great public importance that there should be prompt and efficient means of calling in question the legality of the action of government departments"; and he has passed severe strictures on the haste with which they "take prompt action without any nice consideration as to whether it is legal or not." [5] The generalization, indeed, is probably far too sweeping; most of the strictures passed by the High Court on administrative action build on the exceptional case rather than the habitual practice. But it is clear that such strictures are the basis of a suspicion against which precautions are necessary. It is, obviously, an evil thing for the *bona fides* of government departments to be subject to criticism of this kind, even though it seems disproportionate to the weight of evidence.

I should myself, therefore, like to see the question of *vires* put in the hands of a judge or judges whose independence and detachment are beyond question. It is urgent that they should be able to arrive rapidly and cheaply at their decisions: this, I believe, rules out the ordinary High Court with its slow and costly procedure and its immense hierarchy of possible appeal. It leaves us, I think, with one of three possibilities: (1) a question of *vires* should be referred at once to the House of Lords directly, with the power to secure a prompt decision upon a certificate of urgency from the Attorney-General; (2) alternatively, a special Supreme Administrative Tribunal could be created, staffed by two members of the legal civil service and presided over by a lawyer of administrative experience with the status and tenure of a High Court judge; or (3) a question of *vires* could be sent directly to a High Court judge, set apart for this type of case, as the judges in the revenue and commercial courts are specialized to this type of problem. The first and the third of these methods satisfy, I believe, the classic requirements of the rule of law; and they have the important advantage, in England, that they involve no serious break with the ordinary judicial position. The second method would prove, I think, the most satisfactory, for it would enable the interpretation of statutes to be cut free from the narrow tradition of construction characteristic of the Common Law in recent times. We need to go back to the full implications of the rule in Heydon's case, to look, that is, to the defect the statute seeks to

[5] *Marshall Shipping Co. v. Board of Trade* (1923), 39 T.L.R. at p. 417.

remedy as the basis of its interpretation. The Common Law judge is so accustomed to look at public need only after private property rights have been amply protected as to make it dubious whether he would not, as in the first or third of the methods I have proposed, come to his task in a background unsuitable to its adequate fulfilment.

Nothing in all this lends support to the charges of "despotism" which Lord Hewart thought fit to make against the civil service in so sweeping and comprehensive a way. Both the nature of his charges and the evidence he adduced in their support were rather indications of his inability to understand the nature of the modern administrative process than of a deliberate effort on the part of civil servants to get power into their hands. No one with any grasp of what is implied in the organization and running of social services like our own could assume that rules of law evolved for the *laissez-faire* state would be adequate to their proper operation. We need in our own judiciary a fuller realization than some judges have shown of what the Supreme Court of the United States has termed "the strong presumption that a legislature understands and correctly appreciates the needs of its own people . . . and that its discriminations are based on adequate grounds." [6] In preserving what there is of truth in the doctrine of the separation of powers, we do not want, by a side door, to make the judges the masters of the administrative process. What that implies has been shown only too clearly in the relations between the Supreme Court and the legislatures of America.[7] The rule of law, in the sense in which Lord Hewart and his supporters use that term, would destroy the prospect of affording great bodies of citizens opportunities for a better life which Parliament, in its discretion, has seen fit to confer upon them. There is nothing in the experience of administrative law in this country that affords ground for suspicion that we are in danger of bureaucratic rule. Rather is the manner of the hostility of the courts to this develop-

[6] *Middleton v. Texas Power Co.*, 249 U.S. 157.
[7] Cf., for a good summary, I. Feinstein, *The Court Disposes* (1937).

ment significant evidence of the way in which judicial assumptions are coloured by profound political prejudices of which, often enough, the judges are themselves unaware. I shall deal with the issue this raises in the next chapter.

CHAPTER SEVEN

Parliament and the Courts

1

ACTS of Parliament are not self-operative; they have to be applied by men. And application involves interpretation by a court, since it is a principle of the British constitution that only express and unambiguous words—perhaps not even these—can deprive the citizen of his title to have the meaning of legislative intention settled by a court of law. Thereby we have sought to avoid not merely the obvious dangers of unfettered executive discretion in administration; we have sought, also, to assure that the citizen shall have his rights decided by a body of men whose security of tenure is a safeguard against the shifting currents of political opinion. Statutes are not to mean merely what the ministry of the day may be tempted to make them mean. The intention of Parliament is to be discovered by a body of independent persons, free from any direct interest in the result, and trained by long years of practice to standards of judgment by which that intention may be tested.

This is the famous rule of law which, for something like two hundred years, has been prized by Englishman as the safeguard of their freedom. It is not, indeed, intended to make the judges the masters of Parliament; judicial review, in the American sense is, I think happily unknown to the British constitution. It is always open to Parliament to repeal by statute any decision which it considers unsatisfactory or unwise; the Trades Disputes Act of 1906 [1] repealed the decision in the Taff Vale case; [2] and an

[1] 6 Ed. 7 C. 47.
[2] 1901 A.C. 426.

Act of Parliament amended the difficulties that seem likely to result from *Overtoun v. Assembly of the Free Church of Scotland.*[3]

Ever since the Revolution of 1688 the independence and the incorruptibility of British judges have been beyond dispute in this country. There have been harsh judges and stupid judges; there have been cynics on the Bench and an occasional figure, like Mr. Justice Grantham,[4] whose prejudice in a case of political flavour was so marked as to be matter for serious concern. There have been judges—since there is still no retiring age—who have remained on the court long after it was painfully apparent to the interested public that their powers were inadequate to their function. It is nevertheless true to say that, with the single exception of Lord Macclesfield, the integrity of no English judge has been open to suspicion after his appointment to the Bench at least since the Act of Settlement. Even the exhibition of prejudice of an open kind must be regarded as minimal in character; for not half a dozen times in that period has judicial conduct been the subject of debate in Parliament.

It is nevertheless important to realize that the relation between the legislature and the judiciary is not, and cannot be, a static one. Judges are not separated from the rest of mankind. They are part of, and affected by, the mental climate of the generation to which they belong. They share in the characteristic beliefs by which their age is dominated. A majority of them, in the past hundred years, have played a part in the political life of the country; and these have been the men mostly selected for the highest judicial posts, at any rate since later Victorian times. Law, moreover, may be a logical technique; but it is one the primary assumptions of which are always shaped, in their ultimate form, by the great historical forces of an age. The judge is not an automatic and passionless being who, as he does his work of interpre-

---

[3] 1900 A.C. 515.
[4] Cf. Mr. Asquith's remarks 22 Hansard (5 series) 1911, p. 366; and see 160 *Ibid.* (4 series) 1906, p. 370.

tation, finds a meaning in law which is fixed and invariable. For were the law so fixed and so invariable, men would not go to court; it is the doubt of what the law is that provides the courts with their work. And this means that the judge is, even if incompletely and indirectly, making law not less than merely announcing it. He has the delicate task of finding how a particular set of facts, the significance of which he has to discover, is related either to intentions set out by Parliament, or, in the absence of those intentions, to a somewhat amorphous body of doctrine, itself the product of a long historic process, known as the general principles of the Common Law.

When, as we examine this work of finding such relations, we speak of judicial "impartiality," we must not be led into the assumption that the judges are unmindful of the bearing of the results they reach. They have what Mr. Justice Holmes has called their "inarticulate major premisses" not less fully than other men. Tradition may separate them from formal participation in the political controversies of the time. But as the deposit of those controversies comes to them in the shape of decisions to be made, it is inevitable that they should read into their making, where they consider they justifiably can, the impact of the private philosophy they hold. Just as a good deal of American constitutional law is inexplicable except upon the basis that the Supreme Court did not like the legislation upon which it had to pass, and substituted its own view of the constitution for that of Congress or a state legislature, so the result of a good deal of statutory interpretation in this country is to be explained only upon the assumption either that the judges did not like what Parliament was doing or sought to confine the results of its activity to the narrowest possible area.[5] That is clear in some of the major trade-union decisions;[6] it is clear, also, in a good deal of the interpre-

[5] Cf. Sir F. Pollock, *Essays in Jurisprudence*, p. 85, and my note in the Report of the Committee on Ministers' Powers, (1930) Annex 5; see also the remarkable essay of Sir W. Graham Harrison, *Journal of the Society of Public Teachers of Law* (1935), pp. 9 ff., and especially pp. 35 ff.

[6] Cf. my *Studies in Law and Politics*, Chap. IX, *passim*.

tation of workmen's compensation cases, especially in the first years of legislation which departed widely from the traditional principles of the Common Law.[7] It is now unusual to admit that the decision of the majority in *R. v. Halliday* [8] was predominantly the outcome of a desire upon the part of the judges not to embarrass the action of the executive in time of war. Both the canons of statutory interpretation and the *rationes decidendi* which the judges may select are sufficiently elastic in their possibilities to leave the judges a wide margin for discretionary manœuvre. The driving force behind that manœuvre is likely, in considerable part, to depend upon the political philosophy which, consciously or unconsciously, they hold.

The tradition of the Common Law, it is important to note, has been predominantly shaped by the need to serve the wants of a business civilization founded upon a doubt of positive action by government. Acts of Parliament are scrutinized in the terms of that tradition. The "intent" of Parliament is gathered not, as the layman might naturally expect, from Hansard and such evidence as the reports of Royal Commissions. It depends upon one of three broad canons. There is the grammatical meaning of the words of the statute itself. There is the meaning of those words as they are read in the general context of the statute as a whole. There is the rule in Heydon's case [9] which instructs the judge to give heed to the defect the statute was intended to remedy. The judge may use any or all of these methods to reach his decision. He may use them in the light of past cases by the bearing of which upon any particular set of facts he has to find he may happen to be impressed. Judges may use any one of these methods in the same case, and they may differ entirely in the results they deduce from their application. They may introduce standards of behaviour upon those who come before them which, in fact, have no other source than their private sense that if Par-

---

[7] Cf. my *Studies in Law and Politics*, pp. 286–287.
[8] 1917 A.C. 260.
[9] 3 Coke Rep. 7b.

liament did not improve those standards, it ought to have done so.

That is the only rational explanation of the Taff Vale case; [10] the House of Lords thought it impossible that Parliament should have excused trade unions—despite the plain words of the statute —from liability for the tortious acts of their agents. The idea of "public policy" which runs through the Osborne case [11] hardly conceals the profound bias of the judges against the paid representation of trade unions in the House of Commons; universal payment of members was the outcome of that selective bias. *Roberts v. Hopwood* [12] means, at bottom, simply that the wages paid to the servants of a local authority shall be not, as the statute says, "such wages" as that authority "thinks fit," but such wages as the judges of the House of Lords think it reasonable to pay to working-men; though it is doubtful whether they would interfere with the salary of the County Clerk of Lancashire who, the Lord Chancellor and the Lord Chief Justice apart, is, by a curious anomaly, the highest paid public official in England.

The result of the effort is to make legislative innovation, in Professor Willis's phrase, "moulded into some accord with the old notions." The theory which lies behind a good deal of vital statutory interpretation has no meaning unless it is intended to preserve the Common Law rights of individuals against invasion by statutes which seek to change those rights. Judicial theory builds upon the assumption that, in the absence of express words, the legislature could not have intended to take away a Common Law right; on no other ground can the judgment of Lord Halsbury in *R. v. Leach*,[13] or that of Slesser L.J. in *Rowell v. Pratt*,[14] be explained. We have seen, in recent years, the discovery of a system of assumptions which have the effect of subduing plain legislative intent to a medium of which the judges approve. In the absence of express words, for example, Parliament cannot

[10] 1901 A.C. 426.
[11] 1910 A.C. 87.
[12] 1925 A.C. 578.
[13] 1912 A.C. 305.
[14] 1936 K.B. 226.

have intended to take away property without compensation; the result is to hamstring a good deal of legislation intended to deal with the grim proportions of the housing problem.[15] We are told that all legislation must, if at all possible, be so construed as to give the citizen access to the courts; and this despite the fact that a large and deliberate tendency in modern statutes is to deprive the ordinary courts of jurisdiction in favour of special tribunals. The decision of the House of Lords in *Minister of Health v. R. ex parte Jaffé* [16] is an example of this tendency; and it is illustrated again by the same tribunal's decision that the power of the Wheat Board to regulate the "final" settlement of disputes by an arbitrator did not authorize the Board to exclude a right of appeal from such a "final" settlement on questions of law. This remarkable result was reached by presuming, by reason of the absence of express words, that Parliament did not "intend" to repeal, in this instance, the Arbitration Act of 1889; [17] though what meaning the word "final" can have if this be the case, it is difficult indeed to understand.

The full examination of these tendencies would take us far afield. But it is notable that, in an age of relatively high taxation, the evasion of taxes by rich men has been upheld by the courts through a technique of interpretation which it would be polite to call sophistry; [18] the recent discussion of the House of Lords in the Duke of Westminster's case [19] is merely the high-water mark in a series in which the judges seem to take the view that tax-evasion is merely an exercise in civic casuistry in which the presumption is inevitably against the state. And all this must be read in the light of a curious tenderness towards the executive power in the type of case where challenge to the executive comes from

---

[15] Cf. W. I. Jennings's remarkable article, 49 *Harvard Law Review* (1936) 426, and that of D. Ll. J. Davies, 35 *Columbia Law Review* (1935), p. 519.

[16] 1930 2. K.B. 90 for the amazing remarks of Scrutton L.J. affirmed in 1931 A.C. 494.

[17] *R. W. Paul Ltd. v. Wheat Board* 1937 A.C. 139.

[18] Cf. Professor Willis's brilliant article, 16 *Canadian Bar Review* (1938), p. 1, and especially pp. 25 ff.

[19] 1936 A.C. 1. The incisive dissent of Lord Atkin should be noted.

extreme opinion or is conducted in an atmosphere of political emergency. In *Pasmore v. Elias*,[20] Mr. Justice Horridge, it is true rather by way of *obiter dictum* than by direct decision, so whittled away the effect of *Entick v. Carrington* [21] as to make it dubious whether that classic monument to English freedom has effective meaning any longer. Judges have done nothing to discourage the grave tendency in recent years to the prolonged masstrial arising out of social or political disturbance, in which it is at least dubious whether the jury is able, amid the confusion of numbers, either to follow the relation of the evidence to any particular defendant or to remember the bearing of the accumulation of detailed testimony upon which they are asked to pass judgment.[22] They are allowing unsworn police, in similar cases, to testify as to the opinions of the accused, even when it is patent that the testimony is itself so highly subjective as to have no point save the creation of prejudice. It is not, I think, excessive to say that the majority of contemporary judges approach the trial of a Communist in something of the same spirit as their predecessors who were responsible for the grotesque treason trials under the administration of the younger Pitt. Certainly it is a lamentable thing that a judge who can speak of communism as Lord Hewart has thought fit to do should find no difficulty in trying cases in which the executive has decided to indict the exponents of that doctrine.[23]

The point I am concerned to make is the simple one that the tendencies of the modern state run counter to the main principles upon which the Common Law has been built. The result is an effort upon the part of the judiciary to minimize the consequences of those tendencies in a way which consciously hampers the purpose of the administrator. The judges spare no pains in attacking parliamentary decisions it is not their function to criticize. They are occupied in the construction of what is hardly less than a fun-

[20] (1934) 2. K.B. 134.
[21] (1765) 19 St. Tv. 1030.
[22] Cf. my remarks in the *Manchester Guardian*, January 28, 1937.
[23] Cf. *English Justice* by "Solicitor" (1932), pp. 115 ff.

damental law which they use to confine the ambit of statutes within the limit of policies they happen to approve. The result of this process is to slow down the rate of social change—as notably in housing legislation—or more narrowly to confine the area it covers than a survey of the facts would deem to be justified. The theory upon which they proceed is that they are safeguarding the citizen against the "new despotism"—by which they appear to mean the right of Parliament to confer powers upon the civil service the issues connected with which need not necessarily be determined in an ordinary court of law. They do not appear to consider that Parliament may have had good reason for the decisions it has chosen to make. They do not appear to consider, either, that the grounds for those decisions may lie, in fact, in the very habits of the judges themselves. The whole ethos of their approach is one of hostility to the process of modern administration. They interpret the "rule of law" as though they are themselves the masters of a "higher law" than that of a sovereign legislature the consent of which they themselves determine and the particular relevance of which they themselves decide. It is at least not excessive to say that they bring to the interpretation of the modern state and its processes habits of interpretation which, at least by implication, deny the validity of many of the ends to which its power is devoted.

And they do that, moreover, in an atmosphere which makes it a dangerous adventure to embark upon the criticism of their proceedings. It was a wise remark of Bentham that when the judge had made his decision he was "given over to criticism." But the modern enlargement of the doctrine of constructive contempt—itself historically dubious—has now reached a point where the frank discussion of the habits of any particular judge is, outside Parliament, a dangerous thing.[24] The reader of *R. v. New Statesman*[25] will be tempted to wonder whether such stringent limits of public criticism would have made Bentham's great work

[24] Cf. my *Studies in Law and Politics*, Chap. X.
[25] Cf. verbatim report on 30 *New Statesman*, Feb. 18, 1928, No. 773.

possible if they had then been in force. And this is true of a judiciary which has never itself originated any vital reform of the law, despite the fact that it was the deliberate intention of Parliament that it should make proposals for its amendment. It is true of a judicial system the expense of which is, in its costs to litigants, greater than that of any other save the American; and whose hierarchy of appeal and whose centralization in London put a premium upon all issues where one of the litigants is wealthy and the other poor.[26] It is difficult, in fact, not to feel that the conflict between the premises of the Common Law and those of the modern state in its more positive aspect presages the need for a reconsideration of the whole basis of our judicial institutions.

For it is important to remember that, in England, there is no such thing as a Ministry of Justice. There is no department charged, in a coherent and continuous way, with observation of the working of legal processes and the proposal of necessary amendments. The Lord Chancellor is master of one area of the field; another is the purview of the Home Secretary; another again belongs to the province of the Attorney-General. The judges do not exercise their right to draw attention to desirable changes; and the Council of the Bar has, so far in its history, almost wholly occupied itself with problems of professional etiquette that hardly touch the bearing of the law upon the general public. Not since Bentham's time have the foundations of the British legal system been called into scrutiny. It is yet significant that every other modern state has been driven, since that period, to a thorough overhaul both of doctrines and of institutions. In England, in any comprehensive way, the reform of the law is no one's business. Yet the signs are not wanting that exactly that comprehensive reform is long overdue.

For the danger that confronts England's judicial system, so far as the High Court is concerned, is the profound one that it may find itself in conflict with purposes the legislature is deter-

[26] Cf. *English Justice*, Chap. VI.

mined to further. The result of the ignorance of, and hostility to, the trade unions of the judges of the last age brought the Labour Party into being. The ignorance of, and hostility to, modern social reform of the contemporary Bench may easily make it necessary to build in Great Britain a system of administrative tribunals to prevent it from being wrecked by judges who deny the existence of the defects it seeks to remedy and minimize the power of the efforts made to deal with them. The need is not merely for a greater elasticity in the canons of statutory interpretation; though that is not only great but mainly unrealized by the judges themselves. The need is great also for a far profounder understanding by the judges that the historic philosophy of the Common Law is in considerable part unsuited by its inherent individualism to the necessary implications of a collectivist age. The fact that the judges are both independent and incorruptible does not excuse the complacency with which they approach the wider issues of change. It is significant that every great age of social reform in this country has been one in which judicial conservatism has been a stumbling-block in the way of social progress. That was the case in 1391; it was the case, again, at the time of Jack Cade's rebellion; it was the case in the Commonwealth period; it was the case, finally, in the epoch of Bentham. It is always the mark of the advent of a revolutionary age when the ends of the legislature are at variance with those judicial doctrine is prepared to approve.

To some extent, no doubt, the reality of this problem has been obscured by the fact that, since the close of the World War, no British government has embarked upon a great programme of social reform which it has sought rapidly to implement. But there is much evidence to show that it would not easily encounter sympathy from the judges in that effort. The way in which the courts approached the application of the Trade Boards Act to the catering industry is the symptom of much that heralds danger.[27] The dubious attitude of Mr. Justice Astbury to the general strike of

[27] C.A. (1931) 1. K.B. 1.

1926—an issue which was not before him but upon which he
went out of his way to comment—shows how little the judges
have learned the lesson of the Taff Vale dispute.[28] *Roberts v.
Hopwood* [29] makes it clear that the House of Lords will have no
hesitation in imposing its own view of reasonable standards of
labour upon a progressive local authority. The activities of the
courts in connexion with housing legislation, especially in the
Jaffé case,[30] make it clear, also, that the judges prefer their view
of the claims of private property not merely to those of the legislature but also to those of a civil service the most important part
of which has no interest in the destruction of those claims. Exactly as the Supreme Court of the United States made itself,
above all in its hostility to the New Deal of President Roosevelt,
a kind of super-legislature engaged in the enunciation of political
doctrine under guise of legal procedure, so the High Court in
England is engaged in a similar task. Its opportunities, of course,
are smaller here; it cannot forthrightly annul an Act of Parliament. But it is at least willing to build up a kind of Fourteenth
Amendment in this country, and to use it as fully as it can to set
a barrier across the road of any social change which interferes
with individual rights of which it happens to approve. Latent in
this attitude is a potential conflict between courts and Parliament
of which the result would be the immersion of the judges in political controversy. They would not emerge unscathed from that
experience.

What is the root of this attitude? Above all, I think, it lies in
three things. (1) Our judges are recruited from the ranks of
successful lawyers; and, overwhelmingly, our system makes the
successful lawyer a man who has spent the major part of his life
in serving the interests of property. He comes, therefore, almost
unconsciously, to accept the assumptions of the economic system
in being, and to adopt without examination the legal doctrines

[28] Cf. Prof. Goodhart's pamphlet *The Legality of a General Strike* (1926).
[29] *Ut supra.*
[30] *Ut supra.*

evolved for the protection of those assumptions. When Parliament seeks to change them, he therefore reads into the "intent" of change a presumption that its consequences must leave legal doctrine as evolved by the courts as little altered as possible. Workmen's compensation, trade-union law, and the principles of taxation are all instances of this. The attitude of the courts to each of them is inexplicable save by the assumption that, in changing the Common Law, Parliament was going outside a realm the boundaries of which needed the firmest protection the judges could give them. (2) Partly, I think, the attitude is due to the fact that the education of the barrister (though not of the solicitor) in this country is less an intellectual discipline than a social function. It is significant that it has never occurred to those who choose the judges that a great teacher of law—a Dicey, a Pollock, or a Kenney—would be a natural occupant of the Bench; nor have the teachers of law in British universities (perhaps because of this) the consideration which attaches to their colleagues in Harvard or Paris or pre-Hitler Berlin. It is worth nothing that both legal philosophy and the study of legal administration in this country are at least a generation behind their condition in the United States or in France. Our legal profession is not learned in the sense that it is interested in the examination of foundations. There has been no significant development in English jurisprudence since Austin. There has been no attempt to organize research into the working of legal institutions comparable to efforts abroad.[31] The legal profession itself has displayed no interest in developing law comparable to that of the medical profession in developing medical science or the engineering profession in developing engineering; historically, it has been the least social-minded of all the professions.

(3) The third reason, I believe, for this attitude is more general in nature. The attitude of the courts has reflected the general

---

[31] Lord Maugham L.C. has, however, set up a committee to consider the creation of an Institute of Advanced Legal Studies. Cf. the Annual Report of the Society of Public Teachers of Law in their *Journal* for 1936, p. 58.

atmosphere in which British society has functioned this past hundred years. The Napoleonic wars and the Industrial Revolution compelled a thoroughgoing revision about the time of Bentham which synchronized with the full capture of the state-power by the middle class. Since then, there has not been any vital challenge to the system for the simple reason that it was for so long successful in its general results as to appear to be final in at least its major outlines to the main interests affected by its working. Nothing else, I think, can explain the long indifference to codification, to the tolerance of a system which has both an unnecessary hierarchy of appeal and a centralized jurisdiction which is an intolerable burden on the poor litigant. Nothing else, either, would explain the complacency with which both lawyers and politicians have continually postponed the drastic revision of the costs of law proceedings. Nothing else, again, would explain why we allow whole areas of the law, in divorce, for example, in sexual offences, in obscenity and blasphemy, in the relation between crime and mental disease, to limp haltingly behind general social opinion and scientific knowledge. The very absence, indeed, of any effective permanent machinery for the scrutiny of legal processes, the lawyer's sense that an occasional inquiry is all that is required reflect the attitude of interests which believed that they had made a final bargain with fate. But just as that bargain is destined to be reopened in the fields of economics and politics, so, clearly, law, which is in its ultimate substance dependent upon these, is certain to be profoundly reconstructed in principle. What will be of outstanding interest is to see whether the lawyer can be persuaded to co-operate in that task, or whether, as in the age of Bentham, he will remain indifferent or hostile to its undertaking.

2

In every period of social difficulty, the test of public freedom is the quality of the administration of justice. Men must have confidence that those to whom it is entrusted will be scrupulous to prevent such misuse of authority as may inhibit that freedom of expression and association upon which, ultimately, the effectiveness of parliamentary government depends. For it cannot be too often insisted that the foundation of parliamentary government is ability to respond to the free movement of opinion; and if authority becomes apt to coerce that movement into forms of which it happens to approve, the safeguard of liberty is removed. This is the more particularly the case with a system like our own in which so considerable a part of liberty of expression and association depends upon the habits of the judiciary. The possible range of offences like sedition and seditious conspiracy is so wide in Great Britain that, as Professor Dicey [32] has pointed out, their liberal interpretation would make the kind of political controversy to which we are accustomed practically impossible. "Sedition," says a classic textbook, embraces "all those practices, whether by word, deed, or writing, which fall short of high treason, but directly tend, or have for their object, to excite discontent or dissatisfaction; to excite ill-will between different classes of the King's subjects; to create public disturbance or to lead to civil war; to bring into hatred or contempt the sovereign or his government, the laws or the Constitution of the realm, and generally all endeavours to promote public disorder." [33] Obviously, definitions so vague and wide as these may easily become fatal to public freedom in the hands of a reactionary government unless they are applied with scrupulous care by the judges upon whom their validity depends.

For the most part, since the war of 1914–18, the problems to which these issues have given rise have touched rather the police, the Home Office, and the courts of minor jurisdiction than the High Court itself. In these realms, the evidence makes it clear that there is very considerable ground for dissatisfaction. The

[32] *Law of the Constitution*, p. 240.
[33] Russell on Crimes (9 ed.) 1. 87; cf. Archbold, *Criminal Procedure* (30 ed.) p. 1128.

impartiality of the police has been questioned in case after case where there is not merely no fragment of counterproof, but where, also, as in the notorious Urquhart case,[34] the authorities have denied the alleged bias until it was impossible to do so with hope of success. Almost invariably, also, the Home Secretary has supported the police and refused a public inquiry even where, as in the Thurloe Square case,[35] it is evident that his decision has been wholly built upon the partial testimony of the police themselves. The justices of the peace have constantly shown a tendency to accept unconfirmed police evidence to a degree that has gravely undermined at any rate the confidence of the working-class in the proceedings over which they preside.[36] The extent, particularly, to which, with magisterial sanction, the offence of using "insulting words or behaviour" has been extended by the police to secure the suppression of activities from the Left is ominous. Interference with processions and meetings which were otherwise wholly peaceful has been growingly characteristic of the past ten or fifteen years. It is hardly, I think, an exaggeration to say that the famous principle of *Beatty v. Gillbanks* [37] has become practically a dead letter in the minor courts of law whenever either the unemployed or the Communists have been concerned.

The costs of litigation have made appeal from magisterial decisions in these cases a luxury hardly open to the majority of those involved. It has therefore been infrequent for the High Court to act upon those decisions by way of appeal. But, in so far as it has been put to the test, it can hardly be said to offer reassurance by the care with which it examines the issue. After the notorious Fascist meeting at Olympia in 1934, where many people suffered from the brutality of its promoters, complaints were

---

[34] Cf. the account of this case in W. H. Thompson, *Civil Liberties*, pp. 60 ff.

[35] Cf. the special report of the National Council of Civil Liberties on this case.

[36] Cf. the comments of "Solicitor," *op. cit.*, p. ix and *passim*; and Charles Muir, *Justice in a Depressed Area* (1936), especially Chap. I.

[37] (1882) 9 Q.B.D. 308.

made that the police did not interfere. The Home Secretary explained that "the law provides that unless the promoters of a meeting ask the police to be present in the actual meeting they cannot go in unless they have reason to believe that an actual breach of the peace is being committed." [38] The defence of the police action is striking, for the violence at Olympia seems to have been known to everyone save the police who were on duty outside and saw the constant procession of the wounded being brought out from the building. Three months later, a meeting was held in South Wales to protest against the Incitement to Disaffection Bill. Despite the protests of the chairman, the police insisted on entering the meeting, and resisted removal. The police sergeant was summoned for assault, of which, if the Home Secretary was right, he was plainly guilty. The magistrates dismissed the summons on the ground that the police were entitled to enter any meeting if they had reason to believe that, in their absence, there might be either seditious utterance or a breach of the peace. On appeal to the High Court, the Lord Chief Justice upheld the decision of the magistrates.[39] A principle of law, this is to say, that was unknown to the Home Secretary's legal advisers in June 1934 is enunciated without doubt by the High Court in August of the same year. It is impossible not to note that the speakers at the first meeting were Fascists, while the chairman and chief speaker at the South Wales meeting were Communists. *Thomas v. Sawkins* may be, as one writer puts it, "an instance where the court applied well-known principles to new combinations of facts." It is difficult not to be impressed by the context in which the application was made. The "reasonable apprehension" of the police is curiously selective in its operation; what is certain appears to be that the High Court, as at present minded, will have no difficulty in applying "well-known principles" to those selected issues they have to determine.

I have already referred to *Pasmore v. Elias,* in which Mr. Jus-

---

[38] Letter of June 14, 1934. Cf. Thompson, op. cit.
[39] *Thomas v. Sawkins* (1935), 2. K.B. 249.

tice Horridge deliberately mitigated the rigours of *Entick v. Carrington*.[40] It is important to realize the effect of his judgment. There is no doubt, it should be premised, of the illegality of police action in the case, for damages were awarded against them. But Mr. Justice Horridge also held that "the interests of state excuse the seizure, otherwise unlawful, of documents or articles in the possession or control of the person arrested if subsequently it should appear in fact that they are evidence of a crime committed by anyone." [41] This is, in effect, to legalize the general warrant. It would permit the police, once they can offer ground for the arrest of any person, to search the premises of the organization with which he is connected in the hope of finding evidence not necessarily affecting him, but of a nature liable to incriminate others against whom they have no charges to make. In any time of public excitement it is clear that so wide a power puts anybody whose activities the police may find inconvenient at their mercy.

It is important to read the attitude implied in these decisions in the context of the growing body of repressive legislation which has been put upon the statute-book since 1919. The Emergency Powers Act of 1920 enables the government, subject to parliamentary confirmation, to make such regulations as it thinks necessary if it appears that any body of persons is likely to take action which will interfere with the distribution of food, water, fuel, light, or the means of locomotion or to deprive the community of the essentials of life. The use of those powers during the general strike of 1926 led to imprisonment of men who stated that "the government is out to crush the workers." [42] The Trades Disputes Act of 1927 has probably made illegal any widespread sympathetic strike, and it has so extended the definition of intimidation that a man has been sent to prison for the ironical gesture of raising his hat to a blackleg.[43] The importance of the act lies not

---

[40] *Ut supra.*
[41] *Pasmore v. Elias, ut supra.*
[42] Thompson, op. cit., p. 15.
[43] Ibid.

merely in the width of its provisions; it lies, above all, in the fact that it will be applied, in periods of public excitement, by judges of whom Sir Walter Citrine has said that "with the experience of the past . . . the trade-union movement has little faith in either the competence or the impartiality of the courts in matters affecting organized labour.[44] Nor does Sir Walter Citrine stand alone in this view. Mr. Winston Churchill has said the same thing; [45] so eminent a legal scholar as the late Professor Geldart has insisted upon this thesis with great emphasis; [46] and an ex-Attorney General of England has said that the courts. are prejudiced in labour cases. It is difficult not to feel that, if the Trades Disputes Act of 1927 is invoked, it will do more than any other statute of recent times to undermine confidence in the *bona fides* of the judiciary.

To these two dangerous acts, two others must be added. The necessity for the Incitement to Disaffection Act of 1934 has never been clearly explained. The offences with which it deals were already amply covered by existing legislation. Many of its provisions are so widely and ambiguously drawn that it appears possible to bring within its ambit any speech the pacifist tendency of which might have the result of making a soldier doubt the validity of his calling; certainly I think that the distribution of Peace Pledge Union leaflets to members of the armed forces would bring the distributor within the terms of the statute.[47] The one important case so far brought under its auspices is *R. v. Phillips*,[48] in which a lad of eighteen was sentenced to twelve months' imprisonment by Mr. Justice Singleton for some wild and irresponsible advice to a soldier; the contrast between this sentence and the six months imposed upon Mr. Tom Mann for the famous "Don't Shoot" leaflet of 1912 (Mr. Mann was released after seven weeks' imprisonment) is striking. Not less

[44] *London Times*, May 7, 1927.
[45] 26 Hansard (5 series, 1911), 1022.
[46] *The Present Law of Trade Disputes* (1914), p. 44.
[47] W. I. Jennings, *The Sedition Act Explained* (1935).
[48] See the *London Times* March 10 and March 15, 1937.

drastic in its potentialities is the Uniforms Act of 1936.[49] Most responsible observers will agree that the clauses in the statute which forbade the adoption of uniforms by political bodies were (in the light of continental experiences) salutary. But advantage was taken of the general approval of this prohibition immensely to extend the powers of the police. A wider meaning is given to the offence of "insulting words and behaviour." The Chief of Police may control the route and conduct of any procession about which he has "reasonable ground for apprehending" the possibility of disorder. With the assent of the local authority and the Home Office, he may impose an order banning all processions within the whole, or part, of the area within his jurisdiction for a period not exceeding three months; and the ban may, of course, be renewed. The result is that because Fascist processions have been attended with disorder in the East End of London, Socialist processions, which have been peaceful, have been banned also. Normal political propaganda is thus penalized at the expense of abnormal. The policy, as Mr. W. H. Thompson has remarked,[50] "appears to be equivalent to the prevention of the blowing of all motor-horns because some people blow them unnecessarily."

The cumulative effect of the habits of the post-war epoch in matters concerning public liberty bears an unhappy resemblance to the atmosphere in the period between the end of the Napoleonic wars and the Reform Bill of 1832. In each case there was serious industrial dislocation, and panic among the governing class as its outcome. In each case, the panic led to repressive legislation which was used to limit the right of peaceful political activity to make its impact upon public opinion. In each case, also, the sense of alarm communicated itself to the judiciary which, both in the High Court and in petty sessions, distinguished itself by the severity of its sentences and its tendency to assume that Left Wing agitation was a *malum in se.* In each case, also,

---

[49] 1 Ed. VIII and 1 Geo. VI. c. 6.
[50] *Civil Liberties* (London, 1938), p. 37.

the result of all this has been to undermine the public sense of confidence in the impartiality of the courts. How important is that sense of confidence it is unnecessary to emphasize; upon it rests the ability of the government to rule with the consent of the governed. "Lack of confidence in the administration of justice," an experienced observer has written,[51] "is rapidly growing." That it should have been necessary to set up a National Council of Civil Liberties, and that this body should have found itself fully occupied since its creation, this, after all, is a serious matter in a time when the very difficulties of the age make that confidence a safeguard of peace. The sense grows among the masses that the administration of the law is a weapon in the hands of one class for the repression of the other. "The worker," says one careful observer,[52] "leaves the Court . . . convinced that the Courts are merely a means by which the governing classes grind down working-men." That is a temper which implies grave possibilities. There is too little evidence that a willingness exists to deal with its implications.

3

The greatest of modern American judges has expressed his concern at the tendency of the courts to read into statutes "acceptance of the economic doctrines which prevailed about fifty years ago and a wholesale prohibition of what a tribunal of lawyers does not think about right." [53] The warning is not less needed with ourselves than with the United States. Our judges need to remember, not less than their American brethren, that legal stability depends upon the power to look backwards for certainty, but also forwards for necessary adaptation. They need, not less, to guard themselves against the danger of substituting for the will of Parliament those social and economic doctrines

[51] *English Justice* (2nd ed., 1932) by "Solicitor," p. ix.
[52] Charles Muir, *Justice in a Depressed Area* (1936), p. 27.
[53] Oliver Wendell Holmes, *Collected Legal Papers* (1921), p. 295.

of which they happen to approve. They have to guard against the danger of equating opinions to which they are not accustomed with a threat to the foundations of order. They have to learn that the way to deal with grievance is not by the repression of its incidents, but by the remedy of its cause. They must refuse to believe, as Mr. Lansbury, then leader of the Opposition, warned the Home Secretary in 1933,[54] "the proposition that a government which has to put into force repressive measures is the best judge of what constitutes an infringement of the right of freedom of speech and the right of lawful public meeting."

Every period of rapid social change confronts the danger that its legal habits may not keep pace with the political decisions it has to interpret. That is a danger to which our judiciary is particularly susceptible simply because its methods of interpretation are built predominantly upon a philosophy those political decisions may easily seek to reverse. A judiciary which by this means sought to obstruct, even unconsciously, the programme of a socialist government would open the door to a challenge which might easily threaten the position of independence it has won. Its safety depends upon its ability to persuade not merely the rich but also the poor that it is capable of transcending those "inarticulate major premises" which are written so deeply into the fabric of the Common Law. To be capable of that transcendence, it has to be alert—as it is not now alert—to its failures as well as to its achievements. Overwhelmingly, it has to remember, its ranks are recruited from the upper strata of society; it thinks as it lives. Overwhelmingly, also, it is separated in experience and outlook from the great mass of those upon whose problems it decides. The principles it imposes are largely principles intended to protect a social constitution the foundations of which are challenged; it cannot but be dangerous if, under cover of

---

[54] Letters of January 10, 1933. The occasion was the refusal of Mr. Tom Mann and Mr. Emrys Llewellyn to find sureties against disorderly conduct at a meeting of which they were sponsors. Both were imprisoned for refusing to do so, though no charge had been brought against them.

reverence for the past, it alines its authority unmistakably with those who are defending those foundations. For so to do would, in the circumstances I have described, inevitably appear as a defiance of popular will. Over a period, at any rate, no judiciary can afford the luxury of such a defiance.

This is not, I should add, to speak in alarmist terms. No one who knows the working-class of Great Britain can help being aware that they do not share the confidence of the governing class in either the adequacy or the impartiality of our legal institutions. They are only too conscious that, in large areas of the law, it applies with grim inequality as between rich and poor. They are only too conscious, also, of the difficulty with which their own institutions of economic defence have won their right to recognition from the courts. They know how the hierarchy of appeals works to their disadvantage. They are aware of the pompous humbug that is talked of the poor man's rules.[55] They have little of the confidence in the police which is the faith of their betters, especially in the distressed areas. They have long memories; and the sentences inflicted in the Haworth cases in this generation are not unlikely to do for this century what Tolpuddle did for the last. They see judges and magistrates appointed for no better reason than birth or wealth or service to a political party. They see long-needed reforms postponed, or, when passed, so truncated as to be deprived of half their point. They know how inadequate is magistrates' justice, how profoundly the predominant atmosphere of the police-court is resented by the common man. It is a prediction that may be made with confidence that if ever the judiciary sets itself in antagonism to a progressive government in this country it will arouse a storm of accumulated grievance.

Largely, moreover, it will have brought that storm upon itself. It has had the opportunity to engage in the task of reform; it has never seriously bent its energies to that task. Even in so relatively unimportant a sphere as legal education, most of the

[55] Cf. Muir, op. cit., pp. 138–139, and "Solicitor," op. cit., pp. 213–214, 241.

changes under discussion were urged upon the profession seventy years ago by Lord Westbury.[56] True as it is that British judges stand high for both independence and integrity—and these are great qualities—they do not exhaust the needs of the situation. The right kind of judge is statesman not less than lawyer. He sees the problems he has to confront in the perspective of their political consequence. He realizes that he must not equate his private social philosophy with the implied purpose of legislation. Legal technique as such reaches but a little way in the matters with which we are here concerned. To be, in Blackstone's phrase, the "living oracle of the law," is not enough; he must strive to be the living oracle of a living law. And a living law must look always to the defects which the law can assist in remedying. A search for the *ratio decidendi* is something more than a discovery of an appropriate precedent; it is also a determination of the path along which that precedent is to move. He as judge is to move it; and he cannot move it rightly unless the path he chooses is one that is socially adequate. That, I think, is what Mr. Justice Holmes meant when he said that the life of the law has not been logic but experience.[57]

But in the acceptance of that famous phrase, it is relevant to inquire whose experience is involved. Law is not merely an historical growth, finding its roots always in its own past. It is also a purposive growth whose frame is deliberately altered to serve new needs. The fulfilment of those needs may be settled by men whose experience contradicts the judicial view of what is safe or wise or right. The danger of our British system is that it has led the Bench too often to deny the validity of that contradiction; judicial subjectivity of that kind is the gravest disservice a man can render to the judge's function. To misinterpret the effective mind of his generation is to risk always the confidence of men in the relation of law to justice. There is no passionless and objective law for the judge to impose. Marshall's famous "the

---

[56] Hansard, March 1, 1854.
[57] *The Common Law* (1881), p. 1.

judicial department has no will in any case . . . judicial power is never exercised for the purpose of giving effect to the will of the judge; always for the purpose of giving effect to the will of the legislature; or, in other words, to the will of the law" [58] is a noble myth, but it is still a myth. The judge, even despite himself, cannot but be legislator. His duty is to remember that, as President Theodore Roosevelt said, "every time they [the judges] interpret contract, property, vested rights, due process of law, liberty, they necessarily enact into law parts of a system of social philosophy. . . . The decisions of the courts on economic and social questions depend upon their economic and social philosophy; and for the peaceful progress of our people during the twentieth century, we shall owe most to those judges who hold to a twentieth-century economic and social philosophy, and not to a long-outgrown philosophy which was itself the product of primitive economic conditions." [59]

The call of our time seems likely to be for the enlargement of an old body of legal doctrine with new faith and new principles. That is never an easy task for a judiciary like ours. The influences which have shaped the new faith are alien from those to which they have become accustomed; the logic upon which it is built is opposed to time-honoured formulæ upon which they have relied. The answer to their difficulty is the supreme answer that the successful infusion of the old with the new is likely, as Theodore Roosevelt saw, to be the effective condition of social peace. A judge who rejects, therefore, the call to this attempt is denying the condition upon which his heritage may be preserved.

[58] *Osborne v. Bank of U. S.*, 8 Wheat, 738, 866.
[59] Message of Dec. 8, 1908, 43 *Congressional Record*, Part I, p. 21.

CHAPTER EIGHT

The Monarchy

1

THE metaphysics of limited monarchy does not easily lend itself to critical discussion. On no element in the constitution is our knowledge so inexact; effective documentation upon its functioning ends with the death of Queen Victoria nearly forty years ago. We have no adequate account of the relations between the King and his ministers. We know little of the way in which the officials of the Palace are chosen, or the manner in which their contacts with ministers are organized. We know still less—even after the abdication of Edward VIII—of the important connexions between the Palace and the press. The Court Circular tells us something of the official doings of the Palace day by day; but it gives us, very deliberately, no real insight into the methods by which royal opinion is formed. How scrupulous is the organized silence which surrounds royal activity was shown by the ignorance of the public of King Edward's relations with Mrs. Simpson until the affair reached its remarkable conclusion. Though those relations had been discussed by the whole world for months, no British newspaper referred to them until the third of December 1936; eight days later, Edward VIII signed the Act of Abdication.

It is well known that there has been a vital change in public opinion about the institution of monarchy during the past sixty years. For the first forty years of Queen Victoria's reign, criticism was both vocal and incisive. Men of great eminence in public life, Joseph Chamberlain, for instance, and Sir Charles Dilke, were not afraid to avow their sympathy for republicanism; and the unpopularity of the monarchy had gone so far that the Prince of Wales (Edward VII) was hissed in the streets, and ministers were gravely alarmed by the intensity of public criticism. Since about 1878, there has been no serious republican sentiment in Great Britain and—apart from the brief days of the abdication crisis of 1936—hardly any criticism at all of the institution. It has not merely been taken for granted; eulogy of its habits has reached a level of intensity more comparable with the religious ecstasy of the seventeenth century, when men could still believe in the divine right of kings, than of the scientific temper of the twentieth, which has seen three great imperial houses broken and the King of Spain transformed into a homeless wanderer. Some of the tributes devoted to the person of the monarch since the war would certainly have been more suited to the description of a demi-god than to the actual occupants of the throne in the past sixty years.

What have been the causes of this change? The explanation is inevitably a complicated one. Something, no doubt, is due to the respectability conferred upon the throne by the long devotion of Victoria; after the seventies the nation took pride in her as a kind of national monument. Something, also, was added by the *bonhomie* of Edward VII and his association, especially after he came to the throne, with some of the characteristic pleasures of his people. I think it probable, too, that his unaffected liking for the French was deeply appreciated at a time when his personal antagonism to the Kaiser seemed to symbolize the growing rift between the British and German peoples. Devotion to George V had deeper psychological roots. Quite obviously, especially after broadcasting had given him direct personal contact with millions of his subjects, he was regarded, in a special sense, as the "father of his peoples." He was known to be devoted to his work. He was associated with the nation's victory in the war. It was widely felt that he had steered his way fairly through very difficult political circumstances. His successor ascended the throne with a ready-made popularity which, perhaps, no other monarch in English history has previously enjoyed. To the outside world, at least, he was "Prince Charming"; and, until the very threshold of his abdication, every known gesture he chose to make was applauded with almost hysterical enthusiasm.

What, I think, is notable in this development is less the evolution of this popularity than the case with which its concentration upon a person was broken, in 1936, in the week of the abdication. This suggests that, when everything is said that can be said for the personal qualities of the last five monarchs, they do not explain the change from the attitude before 1878. And even while much is to be explained by a theory like that of Dr. Ernest Jones, which roughly suggests a father-fixation upon the person of the monarch, that applies, also, if in less degree, to the great political leaders of the same period and is even more true of the kind of enthusiasm aroused among their followers by Mussolini, Hitler, and Stalin. Now what is notable in that enthusiasm is the ease with which it can be dissipated. The ruler has only to fall, and there are few so poor as to do him reverence. It therefore appears reasonable to assume that there are two essential reasons for the change. The first is the fact of traditional reverence for the highest position in the state—a reverence which only very special circumstances are able to dissipate. History has made kings almost magical in their impact upon their subjects; most men approach them upon their knees. Granted only a reasonable level of conduct, it is highly unlikely that their conduct will be subject to anything remotely like the scrutiny ordinary men's behaviour must undergo.

But what is, I suspect, of special significance in the change is the date at which it has occurred and the propaganda which has accompanied it since that time. Roughly, the popularity of Queen Victoria dates from her proclamation as Empress of India. It is associated, that is, with the dawning consciousness of an imperial mission in the British people. Since then, it has served two purposes. It has been valuable as a pivot of loyalty for the dominions and colonies; it has made possible a unity of allegiance which would have been far more difficult to secure for the rarely magical personality of an elected President. I do not need to dwell upon the extraordinarily effective propaganda which has been devoted to this end. Ceremonial, pageantry, all the resources of the press, the radio, literature have been lavished upon its production. Whatever may have been the differences between political parties, upon the fact that the Crown is an essential element in imperial unity they have all been agreed. The degree to which this aspect has been important is very great. British imperialism has deliberately elevated the prestige of the Crown as a method of protecting the ends it seeks to serve.

On the domestic side there has been an analogous development. No one can say of the Victorian monarchy that, housing, perhaps, apart, it displayed any serious interest in questions affecting the well-being of the people. Foreign affairs, the Empire, the Church, and the problems of the defence forces were overwhelmingly the Queen's main preoccupations. With the advent of Edward VII, there came a significant, and with that of George V, a striking change. No doubt the changed mental climate of their period is to some extent responsible for this. But no one who looks at the direction of royal interests in this period and compares them with those of the Victorian epoch can, I think, doubt that a conscious effort has been made, again remarkably intensified by adroit propaganda, to associate the royal family with solicitude for those objects upon which working-class interest is bound to concentrate. One prince is specialized to housing; another devotes his attention to industrial welfare; hospitals, the boy scouts, homes for aged miners, the retraining of the unemployed, the value of the settlement movement, all receive their due meed of attention. And since every item of royal activity is blazoned forth by every device that modern publicity can utilize, there is an awareness of this activity different in quality from anything the Victorians knew. The monarchy, to put it bluntly, has been sold to the democracy as the symbol of itself; and so nearly universal has been the chorus of eulogy which has accompanied the process of sale that the rare voices of dissent have hardly been heard. It is not without significance that the official daily newspaper of the Trades Union Congress devotes more space, of news and pictures, to the royal family than does any of its rivals.

Another element of importance must be noted. The Victorian age was still largely an age of aristocracy, in which wealth, of itself, was not a passport to social distinction. With what Mr. Wells has happily termed the "period of generous morality" which supervened on the accession of Edward VII, aristocratic authority in social affairs was largely replaced by plutocratic power. The immense increase in the peerage, the marriage of the aristocracy to business enterprise in general, and to finance in particular, the growing transfer of leadership in the political parties to men of non-aristocratic origin, all these have tended greatly to enhance the social prestige of the royal family. Its patronage has been sought to an extent previously unknown, and this has made it extraordinarily influential in the realm of charitable effort. In this aspect, it is not untrue to say that the royal family is a representative symbol of the nation in a far higher degree than was the case fifty, or even thirty, years ago. It has become, too, far less aloof in public ceremonial than was the case under either Queen Victoria or Edward VII, with the result that a far greater number of persons feel a definite sense of personal connexion with the throne than in the past. Nor is it unimportant that the Crown as the fountain of honour has played more freely in the past generation than at any period in its history; and this has given a sense of its democratization which has had a far-reaching effect. Queen Victoria could refuse a Privy Councillorship to John Bright on the ground that she knew of no public service on his part deserving of so signal an honour; at the time of his jubilee, her grandson gladly acquiesced in the conference of a knighthood of the Order of the British Empire upon the Secretary of the Trades Union Congress. Perhaps nothing so much marks the change in the prestige of the throne than the fact that, despite all the past traditions of the party, the leaders of the first two Labour governments found no difficulty in playing their full part in the ceremonial of the Court. It is even probable that their enjoyment of its splendour far outdistanced the indignation of some of their supporters at their acquiescence.

The restoration of the monarchy's popularity is, on any showing, a remarkable achievement. We must not, indeed, assume that it goes deeper than it does. Very largely, it has been dependent upon the fact that, for the general public at least, it has been politically neutral in character; here, certainly, the debt it owes, particularly under Victoria, to ministers who have enshrouded its occasional vagaries in silence is a heavy one. It is also important that it has so far been consistently successful in war; continental experience makes it at least doubtful whether a dynasty can endure defeat on the battlefield. It is important, also, that the performance of its political functions has not, so far, led it into that difficult area of crisis where the validity of its action is fiercely debated by contending parties. Anyone who saw how nearly, in the week of the abdication of 1936, the nation became divided into "Cavaliers" and "Roundheads" will recognize that the prestige of the Crown is pretty completely a function of that habit of neutrality which is the official Whig legacy of the post-Georgian period. Were that debate to be reopened, it is at least improbable that its authority would remain unimpaired.

It must be noted, too, that the democratic contacts of the throne are in any case superficial, and reach but a little way. The Cabinet apart, practically all those who advise the King are in or about the plutocracy. All its intimate social contacts are of the same kind. The King's knowledge of any life beyond that to which his official dignity entitles him is, at best, remote and second-hand; he cannot have either the experience of the transition from "log cabin to White House" or the constancy of intercourse with all sorts and conditions of men which is the special prerogative of the President of the United States. He is rarely educated for his task in any adequate way; at best, he has that kind of training which marks in this country what we call so curiously a "man of the world." From earliest childhood, members of the royal family are brought up in a highly artificial atmosphere. There is composed for them a kind of public personality, escape from which must be an extraordinarily difficult art. They live constantly in an environment of snobbery and adulation. Their most commonplace utterance is magnified into the quintessence of wisdom. Anyone who reads the *Diaries* of Lord Esher will find it hard to understand how a man of his obvious capacity could live for some forty years in a state of constant genuflexion. It is not insignificant that every occupant of the throne has been, since George III, consistently conservative and imperialist in private opinion. Granted the environment in which he lives, it is difficult to see how it could be otherwise.

Thus far, beyond doubt, the system of limited monarchy has been an unquestionable success in Great Britain. It has, so far, trodden its way with remarkable skill amid the changing habits of the times. Its success, no doubt, has been the outcome of the fact that it has exchanged power for influence; the blame for errors in policy has been laid at the door of ministers, who have paid the penalty by loss of office. An active King, whose opinions were a matter of public concern, is unthinkable within the framework of the British constitution. Even as it is, the system has worked only because political parties have been so largely at one upon matters of fundamental importance. It is, indeed, difficult to imagine what would have happened in Great Britain if, at any of the major crises of the past fifty years, one of the parties had deliberately invoked the support of the Crown against its rival. There have been moments when we have, as we shall see, approached that situation; in 1910–11 over the House of Lords, in 1913–14 over Ulster, perhaps, also (though here we have no certain knowledge), in 1931. Thus far, happily, there has been no such appeal to royal authority in any final way; its part, and its proper part, has been that of a dignified emollient rather than of an active umpire between conflicting interests. That this has been the real source of its growth in influence no one acquainted with the documents will be inclined to deny. A "patriot" King, whatever the character of his opinions, is incompatible with parliamentary democracy in its British form.

2

The King must act upon the advice of his ministers; that is the central theme in the metaphysics of our monarchical system. But it is a postulate from which the most divergent conclusions can be drawn. Does it mean, as Bagehot made it mean, that his authority is limited to "advice, encouragement and warning"? Is he to say his say, to secure, no doubt, an ample consideration for his say, but, that achieved, to accept whatever advice may be offered to him? Is there a reserve of prerogative the exercise of which is in his personal discretion? If so, what are its limits and by whom are they defined? Can he dismiss ministers? Can he refuse a dissolution? Does it still remain within his power to veto a bill which has passed both Houses of Parliament? Is there a difference between the normal functioning of the constitution and an emergency situation, so that in the latter, if needs must be, he should act as that "guardian of the constitution" which Professor Keith evidently believes [1] to be central to the function he now performs? And if this view is correct, how do we define the "normal" working of the constitution? To whom is the definition of an emergency entrusted? Merely to frame these questions is to show how deep in the foundations of the constitution the monarchy lies. We can only attempt to answer them, and to measure the import of our answers, by scrutinizing with care the evidence that now lies at our disposal.

One thing, at the outset, is certain. The famous picture of

[1] Op. cit., Chap. VIII.

the Victorian monarchy drawn by Bagehot seventy years ago is, in the face of the *Letters* of Queen Victoria, no longer a tenable portrait. So far from being, as he imagined, a passive instrument in the hands of her ministers, she was an active and insistent agent in the conduct of government. It is true, and it is important, that she never either refused a dissolution or vetoed a bill. But she played a considerable part in the choice of her ministers; she secured the appointment of some, and prevented the appointment of others. She had no hesitation in forcing her views upon every aspect both of domestic and of foreign policy; the degree to which she made her ministers' lives a burden by her excessive insistences is well borne out by the correspondence of Mr. Gladstone. Against the latter, after 1874, she intrigued incessantly; and her letters to Disraeli, Salisbury, and Lord Wolseley show that she did not shrink from overstepping the elementary decencies of her constitutional position. She interfered constantly in Church appointments, partly by reason of her own strong views, but partly, also, upon the basis of advice given to her by her private and self-chosen ecclesiastical advisers. She had her own views on foreign affairs; and she tried to settle difficult questions of policy behind the backs of the Cabinet. She sought, not seldom successfully, to obtain knowledge of the individual opinions of Cabinet ministers, in the hope of playing off one section against another. She was a consistent obstacle to army reform; and two of the least successful acts of her reign, the Royal Titles Act and the Public Worship Regulation Act, were due to her personal initiative. Movements of the army and the fleet can both be traced to her own responsibility. She sought to control what her ministers should say in their speeches, and to have them rebuked when what they said was not to her liking. She pressed strongly upon Goschen and Forster their obligation to assist in the formation of what became the Liberal-Unionist Party. Those courtiers, of whom Bagehot spoke, who were "agreed as to the magnitude of the royal influence" and supported "the doctrine that the Crown does more than it seems," have ample evidence to support the view his brilliant analysis was intended to refute.

We are able, by the publication of her correspondence, to see Victoria, as it were, working day by day at her task. For Edward VII, we have no such documentation. It is important that Lord Esher, than whom no one save, perhaps, Lord Knollys was better qualified to judge, wrote of his influence, as compared with that of Victoria, that it was "if anything . . . greater and more openly acknowledged." [2] Certainly the material we have points in that direction. He was powerful in influencing appointments. He was a controlling factor in the complicated manœuvres for army and naval reform. He put strong pressure on the Cabinet about his views on the government of India. He was, through Lord Esher, in constant contact both with the leaders of the Opposition to the Liberal government of 1905 and with men like Lord Roberts who opposed bitterly certain aspects of their policy. It is significant that when Asquith, Grey, and Haldane formed their tripartite, but unsuccessful, agreement not to take office unless Sir Henry Campbell-Bannerman retired to the House of Lords, they used King Edward as a medium through which to bring pressure upon their leader. He is kept secretly informed, during the rule of the Liberal government, of the private views of Opposition leaders upon its policy. Through men like Sir Ernest Cassel he has confidential reports upon the state of international opinion. He hears, again through Lord Esher, of private divisions within the ranks of the Cabinet. He causes difficulties with Haldane through the presence about him of the former's "military enemies." [3] He expresses his dislike of Mr. Lloyd George's speeches by refusing to give him hospitality—a differentiation from other ministers which the quidnuncs were quick to note. He has, with difficulty, to be stopped from writing "very tartly" to

[2] Esher, *Journals and Letters*, ii, 107, letter to Lord Knollys, Sept. 2, 1905.
[3] Ibid., ii, 267.

the German Emperor.[4] He decides, after being assured that Mr. Balfour will take office if ministers resign, that he will not agree to create peers to pass the Budget of 1909; and this after the first general election of 1910 had given the government a majority on that specific issue.[5] He uses Lord Esher to try and detach Lord Morley from the rest of his colleagues over the problem of the House of Lords; "It would," Lord Esher told Morley, "be a lamentable outcome of Lord Morley's long training and experience in statesmanship if he were to lend his name and authority to a policy of menace to the Crown and of parliamentary corruption." [6] He uses the Archbishop of Canterbury as a medium of communication with the Opposition and obtains from Mr. Balfour the assurance that he "would come to the King's assistance if His Majesty refused the 'advice' of his present ministers to dissolve Parliament." [7]

Any careful scrutiny of the materials upon which this summary is based makes certain things clear. The King's strong Conservative convictions are apparent throughout. He is for a forward defence policy; he is strongly anti-German; he does his best to prevent Lord Morley from appointing an Indian member of the Secretary of State's Council; he dislikes the radical speeches of Mr. Lloyd George. He interferes in all major appointments in the army and navy. Though, formally, he takes no advice save with the consent of ministers, he is careful throughout the reign to be in constant if informal touch with leaders of the Opposition, and expressions of their views and probable course of action are communicated to him. He constantly uses *éminences grises*, like Lord Esher, to bring individual pressure to bear upon Cabinet ministers whose views are not in accord with his own. That the Cabinet often yielded to his insistence is obvious. But what emerges still

---

[4] Esher, ii, 289.
[5] Ibid., ii, 442, letter of Jan. 25, 1910. The latter was written immediately after a talk with the King.
[6] Ibid., ii, 454–455.
[7] Ibid., ii, 459.

more from the record is the degree of what may be termed prenatal control that is inherent in his position. Ministers obviously refrain from putting forward proposals that are likely to cause difficulty with him. They feel keenly the burden of argument discussion with him entails. They are conscious that what they must put forward is less the view they think right than the view that will enable them to handle him most easily. He is a great stickler for the minutiæ of etiquette which surround his position. There flows in to him a constant series of reports which are made the basis of discussion with ministers. His slightest expression of opinion is received and weighed with immense solemnity. One has no impression of an easy give-and-take in the relations he establishes; even the court favourite, Lord Esher, deals with him in an attitude like that of an eighteenth-century sycophant who fears the withdrawal of the royal smile. It may be, of course, that this impression will be altered when we have, for his reign, a correspondence of similar character to that of Queen Victoria. But, quite certainly, nothing which has so far emerged suggests that Edward VII was a passive instrument in the hands of his ministers. He never overstepped the bounds of constitutional propriety in anything like the ruthless fashion of Queen Victoria. But there is no mistaking the side upon which his influence was thrown.

Naturally enough, our knowledge of the intimate history of George V's reign is even smaller than that of his predecessor; and, save for exceptional circumstances, it is not likely that the essential documents will see the light in the lifetime of the present generation. There are, however, certain problems in his reign upon which at least an oblique light has been cast by biographies and memoirs already available. He came to the throne in the midst of the crisis over the House of Lords, and it is at least probable that the second dissolution of 1910 was due to his unwillingness to agree to a creation of peers to prevent the rejection of the Parliament Act without proof that the country was definitively on the side of the government. There are certain grave problems about his relation to the Ulster crisis of 1913–14 which remain unexplained. It seems probable that he was in touch with the Conservative leaders over the question of Sir Edward Carson's possible arrest for treasonable activities; and we know from the Diaries of Sir Austen Chamberlain [8] that steps were taken by them to communicate their views over the Curragh mutiny of March 1914. It was in this particular controversy that the army officers developed their view that they owed their allegiance, not to the government in office, but to the King personally; a view of which the immense consequences to the civil power are obvious. It was in this controversy, also, that Lord Milner, then a leading figure in the Conservative Party, expressed the view that if "any officers resigned, they would be reinstated when the Conservatives came back to power." [9] It must be added that we know little of the King's views upon the moves and countermoves connected with these grave events. We know only that he had been made aware of the Unionist position; and it is, I think, permissible to assume that he was not backward in pressing its implications upon the government.

Upon the crisis of 1931 there exists little documentation; and the wide divergences of opinion about the King's action during its progress make it difficult to pronounce any opinion upon it with certitude. Certain things, at least, appear to be established. The idea of a coalition government had been mooted in Palace circles for many months before its actual inception; and Mr. Ramsay MacDonald is believed to have been favourable to the idea. Certainly he hinted to colleagues, at least as early as March 1931, that he proposed to embark upon a drastic reconstruction of his government. It is certain that he did not confide the nature of this reconstruction to any of the colleagues who separated from him in 1931. It is certain, also, that none of these supposed, when he went to Buckingham Palace to resign as head of the Labour Cabinet, that he would return almost immediately a

[8] *Politics from Within.*
[9] *Diaries of Sir Henry Wilson,* i, 132.

head of a National Government with the leaders of the Liberal and Conservative Parties serving under him. It is not known whether his emergence in that capacity resulted from advice tendered by him to the King—in view of the tiny minority of his party that he could command this is difficult to believe—or from a suggestion made by the King to him. It appears, in any case, to be universally admitted that the King played a pivotal part in securing the assent of Mr. Baldwin and Sir Herbert Samuel to his assumption of the Premiership. It is notable that, in the formation of the National Government, no attempt was made by the King to elicit the views of the great bulk of the Labour Party who transferred their allegiance from Mr. Mac-Donald to Mr. Arthur Henderson. It appears certain that the impetus to the peculiar form of the new administration came wholly from the King. Mr. MacDonald was as much the personal choice of George V as Lord Bute was the personal choice of George III. He is the sole modern Prime Minister who has been unencumbered by party support in his period of office; he provided only a name, while Mr. Baldwin supplied both the legions and the power that goes with the legions. We need not doubt that the King acted as he did wholly from a conception of patriotic obligation. But since it is known that a Baldwin Premiership was confidently expected at least as late as the night before the break-up of the Labour government, it is not, I think, unreasonable to term Mr. Ramsay MacDonald's emergence as Prime Minister of the National Government a Palace revolution.

It is argued [10] that the King's action was constitutional for two reasons. He was concerned "simply how best to extricate the country from the grave financial difficulties of which the drain from the Bank of England was a clear symptom. He might clearly have accepted the resignation of the Prime Minister when he found he could not command his Cabinet, had that been tendered, and then have sent for Mr. Baldwin to clear up the

[10] Keith, *The King and the Imperial Crown*, p. 136.

situation. But such a course would have had grave disadvantages at a critical moment. The new Prime Minister would undoubtedly have had to face a serious Opposition in the House of Commons, and might at once have been forced to ask for a dissolution, whereas with a National Government that could certainly be delayed, perhaps indefinitely, for there is no reason to suppose that an early dissolution was at first intended. Further, it was easy enough to believe then that the Labour Party did not really represent the Labour voters in the country, and that a National Government would be able to appeal to many Labour voters if and when it did come. It must have been hard to accept the fact that the three Labour leaders [11] really did not represent more than a handful of voters of Labour Party faith. In these circumstances it was inevitable that a co-operative ministry must have seemed ideal to the King, when it was acclaimed by the Conservatives and Liberals alike, and when it offered the chance of maintaining the United Kingdom on the gold standard." This is the first of Professor Keith's arguments in support of the King's action.[12]

It is an argument as notable for its omissions as for what it emphasizes. It omits the fact that Mr. MacDonald deliberately refrained from discussing the step he took with his Cabinet colleagues; that he himself must have known that the party support he could command was meagre, since, at a meeting of the junior ministers in his government, he urged them not to join him and assured them that the coalition was to be of brief duration, and that he never met the parliamentary party—whereby his hold on Labour opinion could have been communicated to the King—at all. It omits the fact, also, that if it was desired to associate Mr. MacDonald with the new combination, he could easily have joined it in another capacity than that of its head, as he did in the reconstructed government of 1935. It omits, also, the fact that, so far as the Labour government itself was

[11] Mr. MacDonald, Mr. Snowden, and Mr. Thomas.
[12] Keith, *The King and the Imperial Crown*, p. 136.

responsible for the crisis, the main burden of that responsibility rested precisely upon Mr. MacDonald and Mr. Snowden. It fails to emphasize the fact that Conservatives and Liberals had, between them, a majority in the House; and that, despite vigorous opposition, they did not dissolve until their main economy measure had been placed on the statute-book; and it omits the fact that, though Sir Herbert Samuel joined the government, his action in doing so was strongly criticized by Mr. Lloyd George. Professor Keith suggests that the primary motive of the King was to secure a government to preserve the gold standard; he omits, therefore, any connexion between its formation and previous rumours of Mr. MacDonald's desire for a coalition. Nor is there any reason to suppose that Mr. Baldwin would, as head of such a coalition, have been driven to dissolve in the midst of the crisis. He would have had his majority in any case, so long as the Liberals were willing to support him; and there is no reason to suppose that they indicated a preference for Mr. MacDonald as leader.

One need not doubt that, given the nature of the coalition, the King could foresee for it a subsequent majority at a general election unlikely to be obtained by Mr. Baldwin; a divided party always goes into a general election under a heavy handicap. But it is surely dangerous doctrine to argue that the King must so concern himself with the inner economy of parties as to attempt to secure a majority for the leader whom he commissions to form a government. From that attitude to Victoria's wholly unsuitable request to Lord Salisbury to know whether he was ready for a general election is a very small step. The implication of Professor Keith's argument is the inescapable one that the King must exert himself to secure a majority for the particular political configuration he happens to approve. That was the policy of George III; and its inherent assumption is that the King is not neutral but engaged in pressing forward a policy of his own. What is striking in the picture drawn for us is the absence of any suggestion that it was not less the duty of the King to inform himself of the mind of that part of the Labour Party—as Professor Keith notes, an overwhelming part—which did not follow Mr. Mac-Donald. In the Ulster crisis he was at pains to inform himself of Opposition opinion; and the Buckingham Palace Conference of 1914 was called out of his desire for accommodation. In 1931 he paid no attention at all to the psychological effects of his action on the Labour Party.

Here Professor Keith's second argument becomes important. The general election, he points out, resulted in an overwhelming majority for the National Government; the inference we are asked to draw is that this is an *ex post facto* justification of the King's decision. But this is to argue that whenever a government formed under the direct auspices of the Crown is able to secure a majority, that makes the action of the King in securing its formation a constitutional action. This is surely dangerous doctrine. It means that the King is entitled to force the resignation of ministers whenever, in his judgment, they have forfeited popular confidence; if the new government obtains a majority at the polls, this is held to validate his action. That, of course, is the position Mr. Balfour played for in the crisis over the House of Lords in 1910–11; and it was implicit in the suggestion, during the Ulster crisis, that the King should refuse his assent to the Home Rule Bill. It is the argument that, if the King does not approve of the advice tendered to him by his ministers, he can always force their resignation and is justified in doing so if the new government obtains a majority.

But what the argument fails adequately to weigh is the position of the King if the new combination does not obtain a majority. His dismissal of ministers is the abandonment of his neutrality; he has, by their dismissal, asked the country to reject their views and has, thereby, proclaimed his own. This is to make him the reserve power in the constitution, and the exercise of that power is bound always to be a difficult, and sometimes a dangerous, adventure. Professor Keith would, I think, agree that it is a weapon to be used only in extraordinary times. But

who is to judge what is an "extraordinary" time? Is it the King
himself? Then he is bound to be a man of exceptional political
discretion and acumen—not always kingly qualities. Is he to take
advice? If so, whose advice is it to be? It cannot seriously be
argued that he should surround himself with a "kitchen Cabinet"
of Lord Eshers, whose counsels he prefers to those of his responsible ministers; no Cabinet would accept such a position. It cannot, either, be urged that he should be in contact with the leaders
of the Opposition whether directly or, as has sometimes been
the case, through the mediation of men like Lord Esher or the
Archbishop of Canterbury. If the King is to decide what ministers he will have, even subject to the results of a general election, his views are bound to be discussed in that election. The
King then inevitably develops a policy of his own, perhaps even
a party of his own; and we are driven back to the technique of
George III. The true picture of this theory is that of Bolingbroke's *Patriot King;* and I doubt whether it is compatible with
the unstated assumptions of the twentieth-century constitution.

3

This is, of course, to take us far beyond the crisis of 1931;
but it is the significant aspect of that crisis that it touches the
foundations of the monarchical power. There are certain pre-
rogatives of the Crown the use of which has been usually regarded as absolete. What is their status at the present time?
Can the King, for instance, veto a bill sent up to him from
Parliament? Can he refuse a dissolution to a Prime Minister who
asks for it? Can he dismiss a Cabinet of whose policy he disapproves? Is he entitled to make his own Prime Minister and
to limit the latter's choice of colleagues?

The Crown has not refused its assent to a bill since 1707, and
it is difficult to feel that this power would now be used save
under conditions akin to those of revolutionary crisis. Its result,
of course, would be the resignation of ministers; and their suc-

cessors, who would have to assume responsibility for the royal decision, would almost certainly have to submit to the hazards of a general election, in which the wisdom of that decision would necessarily be a paramount issue. Clearly, if the new government was defeated, the King would have either to give way or seek to govern outside the terms of the constitution; and, in the former alternative, it is pretty obvious that the new Prime Minister would make it a condition of taking office that the King should pledge himself not to use his power again. It was, indeed, urged by an ex-Lord Chancellor, Lord Halsbury, in 1913 that the refusal of the royal assent was constitutional; and in the heat of the Ulster crisis authorities so eminent as Sir William Anson and Professor Dicey supported this view. In effect, it amounts to saying that the King can dismiss his ministers whenever he disagrees with their policy. The grave personal responsibility which would rest on any monarch who chose to exercise a prerogative power now obsolete for more than two hundred years needs no emphasis. It could not be used without the abandonment of royal neutrality; and that attitude could not be abandoned, in its turn, without making the government formed as a result essentially the personal nominees of the Crown. It is, I think, obvious that once this was the case the centre of the political battle would be the limitation of royal power. That road leads either to the system of George III or to abdication; and it may lead further.

The problem of the prerogative of dissolution is more complicated. It is agreed that the monarch should not dissolve, or refuse to dissolve, save on the advice of ministers; the problem is, however, whether the King may refuse a dissolution that is asked for, or insist upon one that his ministers do not desire. Though the books are emphatic that the decision must rest with the Crown, that this prerogative is, therefore, a living thing, it is well over a hundred years since a dissolution was refused; the revival of so rusty a precedent would be a very delicate operation. And, secondly, if the government which asked for a dissolution and was refused was a majority government, it would obviously resign because its advice was disregarded. Its successor, being in a minority, would sooner, rather than later, be forced to ask for a dissolution; and the King would then be in the delicate position of refusing to one Prime Minister what he agreed to grant to his successor. The precedents, indeed, make it clear that no government which wishes to consult the electorate will be prevented from doing so if, at the time of its request, it has a majority in the House of Commons. Were it otherwise, the Crown would inevitably subject itself to the accusation of discriminating between parties.

Is the situation different where the government is in a minority in the House of Commons? Mr. Asquith, in 1923, took the view that it was. The Labour government of 1924 was in a large minority in the House of Commons; it held only 191 out of 615 seats and, were it to be defeated, Mr. Asquith, as Liberal leader, was prepared to take office in his turn. When, however, the Labour government was defeated and the Prime Minister, Mr. Ramsay MacDonald, asked for a dissolution, the King agreed to his request. And it is difficult to see how it could well be otherwise. For had the King refused and invited Mr. Asquith to form a government, the latter, being head of a party even smaller than that of Mr. MacDonald, would have been bound, in the course of time, to be defeated also, and to have requested a dissolution. To have granted it would have evoked once more the accusation that the King was discriminating between parties. To grant a dissolution automatically is to place the responsibility for the government squarely upon the shoulders of the electorate, where, in the circumstances, it ought to lie. The emphasis upon the automatism of this prerogative is the surest way to the preservation of royal neutrality.

This view has been contested by some eminent authorities, of whom, perhaps, Professor A. F. Pollard is the most notable. To make the right to dissolution automatic, they argue, is to disturb the continuity of government. A government, especially a minority government, may dissolve for a bad reason, or for no reason at all; it may simply be "playing politics" and force a general election on the country because it thinks the situation favourable, or because it believes its opponents to be unprepared. These critics admit that the King ought not to be asked to bear the brunt of refusal; but they think that this difficulty can be overcome by making the assent of Parliament necessary to the grant of the right to dissolve.

It is difficult to see how such a scheme can be made workable. Few Parliaments—if the French Chamber provides any measure of experience—are likely to vote for their own annihilation; a general election is an expensive matter, and most members are eager to hold onto their seats as long as they can. And, clearly, if a government asked for a dissolution which the House, by vote, refused, the blow to the prestige of the government would be so great as to be equivalent to a vote of no confidence. It is hard, in those circumstances, to see how it could retain office; and its resignation would at once involve the necessity of its successor's seeking the support of the country. In any case, it is obvious that the safeguard against an unwise dissolution is the probability, which is great, that the government which seeks it will be forced to pay the penalty by the country for so doing. That was the case with Mr. Baldwin in 1923, and with Mr. MacDonald in 1924. In each instance, from a political angle, the decision to seek a dissolution was precipitate; and in each instance the government paid the penalty of defeat.

The right to compel a dissolution is on a different footing. There have been two occasions in the past thirty years in which a government dissolved at the express desire of the King: over the Budget in 1910, at the desire of Edward VII; and over the power of the Lords in the same year, at the desire of George V. In each case, however, the minister, however reluctantly, acquiesced in the King's desire, and the dissolution was, accordingly, amply surrounded by the cloak of ministerial responsibility; though the King took the initiative in pressing a dissolution upon the government, in each case, also, the government accepted his advice.

What would be the position if the King urged a dissolution and the ministry refused to agree? Clearly, I think, if the King insisted, the government would have no alternative but to resign; a new government would be formed and would at once go to the country. We know, from the memoirs of the time, that George V was constantly pressed to compel a dissolution in this way during the Ulster crisis of 1913–14. He refused; and the onset of the war led to the shelving of the problem of whether he would accept the consequences of the Home Rule Bill. The precedent, however, is of outstanding importance, if only because in an ultimate way it is indecisive upon the matter.

What is clear is the fact that an insistence by the King upon what may fairly be termed a penal dissolution is a variant upon the dismissal of ministers. The last occasion of its use lies in the buried past, and the problem it raises is the difficult one of whether a penal dissolution is justified by the success of the incoming government at the polls. I find it difficult to take this view for two reasons. In the first place, under any circumstances, the King's action is bound to be the subject of electoral controversy, and this is to make his neutrality an issue of the election— as I have argued, a thing at once dangerous and undesirable. In the second place, a penal dissolution could take place only in critical circumstances. But this, it is important to note, places upon the King the grave onus of deciding what "critical circumstances" are; and this raises the problem, once more, of whether he is to rely upon his own judgment or to take counsel other than that of his official advisers. The latter course is patently unconstitutional. The former means a sureness of touch with the electorate which, it may be urged, only an unwise monarch will believe himself to possess. A penal dissolution cannot avoid the result that the supporters of the government formed as a consequence of the ministry he has dismissed will seek to gain power on the pretext that a vote against them is a vote against the Crown; that was even the case in the general election of 1931, where no such factor was present. If the electorate supports the King's view, the precedent becomes established that he may compel a dissolution whenever he thinks the government no longer possesses the confidence of the country. It is, I think, highly unlikely that such a power could be wisely used; and if it were used amid events in which party tempers ran high, the King's position would be a very difficult one. If a penal dissolution resulted in the defeat of the party with which he associated himself by its use, I doubt whether his position would be tenable unless he agreed to the formal abandonment of the right to exercise it in the future.

This view is linked up with the question of whether—apart from penal dissolution—the King has the right to dismiss his ministers. The last occasion upon which this was done was when George III dismissed the Fox-North coalition of 1783; for it is now known that William IV acted on the Prime Minister's advice when he dismissed Lord Melbourne in 1834.[13] It is impossible to suggest that the right is obsolete even though, as Professor Keith puts it, the "power exists only for wise employment in grave circumstances." [14] But the problem is that both "wisdom" and "gravity" are here matters that the King must decide; and it is, at the least, an open question whether the King would, if he were wise, be willing to decide them. To do so is at once to link his fortunes with those of the party he summons to office; as Mr. Bonar Law said during the Ulster crisis, the King runs the risk, whatever he does, of offending half his subjects. And dismissal is the more dangerous adventure because it is more likely to operate against a government of the Left than of the Right—to transform the latter, as it were, into a party of the King's friends. The defeat of that party would inevitably be the defeat of the Crown itself, and the consequences of such a defeat would be necessarily momentous.

The possibility of such a dismissal came into view during the abdication crisis of 1936; though it should be added that nothing exists to show that the Duke of Windsor himself ever contem-

---

[13] Melbourne *Papers*, pp. 220–226.
[14] Keith, op. cit., p. 178.

plated the notion. But it was urged strongly upon him at the time no doubt upon a complex variety of grounds. The suggestion was that Mr. Attlee, as the leader of the Opposition, should declare his disagreement with the hostility of the Baldwin Cabinet to the King's marriage with Mrs. Simpson. The King should then dismiss Mr. Baldwin; Mr. Attlee should be summoned to form a government; and he was then to dissolve and ask for the electorate's approval of the new ministry.

The wisdom or unwisdom of the Duke of Windsor's marriage is, of course, irrelevant to the discussion of the principle here involved. What matters is a twofold fact: in a situation of crisis there was a considerable body of opinion prepared to consider the right to dismissal as an active one, and that its approval (or disapproval) was to depend upon the verdict of the electorate. What was not, I think, clearly seen by those who urged this view was the fact that the subject-matter of the dismissal is irrelevant to the constitutional principle involved. Had the dismissal taken place; had Mr. Attlee formed a government and secured electoral approval for his Cabinet; it would then have followed that, whenever the King did not approve of his ministers' advice, he would be entitled again to dismiss them. He would then have become—what the evolution of the past hundred years has sought to prevent—a vital power in the constitution. Inevitably, powerful influences would have been brought to bear upon him to use his renovated authority. Ministers would have had a perpetual sword of Damocles over their heads—the fear of the King's dismissal. To achieve favour with him would have become an important condition of holding office. We should have gone back, in a word, to the environment of the Hanoverian monarchy; and it is obvious that, once the power of dismissal was unwisely used, the maintenance of the monarchy would have been no easy matter.

Over the choice of ministers, the position is a very different one. The precedents are clear that the King has a certain discretion in the nomination of a Prime Minister. Where, for example,

there is no obvious successor to a Prime Minister who has resigned or died, the personal right of the Crown to offer the post
to the candidate thought to be most available is beyond question;
and the King need not, in these circumstances, consult anyone or
anything but his own discretion. So, in 1894, on Mr. Gladstone's
retirement, Queen Victoria made Lord Rosebery Prime Minister
in preference to three other possible names; so, also, in 1922, on
the resignation of Mr. Bonar Law, George V chose Mr. (now
Lord) Baldwin in preference to Lord Curzon. It is, indeed, clear
that the King's choice of a Prime Minister must be one that
commends itself to the party he is to lead. Not all the efforts of
Queen Victoria to evade the necessity of choosing Mr. Gladstone in 1880 were successful. It was as obvious in 1908, on the
resignation of Sir Henry Campbell-Bannerman, that Mr. Asquith must be summoned to succeed him, as it was, in 1936, to
assume that Mr. Chamberlain must be summoned to succeed
Mr. Baldwin. A King who sought to force his own nomination
upon a party in defiance of its views would find that his nominee
could not secure the support necessary to build a government.
His discretion, therefore, is in fact substantially more limited
than it appears in form. It amounts to the power, when the party
leadership is, exceptionally, in doubt, to choose among a small
number of possible names. The choice made may not be successful; the precedent of 1880 makes it clear that the discretion is,
as it were, experimental rather than decisive in character. It is,
moreover, narrowed by the fact that, as the choice of Mr. Baldwin in 1922 made clear, the Prime Minister must, under modern conditions, be a member of the House of Commons.

The nature of the party system makes it inevitable that a
Cabinet must contain at least its outstanding figures, so far as the
Prime Minister can secure their support. It is, however, obvious
that, beyond half a dozen persons, the Prime Minister himself
has a discretion of choice; old reputations diminish and new
claims are established to which attention must be paid. It is probably true to say that, in any Cabinet, party necessity does not ac-

count for more than half its members; the rest could be replaced by others without making any serious impact on the strength of the government. The King's pleasure is, of course, taken on all these appointments; and the royal influence will count for something in their determination. For how much, it is difficult to say. Victoria took exception, on a number of occasions, to the proposals of her different Prime Ministers; and she was sometimes able to have her way. How far a Prime Minister has been subject to pressure since her time we do not know; though it is not improbable that the offer of the War Office to Lord Esher by Mr. Asquith was due to the desire to please Edward VII. George V is said to have accepted without discussion the proposed membership of both the Labour governments of Mr. Ramsay MacDonald. Since, indeed, a Prime Minister can always have his way by refusing to take office if royal objection to his appointments is insistent, it is obvious that the real power of the King in this realm is simply a function of the degree to which the Prime Minister has made up his mind. Had Sir Charles Dilke not remained under the shadow of the divorce case in which he was co-respondent, it is, I think, obvious that Queen Victoria's objections would not have been able to keep him out of the Cabinet. The King may make representations, and, no doubt, a very considerable weight will attach to them, but the decisive factor in the ultimate choice is, by the nature of the circumstances, the will of the Prime Minister.

4

When the Cabinet has been formed, consultation with the Crown is a continuous process which ceases only with its demise. He has the right to know of vital proposals at a stage early enough to enable him to argue upon them; he has the right to discuss their substance with the relevant ministers; and he has the right, where he takes objection to any course that is proposed, to have it referred back to the Cabinet for reconsideration. The reader of Queen Victoria's *Letters* and the Esher *Papers* will not need to be told that these are rights of high importance, the exercise of which ranges from the minutiæ of military etiquette to the gravest issues of domestic and foreign policy. This is the famous "right to advise, the right to encourage, and the right to warn" of which Bagehot spoke some seventy years ago.

The documents make it clear that the power is more substantial than he conceived it to be. The duty of discussion with the King is, in any circumstances, a heavy one; and a monarch who takes his duties seriously, even more, a monarch who has strong views, may cast a heavy shadow upon the policy of a Cabinet, especially if, like Queen Victoria, he is hostile to the purposes of his government. For his criticisms and suggestions cannot be dismissed lightly. The eminence of his position, the distance which separates him even from the status of his Prime Minister, inhibits that ease of intercourse which is possible between colleagues. It may, perhaps, be doubted whether any recent Prime Minister has had to bear a burden so grim as that which Queen Victoria placed upon the shoulders of Mr. Gladstone. But the fact that royal influence is both constant and pervasive is beyond discussion. The mere rumour that King Edward VIII was dissatisfied with Mr. Baldwin's policy for the distressed areas made that policy a theme of intense, and even angry, national discussion throughout the brief period of his reign. The determination of George V, as he told Lord Esher, to take a special interest in imperial concerns is hardly likely to be unconnected with the emphasis they received from his successive governments. An energetic monarch, skilfully advised, can still play a considerable part in shaping the emphasis of policy.

He must be skilfully advised; and that raises the interesting question, upon which our information is woefully scanty, of the personnel upon whom he depends for advice. That the position of the King's secretary is of vital importance the documents make inescapably clear. The constancy of his personal contact gives him an access to, and an influence over, the royal mind that are of necessarily profound significance. His position gives him whatever access he may desire. He can collect and bring to his master any information he may think desirable. It is only necessary to read the correspondence of Disraeli and Gladstone, of Mr. Asquith and Lord Esher, to see for how much the judgment of the private secretary will count. It is important to note that the private secretary is not a civil servant, but a personal appointee of the King himself; and for nearly a century he has been, if not an aristocrat, at least connected with aristocratic circles, and likely to be elevated to the peerage. He is pretty certain to be aware of the experience of the Palace; and he has, of course, access to all the precedents of the past. I do not think it is going beyond the facts to say that, at least from the time of Sir Henry Ponsonby onwards, the private secretary to the monarch has been the keeper of the King's conscience—certainly the most permanent, and not the least influential, of his advisers. The long years in which each successive holder of the position has been at the Palace have inevitably meant an accumulation of experience which is bound to carry great weight with ministers.

But the King is advised not only by his private secretary. The royal household counts for something—for how much is not precisely known. But it is legitimate to assume that some of them will have ideas and doctrines which carry weight—the great officials, for instance, like the Clerk of the Privy Council, and the heads of the fighting services are in constant contact with the monarch. And the King's personal circle, inevitably, counts for a great deal; people like Lord Esher, and, in a less degree, Sir Ernest Cassel, have made a real impact upon policy through their access to the King's mind. It is not, I think, too much to say that, through them and people like them, whatever opinions are firmly held among the highly placed persons in the country will reach the King, and be communicated, with the authority he alone can attach to them, to the government of the day. It may be taken as certain that whatever is thought, for example, in circles round the Bank of England will find its way to the Palace.

The special relation, too, of the Archbishop of Canterbury makes him a medium for the communication of opinion of exceptional importance. What weight, of course, attaches to what is said and heard, we do not know; we dwell here in a twilight world which prevents anything from assuming clarity of outline. We can only hazard the view that the contacts between the Palace and outside opinion are, even though largely indirect, both constant and pervasive. The King acts upon the advice of his ministers. But he puts to his ministers a corpus of advice and suggestion into which there flow hints, ideas, doctrines, in which the outlook of whatever is both traditional and powerful in Great Britain has an ample and continuous place.

But not, be it noted, any other sort of opinion other than the traditional and powerful in any coherent or organized way. The King will know directly what the great landowner thinks, the great banker, the leaders of the Conservative Party, the heads of the fighting services, the great ecclesiastics of the Church of England. He lives, as it were, with them and among them; his personal circle is built from their number. He will have no such direct knowledge of, or contact with, the other elements in the nation. Unless a Labour government is in office, he has no more knowledge of what the Labour Party or the trade unions are thinking than has any of his subjects. He has no effective social contacts with working-class thought, organized or unorganized; no one is surprised if the King dines with a rich Conservative peer, or goes down to shoot for the week-end at one of the great country-houses; but everyone would be surprised if the King were to dine with one of the leading trade-union officials or spend the week-end at, say, a co-operative holiday home. The inescapable fact is that the social environment of the King is heavily weighted on the Conservative side; and this has been even more emphatically the case since the collapse of the Liberal Party. No doubt an occasional ceremonial function—a dinner to a visiting monarch, for example—gives an opportunity for a formal meeting with the leader of the Labour Party when in opposition. But

356 PARLIAMENTARY GOVERNMENT

that is all. The kind of urgency which led the King to interfere for peace over the House of Lords crisis in 1911, or the Ulster crisis of 1913–14, does not lead him to intervene in a working-class crisis like that over the general strike in 1926, or to seek to learn the views of the Labour Party in 1931. The whole impact of his environment necessarily makes the character of his opinions that of the conventional Englishman, zealous, no doubt, for the general welfare of the poor, but convinced that change must follow the lines of a well-settled tradition.

That this is true is pretty obviously borne out by all the evidence we have. Queen Victoria, in all matters of social change, had essentially that outlook we associate with the London suburbs; there is nothing in her vast correspondence to suggest that she ever understood, much less sympathized with, a single radical idea of her time. She had feelings for the respectable poor; that is evident from her occasional references to housing conditions. But the whole texture of her mind was profoundly aristocratic; and her attitude to Bright (before his Privy Councillorship), to Dilke, and to Chamberlain before 1886, makes it evident that the growing aspirations of democracy were alien to her. There is nothing, either, in the record of Edward VII as monarch to suggest a different conclusion. It is true that he had personal friendships among radicals like Dilke, and it is said, on good authority, that he greatly enjoyed the racy anecdotage of Mr. John Burns. But nothing in the evidence we have suggests that he had any real sense of what lay behind the great growth of the Labour movement in his day; and his notorious social insult to Mr. Keir Hardie showed pretty decisively his sense of the status of the Labour member in the Parliament of his time.

The situation under his successor was different because the political environment was different. After 1918, the British royal family began to devote itself to good works; and the arrival of the Labour Party as the official Opposition in Parliament as well as the government for two brief periods induced a subtle change in the atmosphere. There was, however, nothing in the change which touched the traditional position. It was well known that the King treated his Labour ministers with every consideration and observed in relation to them all the necessary constitutional proprieties. In private life, no doubt, he continued to hold the strong Conservative opinions he always held; but there was little in the programme of either Labour government with which he could have needed profoundly to quarrel. It is said that, on family grounds, he remonstrated strongly with Mr. Arthur Henderson when the latter, as Foreign Secretary, re-established full diplomatic relations with the Soviet Union; but he acquiesced, and it is at least fair to him to note that his doubts of the desirability of that recognition were said to have been shared by the Prime Minister, Mr. Ramsay MacDonald. The main interest of his reign in this regard is, 1931 apart, less his own attitude to his ministers than the effect upon them of the Palace atmosphere; for it is well known that certain members of the two Labour governments were more amenable to its influence than had been any of their contemporaries in Conservative administrations. In any case, no profound question of principle—a conflict, for instance, with the House of Lords—came into view while a Labour Cabinet was in office.

In normal times, indeed, so long as there is continuity of policy between governments of different complexion in matters of primary importance, the problem of the King's power raises no difficulty of a serious kind. At most, like Queen Victoria, he may be a brake upon the wheel of change; so long as there is a general political unity about the foundations, his personality and opinions will not be of essential significance. A weakminded Prime Minister may give way on points of minor importance. The influence of the Crown may be used for beneficent compromise as it was used in the struggle over the Reform Bill of 1884. Such minutiæ apart, so long as the doctrine of continuity holds, the Victorian compromise in the issue of monarchical power seems a workable hypothesis fully suited to the characteristics of ordinary parliamentary government in its classical form.

The real problem that it raises is set by the fact that continuity of policy may not be normal, that the possibility of crisis cannot be ruled out of account. There comes here into view that delicate range of problems which centre around the theory crystallized by Professor Keith in the phrase that the King is, especially nowadays, "the guardian of the constitution." "The Crown remains in fact," he writes, "an authority charged with the final duty of preserving the essentials of the constitution. The passing of the Parliament Act, 1911, has weakened enormously the potency of resistance to change of the Lords; it has only enhanced the importance thus left to the action in emergency of the King." [15]

"Guardian of the constitution" is a noble-sounding phrase; we must be sure that we are fully seised of all the implications it involves. In an emergency, it appears, the King may refuse to act upon the advice of his ministers whenever, in his judgment, what they propose ignores the "essentials of the constitution." Professor Keith does not tell us in detail what those "essentials" are; but we can perhaps gather something of the attitude from the illustrations he provides. If, he argues, the Labour Party were to attempt drastic economic changes which were resisted by the House of Lords, only an "overwhelming" support of the electorate for its projects would justify the King in disregarding "the deliberate settlement which has accorded to the Upper House a power of delay." The King could, on this view, do two things. He could, clearly, refuse to create enough peers to override the veto of the Lords, thus compelling a Labour government either to wait two years for its measures, or to submit to a general election; or he could enforce a penal dissolution in order to assure himself that the Labour government represented the effective will of the electorate. The theory applies, it should be added, not less to Conservative than to Labour measures. "Any Conservative attempt," Professor Keith argues, "to restore the powers of the Lords without first putting the issue to the coun-

[15] Op. cit., p. 183. The whole of this important section (Chap. VIII) should be read.

try would have to be resisted by the King. The duty of maintaining, until otherwise decided by the electorate, the compromise of the Parliament Act applies to Conservative no less than to Labour efforts to defeat it." "It may well be," he insists again, "that the powers of the Crown may have to be invoked to insist that there shall be no fundamental change unless and until the electorate in general has been persuaded of its necessity." [16]

The theory which appears to underlie this view is that the Parliament Act is an "essential" of the British constitution in the sense that the House of Lords can be overridden only by a special electoral decision to that effect. Either the Labour government must pass those measures it rejects on three occasions within a period of two years, or it must dissolve upon the issue; in which case, I take it, the House of Lords is presumably obliged to give way. It is not clear whether Professor Keith takes the view that the issue of the powers of the House of Lords is a separate issue, needing a separate general election if they are to be abridged or abolished. That was the view, at least, taken by George V when he asked Mr. Asquith to submit to the second general election of 1910. His willingness, on that occasion, to create peers if necessary was contingent on the ability of the Asquith government to obtain a majority on the specific issue of limiting the Lords' powers. The first general election was thus interpreted to mean only that the electorate approved the government's view that the Budget of 1909 should not be amended or rejected by the Lords.

We must not underestimate the significance of this attitude. It is the argument that the Lords are entitled to protect the *status quo* in economic (or other matters) for two years, and that if a government of the Left seeks an important alteration in it, it must consult the country. If it asks for the right to create peers, the King must refuse to concede it. In doing so, he acts as the "guardian of the constitution." The theory which underlies this argument is, therefore, that the Parliament Act (intended, as its preamble states, as a temporary measure) has become a kind of

[16] Ibid., pp. 209, 212–213.

fundamental law the procedure of which the King must safe-guard at all costs. Professor Keith does not point out that, reform of the House of Lords apart, this is to apply one form of procedure to measures from Right governments and another to those of the Left. In that procedure, moreover, the King is in effect to make himself the guardian of the economic interests represented by the Conservative Party in the House of Lords. He is to assure himself that the country definitely wants the measures of a Labour government; his doubts on this head are to be aroused by their rejection in the House of Lords. But he has no need for such an assurance in the case of Conservative measures. He may assume, we are to infer, that they do not traverse the "essentials" of the constitution, however drastic they may be, so long as they are not rejected by the Lords.

For we must be clear that the King will not view Conservative legislation as he views that of a Labour government. George V did not, for instance, urge on Lord Baldwin that the electorate ought to be consulted before the passage of the Trade Union Law Amendment Act of 1927, though that drastic statute reversed the direction of a century of legislation. He did not urge the need for a general election in 1932 on the issue of tariff reform, though its proposal split the Cabinet and was widely regarded as a definite breach of the government's mandate. In another realm, Edward VIII did not urge that the country should be consulted upon the rearmament programme of 1936, even though Lord Baldwin admitted that this was a matter upon which he had deliberately withheld his intentions from the electorate at the general election a few months before. As the House of Lords did not object to any of these measures, Professor Keith assumes that nothing arises calling for royal intervention. For that is an "emergency" power which becomes operative only when the House of Lords acts. As it acts only when a government of the Left is in power, it is, on his view, the only institution in the country capable of creating an emergency.

The purpose of a democracy, Professor Keith tells us, is compromise; but, in his judgment, it appears that it is upon the Left only that the duty of compromise is to be incumbent. It is difficult to see how a party, fresh from a victory at the polls, will accept easily the view that its programme is to await fulfilment for two years if the House of Lords objects to it; or that, alternatively, they must prove to the King that a new general election will leave public opinion on their side. It is bound to point out that the result of such a process is devoid of the possibility of equal application. It will insist that, under guise of protecting the "constitution," the King is, in fact, giving to established economic interests a further chance of victory. His action, in fact, if it could be counted upon, would be simply an invitation to the "economic royalists" to exploit the situation by the kind of opposition they have shown to President Roosevelt in the United States and to the Popular Front governments in France. It is, to put it bluntly, to give them an opportunity to organize trade depression, and perhaps even financial panic, in the hope that the electorate may thereby be coerced into returning a Conservative majority. In this context, the King's neutrality is bound, to the Left, to become at best a dubious fiction from which they would necessarily seek to tear aside the veil.

Professor Keith, I submit, has wholly failed to understand that the constitution is not a body of eternal principles operating in a vacuum. The King's relation to its operations cannot be governed by circumstances which were acceptable to his ministers in 1911. Even over the Home Rule Bill of 1913, the suggestion that he might veto the Act unless his ministers submitted it to the country was, as Lord Esher tells us, sufficient to produce a threat from the Cabinet that it would fight the election upon the issue of whether the King or his ministers are to govern the country. To argue that any drastic changes must proceed by general consent, and that the verdict of a packed body like the House of Lords is a necessary part of that general consent, is to say in effect that no drastic changes are possible unless the Conservative Party assents to them. Why should it, since the Parliament Act gives it, on Professor Keith's view, the right to gamble on a general election before it has to admit the need to acquiesce in the earlier victory of its rival?

It must not be forgotten that the proposals of the Labour Party will have been for years a matter of continuous public debate before they are introduced as bills by a Labour government. It must not be forgotten, either, that it will be to put them on the statute-book that the Labour Party will have been returned to power, and, obviously, it will be part of the declared programme of the Labour Party, as it was in 1935, to say forthrightly that they will interpret their election to mean that they have the right to override opposition to their programme from the House of Lords. Is the King to say, in the face of this, that they must either submit to the procedure of the Parliament Act or accept the necessity for a penal dissolution? If ministers refuse to accept the King's interpretation of his function, is he to dismiss them? Does Professor Keith think that an election fought upon the issue of the King's power is likely to strengthen the position of the British monarchy?

Lord Esher, who was an enthusiastic monarchist, saw this danger more clearly, I think, than Professor Keith has done. The King, he insisted, has no option but to accept the advice of his ministers so long as they have a majority. "If the constitutional doctrine of ministerial responsibility means anything at all," he informed George V, "the King would have to sign his own death warrant, if it was presented to him for signature by a minister commanding a majority in Parliament. If there is any tampering with this fundamental principle, the end of the Monarchy is in sight." And a majority in Parliament, clearly, must mean a majority in the House of Commons, since, a priori, a Labour government cannot have a majority in the House of Lords. The King is left, as Lord Esher said, the power of remonstrance. He can expatiate to ministers on the unwisdom of their course; he can picture the grave risks they are running. But, once they have made up their minds upon the advice they propose to tender to him, his constitutional duty is to accept it. The alternative, as I have said, is their dismissal; and that must necessarily lead to a conflict over the prerogative of which the outcome will be on any showing momentous.

It is said that this is to reduce the King to the position of an automaton. Here, distinctions are necessary. My argument is that the King's public acts must be of an automatic character; he must, in the public view, accept the advice of his ministers. In private, no doubt, he can use to the full those rights of advice and encouragement and warning for which his supreme position assures him full consideration. He cannot go beyond them, once ministers have decided upon action, without descending into the full glare of the political arena. If it is said that he does not abandon his neutrality, that his action is limited to the enforcement only of a certain form of procedure, the answer is that this procedure cannot be separated from the substance of the legislation related to it. The House of Lords does not reject legislation merely to assure itself that the country, on reflection, is in favour of the government's plans. It is not a neutral arbitrator between contending parties in the House of Commons. It is, as Lord Balfour remarked, a branch of the Conservative Party charged with the duty of seeing that, whatever be the complexion of the government in office, the Conservative Party is permanently in power. The Parliament Act, no doubt, has modified its authority since Lord Balfour spoke; but the modification still leaves the House of Lords with immense opportunities of wrecking any governmental programme it happens to dislike. To suggest that the King is, in effect, to co-operate with the Lords in its effort to wreck such legislation is to suggest action that is incompatible even with the idea of his neutrality.

The delicacy and danger of the choice of this view of his prerogative calls upon him to take hardly need any emphasis. He is to prevent "drastic" change; he is to safeguard the "essentials" of the constitution. But what is "drastic" change? Is the King to decide upon this by his own judgment? Is he to take advice other than that of his ministers? If so, whose advice is he to take? Obviously, any view of what is "drastic" turns on the premisses of judgment from which we start. There are people to whom the nationalization of the Bank of England is the beginning of the end of all social stability; there are others, Mr. J. M. Keynes, for instance, who regard it as a normal measure of no exceptional importance. What is the standard by which the King is to judge? Is a measure "drastic" because it has been rejected by the House of Lords? That can hardly be a reasonable criterion, since the House of Lords has passed many drastic measures, the Reform Act of 1928, for example, which established universal adult suffrage in England. And what are the "essentials" of the constitution? Not only do they change in time; even in any given time there is no agreement about their content. It has usually been accepted as an "essential" of the constitution that the King shall act on the advice of his ministers; ever since 1688 the general direction of constitutional action has been to establish that principle beyond discussion. It is also true that, at critical moments, those who have objected to the nature of the advice offered have sought to develop the thesis that in a "crisis" the King can ignore that advice if he acts for what he believes to be the safety of the realm. So Lord Balfour expressed his readiness to take office in 1910 if the King chose to dismiss his ministers; he and his party disliked the Lloyd George Budget of 1909 and the Liberal Party's determination to limit the veto of the House of Lords. So, also, the King was urged to veto the Home Rule Act in 1913–14; the Conservative Party disliked the Irish policy of the Liberal government. Those who now dislike the prospect of socialist legislation, if and when the Labour Party returns to power, use the same argument. They ask, in effect, for the suspension of an "essential" constitutional principle because it leads to results of which they profoundly disapprove. A constitutional crisis is, therefore, a situation in which the King is asked to act independently of his government because the Opposition is convinced that the policy of the government is disastrous to the future of the nation.

So to state the implications of the theory is surely to refute it. The volume of actual and active power it would transfer to the King's hands would be enormous. For, clearly, it would give him at once a pre-natal and post-natal control of all government legislation which would arouse deep feelings of hostility in the country; and the House of Lords, that is, the Conservative Party, would be made aware that it has only to use its veto under the Parliament Act to compel either the postponement of government measures or their submission to the electorate. And on Professor Keith's view, this would not apply to a Conservative government unless it proposed to repeal the Parliament Act. The theory is an urgent invitation to the King to place any socialist government in an impossible position. For it suggests that he cooperate with the Lords in wrecking its programme—that is the real result of the two years' delay—while the Conservative Party prepares the best possible atmosphere for the next general election. It takes the initiative in policy from the hands of the government—where the people had placed it—and transfers it to those of the King. And it transfers it, thereby, to an atmosphere in which, at the best, experience shows that the policy will have little chance of being popular. King George V observed with careful scrupulosity all the conventions of the constitution; yet even he told Lord Esher that if he had been compelled to create peers in 1911 he could never have "lifted up his head again." We have, in short, to realize that the King to whom this initiative of emergency action is to be entrusted is practically certain to be hostile to fundamental change. So, too, are the officials of the Palace; their training and environment make it difficult for them to be otherwise. So, also, will be the private circle of the King's own friends; "that whole Tory party," as Lord Esher termed it,[17] "to which he is naturally bound." If the King were to insist

[17] *Journals and Letters of Viscount Esher*, 11, 443 (Jan. 4, 1910).

upon the exercise of personal power in these circumstances, it would be impossible not to conclude that he was seeking, by reason of his own personal sympathies, to prevent a socialist government from realizing the purposes for which it was elected to office.

I am not, it must be noted, arguing that the King will not take the view implicit in Professor Keith's theory; I am arguing only that it will be a breach of vital constitutional convention necessarily fraught with momentous consequences. What they will be it is, of course, impossible to say beyond that hint given by Lord Esher when he wrote of the Budget controversy of 1910 that "the whole situation too perilously resembles that of 1640 for my taste." [18] That the King will be strongly pressed in this direction is hardly doubtful. All the precedents suggest that this will be the case. Indeed, the use of the monarch's personal popularity as a weapon of last instance in political conflict is a familiar technique of the party opposed to fundamental change. That the King is impartial because above the battle; that he is entitled to consult the country before he accepts a policy which is fiercely challenged; that the government is unfair which puts him in the position where he has to choose; that he is justified in seeking ministers prepared, like Sir Robert Peel in 1834, to accept responsibility for a change in policy; that the obsolescence of prerogative does not mean its destruction—all these are the familiar arguments of a party with its back to the wall. Their implication is none the less the clear one that what it chooses to call an emergency must be settled by a procedure not applicable to its own policies when in power. That is not a thesis likely to commend itself to a government which has been given authority to translate its principles into action.

It arises, of course, from the situation I have already discussed in dealing with the changed relation of parties in the post-war epoch. So long, I have argued, as they were agreed upon "fundamentals," they could afford, in Lord Balfour's phrase, to bicker

[18] *Journals and Letters of Viscount Esher*, ii, 408.

safely; their quarrels have only twice, since 1832, touched the ultimate conventions of the constitution. The power of the monarchy did not, save on those occasions, need to be invoked because neither side needed to have a view of its extent in order to carry its policies into operation. Contingently, at least, this is no longer the case. The whole trend of social and economic evolution since the war has brought into discussion the foundations of social organization. To take a wide view of the royal authority is to invoke it as a weapon capable at least of postponing, and perhaps of preventing, any change in the nature of those foundations. There is no reason to doubt that the prerogative of the King seems to men of both eminence and experience in politics above all a means of delaying the coming of socialism. They believe, no doubt quite sincerely, that socialism is a synonym for national disaster. They look, therefore, to the King to save the nation from its consequences. That those who believe in socialism are unable to share their view of the prerogative does not appear to change their outlook. Nor, indeed, are they moved by the fact that many who dislike socialism equally with themselves would, as Lord Esher did, view with alarm any attempt to make the King an active agent in political decisions. They are prepared to risk its authority in the struggle for economic power.

There are even those who represent the use of that power as essentially democratic in its nature. "What could be more democratic," they say, "than to consult the nation when it is deeply divided?" But every government is responsible for a mass of measures which deeply divide the nation; it does not, nevertheless, regard it as necessary to consult the nation upon them. Few measures are more fundamental to the life of a nation than a declaration of war; yet everybody in his senses is aware that it is a misuse of the democratic principle to ask for a referendum before war is declared. Or the argument takes the form of insisting that in measures of really vital importance we ought to be sure that the people has made up its mind before they are finally accepted. Here, of course, "measures of really vital importance" are only those measures which emanate from a government of the Left; it is not suggested that the King should force a dissolution upon a government of the Right in order that its "vital measures" should be submitted to the people for reconsideration. And the reason that the Crown is invoked to assume responsibility for a popular verdict is a simple one. No one now defends the anachronism of the House of Lords. In a straight conflict between it and the House of Commons, there is no sort of doubt on which side the popular judgment will be. But a Conservative strategy conducted under the auspices of the Crown may serve to confuse the situation. Above all, it will enable the popularity of the throne to be used against the forces of the Left. It is a powerful card in the hands of the Conservative interests; it may, with a King as beloved as George V, be a trump card. At the best, an election won with the King as the virtual leader of the Conservative forces can be represented as a triumph for the forces of democratic sanity; at the worst, their defeat will transfer the scene of the battle from the economic to the constitutional field. The outcome of that transfer it is impossible to predict, for the roots of monarchy lie deep in human experience. To bring its foundations into dispute is to raise controversies of which no one can foresee the end.

One final point in this context may be made. It is notable that, during the abdication crisis of 1936, no authoritative voice on the Conservative side asked that the decision of the Cabinet against the Duke of Windsor's proposed marriage should be confirmed by an electoral decision, though there was, of course, no sort of mandate for the view it took. Mr. Churchill, indeed, pleaded for delay; but he does not appear to have meant more than the opportunity for further consultations. It is notable, too, that no authoritative voice raised the issue that the King had the right, even in so intimate a matter, to reject the advice of his ministers. The Labour Party, moreover, which insisted throughout that he had no such power of rejection was warmly praised by Conservatives for the constitutional correctness of its attitude.

The gravity of the abdication crisis is universally admitted; and if ever there was a case in which the King might have acted independently of his Cabinet, a matter of such personal intimacy as his marriage would appear to be that case. Yet the theory of an independent royal prerogative in an emergency was never raised on that occasion save, it is important to note, by the Fascists and Lord Rothermere, on the one hand, and by the Communist Party, on the other. Neither of these elements, I suggest, is interested in the due observance of constitutional forms. The purpose of the first was to injure the party system by placing the King in opposition to the Baldwin government, in the hope of profiting from the resultant confusion. The Communist Party hoped that, if the King could be persuaded to form a Labour government, his popularity might help to win a general election for socialism. It failed, of course, to realize, what Conservatives were quick to point out, that if the King had the right to dismiss his ministers for one cause, he had the right, also, to dismiss them for another. In any case, we have the Prime Minister's assurance that such a step was never contemplated by the King. He could not accept the consequence of his ministers' advice; and he abdicated rather than set himself in opposition to them. That was a view overwhelmingly approved by the vote of both Houses of Parliament. It is a precedent the significance of which for the coming years it is impossible to overestimate.

5

There is one element in the functioning of the monarchy which the abdication of 1936 brought into view that deserves a brief treatment. The records make it clear that the exercise by the King of his function of criticism and comment very largely depends upon the quality of his private secretary and his assistants, and, to some extent, at least, upon the personnel of the royal household through the members of which a good deal of information reaches the King. It is well known that, so far, the royal secretaries have done their work admirably. Mr. Gladstone paid a high tribute to the services of Sir H. Taylor; and the devotion of Sir Henry Ponsonby is attested by the volume compiled from his records.

When Edward VIII ascended the throne, sweeping changes were made in both the secretarial and household appointments, and few of those whom he chose to replace the former officials possessed the training for their delicate task which experience has proved to be essential. It may, indeed, be urged that some, at least, of the problems of his brief reign were not unrelated to the inexperience of his personal advisers. I believe the time has come when all the posts at the Palace should be made civil service positions in the ordinary way. There is no difficulty at all in finding in the various government departments officials of the requisite experience and character. Their training will have given them a fuller appreciation of the constitutional problems they have to handle than any other section of the community. There is likely to be in their work that atmosphere of impersonality and detachment the importance of which is so clear. They are more likely to be a safeguard, than are those appointed under the present system, against the exercise of undue influence by *éminences grises* like Lord Esher, or ex-ministers willing to outstep the bounds of constitutional propriety like Beaconsfield and Salisbury. Their immersion in the general civil service tradition, as distinct from that of the Palace, is itself an important argument for their special availability for this kind of work.

It is, I think, clear that all persons in official positions about the King should be as non-political as possible. A situation like that confronted by Sir Robert Peel over the Whig ladies of the household is unlikely to occur again; but it is certainly undesirable that one of the King's military aides, as in 1913, should be closely linked with the threat of an Ulster rebellion, especially when it is clear that his attitude influenced the King's mind.[19] No doubt, it is useful for information to come to the Palace from

[19] Esher, *Sunday Times*, January 30, 1938.

sources as wide as the interests of the nation. But it is important
to emphasize that its evaluation for use by the King is a difficult
and delicate matter for which the previous training of his officials
does not always fit them. Labour members of the government of
1929-31 were rightly disturbed at the constant hints they received when in attendance at the Palace of the desirability of a
coalition government. Judgments of this kind are, clearly, outside any function these officials have to perform. The whole ethos
of the civil service is a training against such an attitude; and
the transformation of posts in the Palace to this basis would be
an assurance that, so far as is humanly possible, the connexions
of Palace officials would give no ground for suspicion.

6

A word is desirable upon the place of the Crown through the
change in the status of the Dominions. Writers of the authority
of Lord Balfour have written as though the result of the change
is, somehow, to advance the power of the Crown as the bond or
unit to which the different pacts of the Empire owe their allegiance.[20] It is difficult to see that this is the case. Broadly speaking, it is true to say that the Dominions are now free from any
control from London; the King, or his Governor-General, acts
upon the advice of his Dominion Prime Minister in exactly the
same way as he acts upon the advice of his Prime Minister in
London. What would happen if two of his Prime Ministers gave
him advice which was in conflict, it is difficult, of course, to know.
Obviously, the good offices of the King would be invoked to arrive as best might be at a solution of the difference. The problem, it should be added, is real in the case of Eire; and it might,
in the event of war, give rise to difficult problems in the case of
South Africa. But it is not easy to see how, in any real way, this
multiple personality of the Crown adds to its power.

[20] Introduction to Bagehot, *The English Constitution* (World's Classics edi-
tion); and see also Keith, op. cit., p. 452.

It is no doubt true that the psychological bond of allegiance constituted by the institution of a monarchy strikes deeper roots than are easily available by other means. But the roots of the British Commonwealth of Nations remain, far more deeply, those of which Edmund Burke spoke in his speech on conciliation with America. The psychological superstructure of empire rests, inevitably, on an unmistakable material foundation. If that is held inadequate, as it was held inadequate by the American colonies in 1776, the institution of kingship will prove but a frail barrier against secession. The person of the Crown is valuable while the material foundation remains. It is associated, clearly enough, with profound traditions which make for a common outlook, and tend, therefore, to render easier the solution of differences. It is also true, as Professor Keith points out, that "were it not for the Crown it would become necessary to seek to formulate definitely the relation between the several parts" of the Commonwealth; and it is at least doubtful whether the time is ripe for this formulation. But it is interesting to note that the need for such a formulation has been urged with great power by high authority; and problems like the intricate question of the right to secede, or whether the relations between Great Britain and the Dominions are part of the proper subject matter of international law, are really independent altogether of the King's person. They will be solved by the interplay of British and Dominion interests as these seem to make desirable to the parties a solution in one direction rather than another. It may even be doubted, in view of the discussions over the meaning of allegiance during the Irish treaty negotiations of 1921, whether the person of the King as a bond of unity has not been a hindrance rather than a help to the solution of some of the delicate problems involved. And it is not impossible that the special position of the Governor General of a Dominion, as the personal representative of the Crown, may raise issues in the future.[21] George V

[21] See the illuminating volume of Mr. Justice Evatt, *The King and His Dominion Governors.*

did not easily accept the appointment of Sir Isaac Isaacs as the first Australian-born Governor-General of the Commonwealth; and the future of India, in this context, contains the germ of problems it will not be easy to solve.

Those, it may be urged, who see in the imperial position of the Crown a proof of its indispensability are concerned chiefly with two things. They seek, first, the enhancement of monarchical prestige abroad as a means of strengthening the idea of imperial unity; the oath of allegiance has deep, even mystical roots in the history of human nature. But they seek, secondly, to enhance the prestige of the Crown at home. They are concerned to emphasize its indispensability in order to safeguard its right to a wide prerogative in domestic affairs. A criticism of royal action can thus be represented as a blow at imperial unity. To risk the position of the King is to risk the maintenance of the Empire; and the more firmly this can be driven home to the electorate, the more urgent does it then seem to screen all royal action from public examination. We are told that the Crown is of pivotal importance to our retention of India, for example; and it is assumed that, without its pageantry, our power over the Indian mind would somehow diminish.

It is not necessary to deny the value of either pageantry or symbolism to doubt whether this is the case. It is relevant in this connexion to remember that the elevation of the Crown's imperial prestige dates from the discovery of the commercial value of India; we did not hear of this aspect of its importance when the colonies were "like wretched millstones round our necks." The unity of the Empire will be maintained so long as it is valuable to its constituent parts to maintain it. While that value persists, the Crown will necessarily have value as the symbolic representation of that unity. The part he plays in the Empire will be determined by the interplay of the political and economic forces which now exercise a centripetal influence upon its interrelations. No amount of turgid rhetoric will conceal the fact that he has not, and cannot have, an imperial policy of his own. What he says and does will be what his ministers in the Empire advise him to say and do. The rise and fall of empires depend on causes which a constitutional monarch can do little to influence, much less to control. The more fully this is realized, the clearer will be the perspective in which the position of the King is reviewed.

Index

Index

377

380 INDEX